U.S. ARMY DIVISIONS OF THE PACIFIC WAR

U.S. ARMY DIVISIONS OF THE PACIFIC WAR

STEPHEN R. TAAFFE

CASEMATE

Pennsylvania & Yorkshire

Published in the United States of America and Great Britain in 2024 by
CASEMATE PUBLISHERS
1950 Lawrence Road, Havertown, PA 19083
and
47 Church Street, Barnsley, S70 2AS, UK

Hardback Edition: ISBN 978-1-63624-449-5
Digital Edition: ISBN 978-1-63624-450-1

A CIP record for this book is available from the British Library

Printed and bound in the United States of America by Integrated Books International

Typeset in India by Lapiz Digital Services, Chennai.

For a complete list of Casemate titles, please contact:

CASEMATE PUBLISHERS (US)
Telephone (610) 853-9131
Fax (610) 853-9146
Email: casemate@casematepublishers.com
www.casematepublishers.com

CASEMATE PUBLISHERS (UK)
Telephone (0)1226 734350
Email: casemate@casemateuk.com
www.casemateuk.com

All maps reproduced courtesy of U.S. Army and U.S. Army Center of Military History.

Contents

Acknowledgments   vii
Introduction   ix

1   South Pacific Maelstrom   1
2   The Central Pacific Offensive   45
3   MacArthur's New Guinea Road   81
4   Liberation of the Philippines   105
5   Closing in on Japan   155

Conclusions   167
Appendix: List of Pacific War Army Divisions   177
Endnotes   189
Bibliography   203
Index   211

Acknowledgments

Solitude is, at least for the introverts among us, one of the few charms of the otherwise tedious chore of writing. However, even the most cloistered writer must occasionally work with others. Fortunately, my interactions in writing this book have been mostly pleasant and productive. James Zobel at the Douglas MacArthur Memorial Archive, Riley Johnson at the United States Army Heritage and Education Center, and Kirsten Cooper at the United States Military Academy were particularly cooperative. Bill Kimok and Judy Markins at Ohio University helped me procure materials that my university was unable to obtain. Two of my colleagues and friends, Dr. Philip Catton and Dr. Brookford Livingston Poston III, read through the manuscript and offered perceptive suggestions. My dean at Stephen F. Austin State University, Dr. Dustin Knepp, awarded me a grant that funded two of my research trips. And, as usual and most of all, I am thankful for the continuing kindness of my wife and travelling companion, Cynthia, who tolerated my moodiness and broodiness with more patience than I would have exhibited had our roles been reversed.

Introduction

On 6 July 1945, General Robert Eichelberger, the commander of the American Eighth Army, visited the 37th Infantry Division headquarters near Tuguegarao on the Philippine island of Luzon. The 37th Division was a National Guard outfit from Ohio with a fine reputation that had been overseas for three and a half years. During that time it had seen plenty of combat, most notably in clearing die-hard Japanese defenders from the Philippine capital of Manila during the previous February–March in a brutal battle that completely wrecked the city and cost the division 3,732 casualties. After inspecting the troops, Eichelberger gave the divisional staff a pep talk in which he praised the 37th for its performance. By the time he finished, the head of the division, General Robert Beightler, had tears in his eyes. Beightler was a wartime anomaly. Although he had led the 37th Division for the entire conflict, he was not a Regular Army officer. He was instead a National Guardsman who, before the war, had been a civil engineer and director of Ohio's highway system. In its efforts to professionalize the army, the War Department had systematically weeded out almost every single high-ranking National Guard combat commander, so Beightler's survival was testament to both his ability and the respect that Regular Army officers such as Eichelberger had for him. Beightler's tears resulted from his conviction that his division had not received the recognition it merited for its wartime exploits. The 37th, he believed, deserved better from both the army and the public, and he was grateful that Eichelberger had made at least a down payment in that direction.[1]

Beightler's sentiments reflected a feeling held by many GIs that the army did not receive sufficient credit for its role in winning the Pacific War against Japan. They resented the prevailing view that the Marine Corps bore the brunt of the ground war, as evidenced by the accolades that leathernecks received for their courageous actions at Guadalcanal, Tarawa, Iwo Jima, and elsewhere. Moreover, General Douglas MacArthur, the Pacific War's highest-ranking army general, monopolized whatever limelight did spill onto the army. The reality, though, was that the army did most of the heavy lifting in the Pacific War's land campaigns. By the conflict's end, the army had 1.77 million troops in the Pacific and Asia, considerably more than the 484,000 Marines involved at that time. The army's contribution was more than numeric. It also conducted more amphibious assaults and prosecuted more operations than the Marines. Indeed, the army sometimes had to help the Marines fulfill their missions. The Pacific War, in short, was as much the army's war as the concurrent struggle in Europe against Germany and Italy.

The army deployed ninety combat divisions in World War II. Of these, it sent twenty to the Pacific to fight Japan, nineteen of which were infantry divisions and one an airborne outfit. A World War II-era army combat division was a self-contained unit of around 15,000 men led by a major general and capable of conducting independent missions. Before the United States entered the conflict, the army's infantry divisions were, at least on paper, large units of almost 28,000 troops composed of two brigades of two regiments apiece. Although their size enabled them to sustain heavy losses and remain combat effective, it also limited their responsiveness. After World War II began, the army gradually transformed these so-called "square" divisions into "triangular" ones by eliminating the brigades and reducing the regiments from four to three. Their triangular organization meant that every unit possessed three maneuver elements—each regiment contained three battalions apiece, each battalion three companies, each company three platoons, and each platoon three squads. To increase their firepower, the army gave each maneuver element a fire support unit of machine guns, mortars, or howitzers. Each regiment, for example, received a battalion of 105 mm howitzers with a range of 7,000 yards. As for mobility, the army motorized its divisions and eliminated the need for horses. A headquarters company, reconnaissance troop, engineer battalion, medical battalion, ordnance company, quartermaster company, signal company, military police platoon, and various other odds and ends rounded out the division. The result was, in theory anyway, a balanced organization large enough to survive prolonged combat, but with sufficient mobility and firepower to outmaneuver and destroy enemy formations.

These divisions did not, however, operate alone. They were usually grouped into corps. A World War II corps was a flexible outfit that typically contained at least two divisions. It consisted of little more than a major general or lieutenant general and his headquarters. Corps commanders' responsibilities were completely tactical, enabling them to focus exclusively on combat operations. Five of these corps served in the Pacific during the conflict. Corps, in turn, were part of field armies led by full generals with significant combat and administrative duties. The army deployed three of them to the Pacific during

World War II. Finally, field army chiefs answered to theater commanders such as MacArthur who oversaw large geographic areas.

Although almost all the divisions the army deployed to the Pacific were infantry, their origins varied. Those divisions numbered between one and twenty-five were Regular Army ones built around professional soldiers with years of experience. They included famous outfits such as the 24th "Victory" and 25th "Tropic Lightning" Divisions. Although the army skimmed off many of these men as cadres for constructing new divisions and replaced them with draftees, these units maintained an aura of professionalism, pride, and discipline. In theory, they should have been, and often were, some of the army's best units. However, frequent turnover and inadequate leadership sometimes undermined or diluted esprit de corps and led to problems that did not become apparent until these divisions were committed to combat. In addition, the army occasionally attached entire National Guard regiments to them to bring them up to strength. Six of these Regular Army divisions served in the Pacific during the conflict.

During the war the army also mobilized nineteen National Guard divisions, most of which were numbered between twenty-six and forty-five. Ten of them served in the Pacific War. Each state possessed a National Guard that was composed of citizens who joined out of military interest or to supplement their incomes. During peacetime the National Guard and the Regular Army cooperated to give guardsmen periodic and standardized training similar to that of fulltime soldiers. National Guard officers, for example, had to meet Regular Army expectations. In an emergency the federal government could call out the National Guard to augment the Regular Army. When President Franklin Roosevelt did so in September 1940, the National Guard added an additional 278,000 soldiers to the army. Although National Guard divisions lost some of their regional identity when the army transferred personnel in and out, they retained their statehood ties, culture, and ethos until the war's end.

The National Guard should theoretically have been ready for the war. The reality, though, was something else. Prewar state National Guards were usually underfunded, underequipped, and undertrained because the small defense budget only stretched so far. Moreover, like their Regular Army divisional counterparts, the War Department often cannibalized National Guard divisions to provide cadres and replacements for other outfits. Although many claimed that the National Guard possessed great esprit de corps because it contained friends and neighbors who were familiar with each other and had worked together for years, this created its own set of problems. Some National Guard units were close-knit cliques in which advancement was based on political connections, popularity, and status, not on military ability. Officers were therefore not necessarily the most militarily proficient men available. Under those circumstances, it was difficult for officers to make hard and contentious decisions that might anger old buddies. As one Regular Army officer stated, "The problem with the Guard is that the kind of a person that you need to hold a unit together as an inactive National Guard unit is not the kind of person that you need to command in combat."[2]

To rectify these defects, the War Department tried to improve National Guard divisions by breaking up cliques, transferring in soldiers who possessed no previous Guard connections, replacing underperforming high-level commanders with Regular Army officers, and holding guardsmen accountable. Unfortunately, such efforts were only partially successful. They often alienated guardsmen who felt that the Regular Army was prejudiced against them. And, in fact, some Regular Army generals did believe that National Guard divisions were second rate outfits best avoided. These attempts to transform the National Guard gradually diluted its regional identities and loyalties, but never completely erased them. National Guardsmen were just as likely to coopt outsiders as outsiders were to reform the guardsmen. The upshot was that National Guard divisions and their officers were something of an unknown quality before they entered combat. The army chief of staff, General George C. Marshall, inarticulately remembered:

> [I]t was very hard to get a correct judgment of [the National Guard's] efficiency, their qualifications, because here you stepped into the realm of politics....And in their handling of the men and all, it is very difficult, short of a war basis, to have men discipline their neighbors during the peacetime training in a manner that is required in order to get a strict compliance with the orders that are so necessary to build up a satisfying state of discipline. In the main the weakness was the complete lack of time to basically train the individuals in the Guard, the political influences involved in the officer corps, and the lack of method of firmly establishing the qualifications of the candidates for promotions or commissions.[3]

Marshall later complained, with some hyperbole, that overcoming the National Guard's inherent parochialism and bringing it up to snuff delayed war preparedness by a year.[4]

The majority of the army's wartime infantry divisions were not Regular Army or National Guard, but so-called "draftee" or "selectee" divisions composed of men conscripted for the conflict. Numbered from forty-six to 106, these draftee divisions lacked the history and discipline of Regular Army outfits or the community ties of National Guard units. On the other hand, this made them blank slates upon which the army could inscribe its wartime doctrines, procedures, and values. Such efforts, though, sometimes wilted in the wartime heat. As with their Regular Army and National Guard counterparts, no two draftee divisions were alike. Those created in 1942 tended to perform better than those activated later because they usually had more time to train before deployment and were less subject to turnover, which preserved unit cohesion. The later ones were sometimes cannibalized or altered not only during training, but also once they arrived overseas in order to maintain veteran outfits that had suffered severe losses. Although the vast majority of these units served in Europe against the Germans and Italians, the army sent five of them to the Pacific.

It is only natural to compare and contrast the battlefield records of the twenty divisions the army mobilized against the Japanese. Doing so provides a better understanding of the war by helping to explain the army's victories and setbacks. There are innumerable factors that influenced each division's combat performance. One is the quality and quantity of the resources available to divisions. A division committed to action that had plenty of ammunition, manpower, rations, artillery, tanks, and so on had an edge over a less endowed opponent and was likely to fight better. Because it took some time for the American economy to provide the army with sufficient tools to wage war effectively, divisions committed to combat early in the conflict were often less successful initially than those subsequently deployed with an abundance of materiel. Similarly, a division with secure supply lines and easy access to resources usually acquired a more impressive reputation than one without strong logistical support. Quantity, in short, had a quality of its own.

There were some factors that affected a division's battlefield performance over which the army often had little control. One was the quality of the enemy. Although the Japanese propensity to fight to the death made them extremely dangerous opponents at all times and under all circumstances, the condition of these Japanese soldiers was relevant. It was easier for American divisions to overcome isolated and starving Japanese troops than well-supplied and well-prepared ones. Moreover, it mattered *when* a division was sent into combat. A division deployed earlier in the war, before the army learned how to fight the Japanese, had a more difficult time than one committed later that benefited from more realistic training, expectations, and preparation. Finally, terrain and geography were important. Divisions maneuvering in open terrain with an adequate road network at their disposal had a better chance of fulfilling their missions than those operating in mountains and jungle in heavy rains, oppressive heat, and bottomless mud. As a result, a good division might struggle more earlier in the conflict in unfavorable terrain and inclement weather against experienced Japanese soldiers than a mediocre division mopping up demoralized and hungry Japanese later in the war.

Experience also played a major role in a division's battlefield performance. Those divisions that had previously seen action had a substantially better chance of achieving their objectives than those that had not. Combat is among the most confusing of human activities. Soldiers under fire must cope with insufficient information, deafening noise, paralyzing fear, shortages, chaos, horrific sights, and inclement weather. They must make split-second decisions upon which lives depend. Functioning well under those circumstances is difficult enough, but collectively there is an exponential increase in the number of things that can go wrong. It is therefore unsurprising that many divisions fought poorly in their first actions. Experience, though, is a first-rate teacher, so most divisions improved considerably as time went on and the surviving soldiers learned from their mistakes. Coordination, planning, logistics, and tactics got better as the troops became increasingly skilled at their tasks. This proficiency continued even after a division sustained enormous losses. Because they were under direct fire, riflemen suffered a disproportionate number of casualties, but the supply officers, staffers, artillerymen, engineers, headquarters personnel, and others operating behind the front lines remained extant and continued to function effectively. Furthermore, enough riflemen survived to pass their hard-won knowledge on to raw replacements. As General George Patton noted, "[T]here is a great difference between an old division, irrespective of the individuals composing it, and a new division. War develops a soul in a fighting unit, and while there may not be many of the old men left, it takes very little yeast to leaven a lump of dough."[5] It is therefore small wonder that the best divisions were almost always among the most experienced.

No one would deny that resources, quality of opposition, geography and terrain, weather conditions, and experience all impacted a division's combat record. However, as far as many officers were concerned, good leadership constituted *the* determining factor in a division's value. Indeed, many believed that the caliber of a division commander was directly proportional to a division's ability to achieve its missions. As General Dwight D. Eisenhower put it:

> I have developed almost an obsession as to the certainty with which you can judge a division, or any other large unit, merely by knowing its commander intimately. Of course, we have had pounded into us all throughout school courses that the exact level of a commander's personality and ability is always reflected in his unit—but I did not realize, until opportunity came for comparisons on a rather large scale, how infallibly the commander and unit are almost one and the same thing.[6]

By this thinking, a good commander could, through personal example and force of character, overcome all reasonable obstacles to fulfill his division's objectives. Quality division leaders might be phlegmatic or energetic, intellectual or common sensical, outgoing or taciturn, self-disciplined or free-wheeling, expressive or self-controlled. However, they all knew what they wanted from their divisions, how to attain it, and could go about it in a way that made it look easy to an outsider. On the other hand, ineffective division commanders failed to manage their divisions in such a way to achieve battlefield victory. There was, in short, a symbiotic relationship between a division and its commander that went a long way in explaining the division's battlefield record.

Leadership was undoubtedly important in molding good combat divisions. However, sometimes even good commanders were unable to subdue organizational culture. Although the army tried to make its divisions as uniform as possible, the reality was that every organization has its own distinct ethos based on its formal and informal rules, traditions, hierarchies, and values. An organization's culture can sometimes help it overcome obstacles such as poor leadership when it aligns with and reinforces its stated goals. On the other hand, organizations become inefficient and dysfunctional when their overt objectives conflict with the informal ones held by many members. It can be extraordinarily difficult for leaders to reform such dysfunctional organizations, even those over which they possess extraordinary power such as military units. This was true of army divisions during World War II. The high turnover rate among division leaders before those outfits deployed overseas made rooting out dysfunction even harder. The result was that no matter how much the army tried to make its divisions interchangeable and efficient, organizational culture inevitably differentiated them from each other for good or ill. Some leaders were able to surmount these differences and problems, but others could not.

Many have criticized the army's performance in World War II. Some of these critics contend that the army only defeated its enemies because of overwhelming materiel superiority. Without its advantages in firepower, air and naval support, and logistics, the low-quality personnel who made up the bulk of the riflemen could never have defeated their opponents because they lacked aggressiveness and initiative. As a result, they did little more than seize ground obliterated beforehand by artillery, naval, and air power. Such comparisons, though, are unfair and misunderstand army doctrine. Army officers designed their divisions to integrate combined arms in cooperation with technology, logistics, firepower, and motorization to destroy the enemy in a short amount of time with minimal casualties. It was a perfectly logical doctrine for a wealthy democratic society fielding a mass-based citizen army with little familiarity with the profession. The army did not need brilliant generals leading elite units to win against overwhelming numbers, but rather competent commanders and battleworthy divisions capable of applying army doctrine in a professional and methodical manner that took full advantage of American power. The fact that the army ground units required less than four years and only approximately 188,000 casualties to defeat the Japanese is evidence of the wisdom of this approach.

Almost all accounts of the army's Pacific War campaigns mention its combat divisions. After all, the divisions were the pieces that theater, field army, and corps commanders deployed and maneuvered around the Pacific's geostrategic chessboard to battle and defeat the Japanese. The army may have wanted its divisions to be interchangeable and uniform, but this proved impossible. Their quality and performance depended upon their resources, the geography and terrain on which they fought, experience, leadership, and organizational culture. Historians, though, have made little effort to examine their records in a systematic way. Almost all of the army's divisions, some after admittedly rocky starts, became units capable of winning their engagements. Indeed, not a single army division fighting the Japanese during the American counteroffensive across the Pacific was completely destroyed in combat. Whatever problems these divisions faced tended to grow out of the society that produced them, not fundamental flaws in army doctrine. This is a tribute to the army as a whole and to the twenty divisions that the army deployed against the Japanese.

CHAPTER ONE

South Pacific Maelstrom

An Enormous and Complicated Arena of War

The Pacific War against Japan was unlike any conflict the American military had ever fought. The United States had dispatched large military forces overseas before, and would again, but in this instance the conflict's dimensions were beyond anything army and navy officers had ever previously contemplated. For one thing, the distances involved were staggering. The Pacific Ocean was enormous, encompassing 63.8 million square miles, or twenty times the size of the continental United States. It was in fact larger than the landmass of all the continents combined, and covered almost a third of the globe's surface. It was 2,400 miles from San Francisco to Honolulu, and from there another 5,300 miles to Manila, 5,500 miles to Melbourne, 3,850 miles to Tokyo, and 6,700 miles to Singapore. During the war it took weeks for ships to cross the Pacific, and even flights over the trackless ocean required days of hopping from one rudimentary island-bound airfield to another. Small wonder so many servicemen compared their voyage across the Pacific to journeying to the very ends of the planet. If technology was shrinking the earth, it still had a ways to go to make the Pacific seem anything other than huge and intimidating.

The Pacific's prewar cultural and physical geography was as expansive as its size. Approximately 30,000 islands dotted the ocean and varied in magnitude from tiny unnamed stadium-sized atolls to gigantic New Guinea, which was larger than Texas. Most were part of island chains that could stretch for hundreds of miles. The climate was equally diverse. The North Pacific's Aleutian Islands were cold, foggy, and mountainous. The Central Pacific, on the other hand, was full of balmy flat barren atolls surrounded by dangerous coral reefs. As for the South Pacific, it contained steamy jungle-covered mountainous islands riddled with exotic animals and deadly

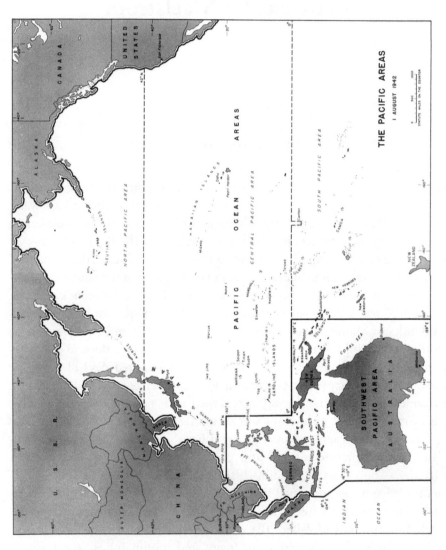

The Pacific Theater

diseases. Finally, the western Pacific possessed millions of inhabitants living in the thousands of islands that constituted the Philippines archipelago and the vast Dutch East Indies. Culturally, the Pacific Ocean's indigenous population of Melanesians, Polynesians, and Micronesians was augmented by Chinese, Japanese, Americans, and others who had filtered in during the nineteenth and early twentieth centuries. Most of these native peoples lived in small villages before the war, but there were a few larger cities as well. The local population, though, usually possessed little political power because the Japanese, Americans, and Europeans had occupied the Pacific Ocean islands as part of the turn-of-the-century empire-building scramble.

In part because of its enormous size, the Pacific during World War II was one of the world's most primitive areas. Most of the islands over which the Japanese and Americans fought possessed little or no infrastructure. There were few railroads, port facilities, airfields, power plants, warehouses, and all the other accoutrements that a modern army needed to wage war effectively. This meant that the army had to bring or build its own supply network while simultaneously fighting the Japanese. That it succeeded in doing so in such a short time was a tribute to the army's logistical prowess and played no small role in its victory over Japan. Once it had transformed these islands into suitable military bases, the army used them to project its power to the next target. For the soldiers stationed on these islands, though, life when not in combat was usually a monotonous routine bereft of women, alcohol, and other luxuries to which they had been accustomed back home. However, this was preferable to the nightmarish living conditions that prevailed at the front.

For American GIs, the Pacific War's primitive living conditions, hostile and unfamiliar terrain, and daunting distances were bad enough, but their baffling, tenacious, and formidable enemy could make life downright terrifying. Indeed, Japanese soldiers were so culturally alien as to seem almost unearthly. Weaned in a society that valued conformity and harmony, inculcated with a bushido warrior code that saw surrender as dishonorable, and led by a fascistic government convinced of Japan's imperial destiny, Japanese troops routinely conducted unspeakable atrocities and fought to the death on even the most remote and strategically insignificant islands. Because of this ethos, Pacific War engagements often degenerated into grueling battles of attrition in which neither side gave or expected quarter. Cruelty and barbarism toward the enemy, while never officially condoned by the army, was commonplace. Even mopping up operations were dangerous because surrounded Japanese soldiers would not be rounded up and imprisoned, but rather had to be hunted down and killed. It was an environment tailor-made for racist assumptions and stereotyping by both sides. Small wonder so many GIs dehumanized the Japanese and treated them as little more than vicious and dangerous animals to be exterminated. This inherent brutality contributed to the otherworldly and desperate nature of the conflict.

Because it invested the bulk of Allied resources toward defeating Japan, the United States determined Pacific War strategy. The chief difficulty the American military had in formulating its plans for waging the conflict was therefore not *international*, but rather *interservice*. The problem was that the army and navy were independent and co-equal branches of the American military, meaning that neither could boss the other around. Only the president as commander in chief had authority over both services. Like the army, the navy had its own traditions, culture, and doctrine. It even had its own army: the Marine Corps. Unfortunately, but unsurprisingly, army and navy officers did not always see eye to eye on the best way to prosecute the war against Japan. In an effort to facilitate interservice coordination, at the conflict's start the two branches established the Joint Chiefs of Staff (JCS). The JCS consisted of four members, two from each branch: army chief of staff General George C. Marshall, Army Air Forces commander General Henry H. Arnold, navy chief of naval operations Admiral Ernest J. King, and retired chief of naval operations Admiral William D. Leahy. It had no statutory authority and made decisions by consensus, so no one member could compel the others to do anything. This might ordinarily have been a recipe for irresolution and obstruction, but during the war the JCS had a powerful incentive to come to decisions acceptable to all: President Franklin Roosevelt. If the Joint Chiefs failed to reach an agreement, their only recourse was to appeal to the unpredictable Roosevelt, whose strategic judgment all four members of the JCS distrusted. The upshot was that the Joint Chiefs had to go along to get along, and that basic truth provided sufficient motivation for the army and navy to cooperate effectively in making the compromises necessary to wage the Pacific War.

Preserving interservice relations sometimes came at the expense of sound military strategy. This unhappy reality manifested itself numerous times during the Pacific War, starting with the organization of geographic theaters for the conflict. In March 1942, the Combined Chiefs of Staff—a high-level Anglo-American committee composed of the JCS and its British counterpart that met periodically to develop Anglo-American grand strategy—agreed that the United States would control the Pacific War. Instead of creating one big theater out of the Pacific under one person's authority, the JCS divided it into two theaters, one led by a navy admiral and the other by an army general. The JCS assigned Admiral Chester W. Nimitz the head of the Pacific Ocean Areas (POA), which encompassed subordinate commands in the north, central, and south Pacific. To oversee the Southwest Pacific Area (SWPA), the JCS appointed General Douglas MacArthur. His purview included Australia, New Guinea, the Philippines, and all of the Dutch East Indies except for the island of Sumatra. Both theaters contained significant army and navy assets, but the navy dominated the former and the army the latter. Separating the Pacific into two theaters dispersed American resources, amplified inefficiencies, increased coordination problems, and complicated strategy, but it also maintained interservice harmony by giving each branch its own arena from which to prosecute the war more or less on its own terms and based on its own doctrine. It worked well enough in the end in large part because MacArthur and Nimitz obeyed JCS directives to get along, but there was nothing easy or inevitable about it.

Guadalcanal

Japan's surprise assault on the American naval base at Pearl Harbor, Hawaii, on 7 December 1941 was merely one part of its multifaceted offensive against British, Dutch, and American possessions throughout the Pacific and East Asia designed to establish a self-sufficient empire. By crippling the main American fleet at Pearl Harbor, the Japanese opened up the entire Pacific to attack. In subsequent weeks and months, the Japanese outmaneuvered and overwhelmed the stunned Allies in a series of well-coordinated and rapid operations. One by one, the Philippines, Dutch East Indies, Malaya and Singapore, Hong Kong, Burma, and innumerable Pacific islands fell to the Japanese onslaught. The Japanese navy ranged throughout the Pacific and into the Indian Ocean, crushing all opposition it encountered. Japanese soldiers repeatedly emerged victorious in their battles with their disorganized opponents. Eighty thousand British empire troops surrendered at Singapore in February 1942, followed two months later by an additional 78,000 Americans and Filipinos at Bataan on the Philippine island of Luzon. The Japanese added all this newly acquired territory to an extensive empire that already included their Home Islands, Manchuria, much of eastern China, Indochina, Formosa, and scattered islands in the Pacific. Indeed, by May 1942, the Japanese controlled a quarter of the world's surface and had defeated the Allies in almost every engagement. It was an impressive achievement for a nation which had less than a century earlier been isolated and technologically backwards.

Unfortunately for the Japanese, their free rein in the Pacific came to an abrupt and disastrous end at the hands of a surprisingly resilient American navy. In early May, an American naval task force thwarted a Japanese attempt to seize Port Moresby in New Guinea at the Battle of Coral Sea. Although the Japanese inflicted more damage than they sustained, they turned tactical victory into strategic defeat by retreating. Then, in an effort to tempt the remainder of the American navy into a decisive battle, the Japanese targeted Midway Island, 1,100 miles west of Hawaii. American intelligence discerned Japanese intentions, enabling the American navy to ambush the unsuspecting Japanese fleet in a brouhaha in which luck played more than a small role in American victory. By the time the four-day Battle of Midway ended on 7 June, the cream of the Japanese navy, including four aircraft carriers, 250 planes, and 3,000 personnel, was at the bottom of the ocean. American losses, for their part, amounted to one carrier, 150 planes, and 300 airmen and sailors. This crushing defeat turned the war's tide by costing the Japanese the strategic initiative.

The navy may have blunted the Japanese offensive at Coral Sea and Midway, but the army had not been idle during this time. Even before the United States entered the conflict, American and British policymakers had agreed that defeating Germany should be their top priority, with everything else, including Japan, a secondary concern. Japan's initial stunning successes, however, compelled the War Department to divert more resources to the Pacific than it had intended. The old Hawaii Division had been triangularized before the Japanese attacked Pearl Harbor, and out of it the army, on 1 October 1941, created two new divisions, the 24th and 25th. Both were available to protect Oahu and Pearl Harbor. Two National Guard regiments, dubbed Task Force 6814, disembarked at New Caledonia in March 1942. Another National Guard outfit, the 27th Division, arrived in Hawaii on 21 May to defend its Outer Islands. As part of a deal with the British and Australians to keep Australian troops in the Middle East, the army dispatched two National Guard divisions to Down Under. The 41st reached Melbourne in April–May and the 32nd followed a month later at Port Adelaide. Finally, the 37th Division put ashore on Fiji Island in June. None of these units was by any stretch of the imagination ready for combat, but it was the best the army could do for now.

After losing the Battle of Midway, the Japanese decided to round out and consolidate their empire to better resist any American counteroffensive. Doing so may have meant surrendering the strategic initiative to the United States, but the Japanese figured that the Americans lacked the collective will to wrest away all the territory protecting their Home Islands. As part of this

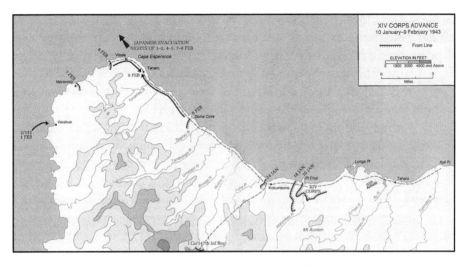

The Guadalcanal Campaign, August 1942–February 1943.

new strategy, the Japanese hurriedly secured their partial grip over the Solomon Islands. Located east of New Guinea in the South Pacific, the Solomons were a chain of six major and some 900 smaller islands that stretched 930 miles from northwest to southeast. The Japanese had started the process of occupying them even before the Battle of Coral Sea. On 3 May 1942, they landed on the small island of Tulagi and then, in July, crossed over Sealark Channel to Lunga Point on Guadalcanal and began constructing an airfield there. At ninety miles long and twenty-five miles wide, Guadalcanal was the second largest island in the Solomons, with jungle-covered mountains up to 8,000 feet high. It was not worth much strategically, at least not until the Japanese commenced building their airfield there which would, when and if completed, enable them to project their power southward and eastward to threaten the supply and communication links between Australia and the United States.

Ernest King, the navy's hard-bitten and irascible chief of naval operations, certainly saw it that way. He did not want to surrender the strategic initiative that his sailors had so decisively grabbed at Midway, so he was open to any opportunity to assume the offensive. Japanese airfield construction on Guadalcanal alarmed him so much that he wanted to launch a counterattack as soon as possible to reclaim the island. However, because defeating Germany was its top priority, the army was investing its limited resources in its upcoming invasion of French North Africa. King therefore decided that if the army was unwilling to take the lead on Guadalcanal, the navy would. He persuaded the JCS to authorize a navy-dominated operation against the island with

General Alexander Archer Vandegrift's 1st Marine Division, and to readjust theater boundaries to put Guadalcanal in Nimitz's POA. After hurried and slapdash preparations, the Marines landed on Guadalcanal and nearby Tulagi on 7 August. They easily scattered Japanese construction crews and seized the airfield the next day, but had to fight a fierce three-day battle to overcome and obliterate those enemy troops dug in on tiny Tulagi.

The Marine landing on Guadalcanal provoked a furious Japanese response. Indeed, the island quickly became a vortex that sucked in Japanese and American resources from across the Pacific. For six months the Japanese and American navies slugged it out in the waters around Guadalcanal, the former to sever and the latter to maintain the Marines' tenuous communication and supply lines to the island. These confused and vicious engagements included all varieties of ships from submarines and patrol boats to battleships and aircraft carriers. Because they could more easily replace their losses, the Americans gradually gained the upper hand through painful trial and error. On land, Vandegrift decided that he lacked the resources to occupy all of Guadalcanal, so he concentrated his leathernecks on protecting the only piece of real estate that mattered: the newly named Henderson Airfield. By doing so, however, he made it possible for the Japanese to land troops elsewhere on the island who could assail the Marines defending the airfield. Happily for the Americans, the Japanese repeatedly underestimated Marine strength and determination, so their ferocious but piecemeal attacks broke down in the face of Marine firepower. Despite these successes, there was nothing easy about the Marines' ordeal. They were periodically cut off and isolated from outside assistance, exposed to Japanese naval and air bombardment, and subject to disease and awful living conditions. By late October, the outcome of the campaign remained in serious doubt.

Marine Corps units lacked the logistical support for prolonged combat because they were designed for short and violent amphibious assaults. As a result, by late September the 1st Marine Division was so exhausted from casualties and disease—especially malaria—that Vandegrift suggested withdrawing the outfit. The problem was not only getting replacements and reinforcements past the Japanese navy to Guadalcanal, but also finding them in the first place. Although the Marines planned to commit their 2nd Marine Division to Guadalcanal, one of its regiments had been attached to the 1st Marine Division since the operation began and was just as depleted as the rest of that outfit. Besides, an understrength Marine division did not possess the combat power needed to drive the approximately 25,000 Japanese troops off the island. It was increasingly obvious that only the army could do that. In early October, the commander of all army forces in the South Pacific, General Millard F. Harmon, recommended deploying an army regiment from New Caledonia to reinforce the beleaguered Marines. The new head of the South Pacific Area (SOPAC), Admiral William F. Halsey, Jr., liked the idea and provided the shipping necessary to bring the 164th Regiment to Guadalcanal on 13 October. The arrival of the 43rd Division at New Caledonia and growing American naval and air power in the region soon made it possible to deploy more soldiers to Guadalcanal. On 12 November, the 182nd Regiment disembarked there, followed by the 132nd Regiment on 8 December. All three regiments were part of one of the army's strangest divisions: The Americal.

Within a month after the Japanese attacked Pearl Harbor, the army hastily dispatched two National Guard regiments, later joined by a third, to occupy the French island of New Caledonia in the South Pacific. They arrived in mid-March after a stopover in Australia. All three regiments—one each from North Dakota, Illinois, and Massachusetts—were leftovers from the army's ongoing triangularization transformation of its divisions. Spare, ascetic, and enigmatic General Alexander M. Patch led the force and proved proficient at handling the touchy French officials with whom he dealt. In May, the War Department decided to organize the three regiments into a new division. For whatever reason, though, it did not assign it a number, but instead suggested "Necal," the then codename for New Caledonia, to Patch. Patch countered with "Bush Division," but, perhaps recognizing that nomenclature was not his forte, he asked the new division's personnel for recommendations. One private suggested "Americal," an amalgamation of "American" and "New Caledonia," and the name stuck. After the conflict, the War Department attempted to redesignate it as the 23rd Division, but it did not take. A year later, the Americal adopted as its official patch a representation of the Southern Cross of four white stars on a blue background to mark its exotic origins. In addition to its peculiar nonordinal name, the Americal Division was also unique in that it was the only army division created outside of American territory during the conflict. Although Patch initially lacked sufficient equipment, weapons, and personnel, he succeeded in breathing life into his new outfit. The division moved to Guadalcanal gradually as shipping became available, one regiment at a time, with the last departing at the end of the year. The division got off to a good start when its 164th Regiment helped the Marines repel the climactic Japanese assault on Henderson Airfield on 24–26 October. Although the Marines were thankful for the timely assistance, this gratitude did not prevent them from robbing the soldiers blind in the following weeks.[1]

The army and Marine Corps spent the rest of the year attempting to expand their defensive perimeter far enough to stop Japanese artillery from hitting the all-important airstrip. The key to doing so was Mount Austen, located about six miles southwest of Henderson Field. At 1,500 feet tall, the mountain was actually a series of jungle-covered heights in the area on which the Japanese had deployed their guns. Unfortunately, soldiers and leathernecks soon learned that assuming the offensive was more complicated and difficult than fighting from behind fortifications. An army-Marine attack on the Japanese army headquarters at Kokumbona, on the coast nine miles west of Henderson Airfield, failed in mid-November. One Marine officer monitoring the action recalled:

> After about a day, I discovered that the operation was going very poorly. I got in a jeep and went out there, beyond the Matanikau [River], went up with the 182nd Infantry [Regiment] which was supposed to be attacking …. There weren't any officers around. But I went on back to Patch's headquarters, and I told him that … and he was very downcast, and he said, "I realize that that regiment that I have up there's not doing well."[2]

Then Americal Division troops pushing toward Mount Austen in mid-December ran afoul of a Japanese strongpoint called Gifu that they were unable to completely overcome. Navigating, coordinating, maneuvering, and supplying their men through the jungle, often under fire, proved too much for some battalion commanders. Three weeks of combat around the mountain cost the Americal Division's 132nd Regiment alone nearly 400 casualties. Discouraged by his division's performance and cognizant of the impact of disease on his men, Patch decided to suspend operations until more reinforcements arrived. It was hardly an auspicious offensive debut for the Americal Division.[3]

The new year brought important changes to Guadalcanal. On 2 January 1943, Patch activated and assumed command of the new XIV Corps, which would henceforth oversee what now became an army-directed campaign. Patch's former chief of staff, General Edmund B. Sebree, replaced Patch at the head of the Americal Division. Although the 1st Marine Division had left Guadalcanal for Australia on 8 December and the Americal Division was severely understrength due to casualties and disease, reinforcements were on their way. The 2nd Marine Division arrived in early January, at about the same time as the 25th Division finished deploying to the island.

The 25th Division was one of the two divisions created out of the old Hawaiian Division. Two of its regiments were Regular Army, but the third, the 161st, was based on the Washington State National Guard. Because the Hawaiian Division had a reputation as a second-rate outfit, there was reason to believe that the 25th might go the same way. That it did not was due in large part to its second commander, General J. Lawton Collins. Brash, energetic, focused, and smart, Collins gave his undivided attention to whipping the 25th Division into shape. Considering his breezy self-assuredness, it was unsurprising that Collins soon boasted that he led the best division in the army. Collins was hardly an objective observer, but others agreed, including POA chief Chester Nimitz. Indeed, when Nimitz learned that the Joint Chiefs were thinking about sending the 25th Division to Australia to serve in MacArthur's SWPA theater, he told Collins, "You have too good of a division and I'm not going to let you get out of my control."⁴ Nimitz subsequently prevailed upon the JCS and MacArthur to swap the 25th Division for the 1st Marine Division. With that flank secured, in November–December 1942 Nimitz sent the division to Guadalcanal via New Caledonia and Fiji. When Collins arrived at the New Caledonian capital of Noumea, he bragged to the head of SOPAC, William Halsey, that his division would be ready for action anywhere as soon as it had a few weeks to get combat loaded. Halsey smiled and told Collins that he was dispatching the 25th Division to Guadalcanal the very next day. As things turned out, it took several weeks to get the entire division to the island, but by early January it was on hand and ready to go.⁵

These reinforcements gave Patch 50,000 soldiers and Marines in more than three divisions—the 2nd Marine, the Americal, the 25th, and the army's independent 147th Regiment—with which to undertake a full-scale offensive to destroy the Japanese on Guadalcanal. On 10 January 1943, Patch sent the 25th Division to mop up the Mount Austen area while the 2nd Marine Division advanced westward along the coast to Kokumbona. As for the Americal Division, Patch left it behind to guard Henderson Airfield. Collins' soldiers spent the next two weeks in heavy combat methodically taking apart the Japanese defenses at Gifu, Mount Austen, and a group of hills dubbed the Galloping Horse. When the Marines encountered stiff opposition, Patch pulled them out and replaced them with a bizarre ad hoc outfit dubbed the Composite Army-Marine (CAM) Division composed of the 6th Marine Regiment, the Americal's 182nd Regiment, and the independent 147th Regiment to pick up where the 2nd Marine Division had left off. By the time Patch renewed his offensive on 22 January, the Japanese had decided to evacuate their troops from the island. Even so, their rear guard fought hard to buy time for their comrades to get away. Attacking to the northwest, one of the 25th Division's regiments found a gap in the Japanese line that Collins rapidly exploited to trap 1,000 Japanese in and around Kokumbona. That village fell on 23 January, at which point the CAM Division took the lead in marching westward to Cape Esperance, where the Japanese were extracting their remaining soldiers. Meanwhile, the rest of the XIV Corps stayed in position to guard against a renewed Japanese assault on Henderson Airfield that Patch mistakenly believed was in the offing. When the Americans reached Cape Esperance on 9 February, the Japanese were gone.

The Guadalcanal campaign was a crushing defeat for the Japanese not so much because they failed to secure the island, but rather because of the enormous resources they expended in their unsuccessful efforts to do so. By challenging the Marine landing, the Japanese instigated a brutal six-month-long war of attrition that cost them more than they could afford. Of the 36,000 Japanese soldiers committed to Guadalcanal, 14,800 were killed in action, another 9,000 died of disease, and 1,000 were captured. Only 10,600 escaped to fight another day. The Americans, for their part, dispatched about 60,000 troops to the island, of whom 1,600 were killed and 4,245 wounded, mostly Marines. The Americal and 25th Divisions suffered 1,200 and 655 casualties, respectively. Both sides also lost twenty-four warships and around 600 planes. The big difference, though, was that the Americans could more easily afford to replace their men and materiel than the Japanese. The American victory secured Australia's communication and supply lines to the United States, provided a base for further offensives in the Solomons, and gave two army and two Marine divisions valuable combat experience that they put to good use in subsequent operations.

The Marine Corps then and later garnered an outsized amount of credit for victory at Guadalcanal. After all, it was the 1st Marine Division that seized and tenaciously held onto Henderson Airfield for three long lonely months despite ferocious Japanese opposition, debilitating disease, and erratic logistical support. Even so, it was primarily the army that finally drove the Japanese from the island. Those who recognized the army's contribution were quick to give credit to the Americal and 25th Divisions for jobs well done. George Marshall, for instance, later praised both divisions for their efforts. Patch felt the same way. A closer look, though, presents a more complicated picture. It is hard to criticize the green 25th Division's performance. Led by the dynamic Collins, the 25th provided the Sunday punch that broke the back of Japanese resistance on the island. It was the 25th that finally occupied all of Mount Austen, that overcame the Galloping Horse, and that unlocked the door to seize Kokumbona. It fought professionally, skillfully, and creatively by, for example, using time on target fire support so that shells from many artillery pieces exploded simultaneously over enemy positions. As Nimitz put it, "It was largely through the sustained drive of the 25th Infantry Division that the last vestige of organized resistance on Guadalcanal was crushed and possession of this strategically important island, so vital to projected operations, was finally wrested from the hands of the Japanese."[6] Subsequent historians echoed this positive view. Eric Bergerud, for instance, noted, "Yet the 25th dismantled the Japanese wherever it faced them. A mountain of supplies and great firepower are not worth much if a unit does not know how to use them. The 25th knew the craft of war very well."[7] It was, in short, an impressive debut for an inexperienced division plunged so violently into Pacific War combat, one that earned the outfit its new nickname, "Tropic Lightning."[8]

On the other hand, the Americal Division's performance left something to be desired. Although the 164th Regiment earned kudos for assisting the Marines in repulsing the last big Japanese assault on Henderson Airfield, the division had a more difficult time in an offensive role. Its efforts to expand the American perimeter around the airfield and to seize Mount Austen sputtered out. Indeed, from that point on Patch deployed the bulk of the division on the defensive guarding Henderson Airfield while relying on the 25th Division to do the heavy lifting necessary to drive the Japanese from the island. In the warm afterglow of victory, it was easy to gloss over the division's difficulties and focus on the positive. Even Marine observers downplayed the division's problems. The fact was, though, that the Americal failed in its first offensive mission. In the division's defense, it is hardly surprising that three different National Guard regiments from three different states hastily thrown together and organized on a remote island would not fight as skillfully as a well-trained Regular Army division such as the 25th. It is also important to remember that those Japanese troops the Americal Division confronted in November–December 1942 were fresher and more determined than those Collins' soldiers faced shortly thereafter. As things turned out, the Americal Division's lackluster response to its baptism of fire proved more common in the Pacific than the 25th Division's impressive debut.

Crawling Up New Guinea

At about the same time that the Japanese landed on Guadalcanal and began construction of the airfield there, other Japanese soldiers splashed ashore at Buna–Gona on Papua New Guinea's northern shore. As with Guadalcanal, this invasion was intended to round out and consolidate Japan's empire after its naval defeat at the Battle of Midway. Although Buna–Gona was the Japanese army's immediate target, its real objective was Port Moresby. Located on New Guinea's southern coast about 100 miles from Buna–Gona, Port Moresby was the nexus of nascent Allied operations on the big island. Seizing the town would in effect deny New Guinea to the Allies and go a long way toward securing Japan's defensive perimeter. The Japanese had attempted to take Port Moresby the previous May in a seaborne operation that foundered at the Battle of Coral Sea. This time, though, the Japanese planned to march overland across the formidable Owen Stanley Mountains via the primitive Kokoda Track to storm Port Moresby from that direction. Their approximately 6,000 soldiers pushed southward against increasingly stubborn Australian resistance until halted in late September at Ioribaiwa, about twenty-five miles from Port Moresby. Deprivation and disease, as well as growing Australian opposition, forced the Japanese to retreat back to their starting point. Less than 1,000 of them made it back to Buna–Gona, where they joined their comrades, dug themselves in, and awaited the Allies' next move.

The Australians may have been the ones who stopped the Japanese assault on Port Moresby, but they did not determine regional strategy. That was the purview of the SWPA commander, General Douglas MacArthur. MacArthur had led American and Filipino troops in East Asia when the war began. His ill-equipped and undertrained army failed to halt the Japanese invasion of the Philippines that began in earnest several weeks after Pearl Harbor. Instead, the Japanese drove MacArthur's soldiers southward in disarray to the Bataan Peninsula near the Philippine capital of Manila. President Roosevelt thwarted MacArthur's plan to stay there and share the fate of his 80,000 soldiers by ordering him, his family, and selected staff members to leave, so MacArthur was not on hand to see his men surrender on 10 April 1942. Instead, he was in Australia, from where he promised to return to the Philippines to free the archipelago from Japanese control. As commander of the newly organized Southwest Pacific Area theater, he pursued the Philippines' liberation with a single-minded determination bordering on obsession. Egotistical, charismatic, intelligent, and absolutely certain of himself and his opinions, MacArthur jealously guarded his prerogatives. Whatever his less admirable traits, no one doubted MacArthur's decisiveness and initiative. As far as he was concerned, the best place from which to defend Australia was in New Guinea. That being the case, he decided to commit American ground troops to the island, first in a defensive role and then, when the Japanese threat to Port Moresby receded, to seize Buna–Gona as a springboard for further operations up the Papua New Guinea coast toward the big Japanese base of Rabaul on New Britain Island.

MacArthur had at his disposal in Australia two American army divisions, the 32nd and 41st, available for deployment to New Guinea. Unfortunately, he lacked the logistical wherewithal to send both of them. He left the decision as to which one to use to his I Corps commander, General Robert L. Eichelberger. Eichelberger was a genial, glib, gossipy, and intelligent man perfectly at home in a comfortable headquarters or a primitive command post. Although Eichelberger believed that the 41st was the better trained outfit, he picked the 32nd because it would eventually have to move from its inadequate camp near Brisbane anyway. The 32nd Division, built out of the Michigan and Wisconsin National Guards, was referred to as the Red Arrow Division and had earned a good reputation in World War I. Federalized in October 1940, it had originally been slated to go to Europe, but at the last minute the War Department dispatched it to the Pacific instead. It had been led by General Edwin Forrest Harding since the previous March.[9]

Eichelberger's selection of the 32nd Division was not based on confidence in the unit. In fact, after preliminary inspections, he and his staff had concluded that the 32nd was unready for action, and Eichelberger had given the division a barely satisfactory rating for combat efficiency in his report. The reality was that the 32nd Division had all the problems common to National Guard units, as well as some unique ones of its own. Many of its line officers included men who got their positions for reasons other than competency, and its staff work was sloppy. The division had not been trained in jungle warfare and lacked the weapons and equipment needed for that kind of fighting. Although it had required 8,000 draftees to bring it up to par when stateside, it was still understrength even before it left Australia. As Eichelberger later put it, "All the sins of poorly trained troops came to the front during this campaign."[10] The one thing the 32nd Division officers and men did possess, according to many outside observers, was plenty of misplaced confidence in themselves. By any objective measurement, they were not prepared to engage the Japanese. MacArthur, though, was in a hurry to stop the Japanese, seize the initiative, and assume the offensive, so he brushed aside Eichelberger's warnings and ordered the division sent to New Guinea.[11]

Two of the 32nd Division's regiments, the 126th and 128th, deployed to New Guinea by boat and plane in late September, just as the Japanese offensive toward Port Moresby sputtered to a halt. Eager to capitalize on this good fortune, MacArthur approved of plans to swing the two regiments around the left flank of the retreating Japanese to strike Buna while the Australians pursued the enemy along the Kokoda Trail. Although some of the American units marched overland, most went by air and sea. Getting all these pieces in place took time, though, and stretched SWPA logistics to the breaking point. Worse yet, exhaustion and disease—especially dysentery and malaria—thinned out the ranks of the Red Arrow soldiers even before they

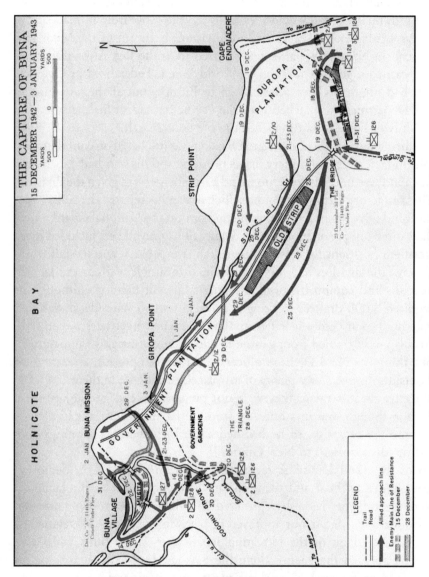

Battle of Buna–Gona, November 1942–January 1943.

engaged the Japanese in earnest. Allied troops were not in position to assail Buna–Gona until mid-November, with the Americans facing Buna and the Australian 7th Division before Gona.

As the Australian diggers and American GIs were about to discover, Buna–Gona was an awful place for a battle. Dense jungle, coconut groves, waist-deep mangrove swamps, swift-moving streams, and an occasional open field full of razer-sharp kunai grass dotted the area. Dry ground was rare, roads even more so, and visibility was almost zero. There were also plenty of insects around, especially malaria-carrying mosquitoes, to make life miserable for everyone. The rainy season had not yet arrived, but the humidity remained oppressive. Merely subsisting was difficult enough before the approximately 6,500 Japanese there got busy turning the place into a fortress. Their defensive line was around eleven miles long, but centered on three strongholds at Buna, Sanananda, and Gona. To defend themselves, the Japanese built dozens of camouflaged bunkers made of coconut logs and sand-filled barrels that were almost impervious to anything short of direct artillery fire. These bunkers, next to impossible to spot from any distance, were mutually supporting with interlocking fields of fire, and were placed to channel attacking American and Australian troops into deadly cul-de-sacs. It would be difficult to conceive of a tougher assignment for the inexperienced Red Arrow soldiers.

The American attack on Buna began on 19 November and immediately ran into trouble. Japanese resistance proved far more formidable than expected. Many of those soldiers not cut down by Japanese fire froze and refused to advance. Snipers seemed everywhere and nowhere. Even when the GIs were able to locate Japanese bunkers, they lacked the heavy weapons they needed to destroy them. Many officers demonstrated little initiative and lost control of units that soon became hopelessly intermixed. The rickety logistical system broke down to the point that soldiers ran short of food. Disease spread, and eventually almost everyone had malaria to one degree or another. No one doubted Harding's conscientiousness, but he seemed unwilling to relieve substandard commanders or really take control of the battle. Within a couple weeks the division's battalions were at half strength. One officer remembered, "The Allied troops were no longer fresh. Heat, humidity, mud, and disease had taken a heavy toll. In jungle fighting nature is against the weary. Malaria, dengue fever, and dysentery were prevalent …. Supply was inadequate. Meals were down to two a day, and meager at that. Platoons and companies were mixed with other units of different commands. Morale was low."[12] Australian observers were soon sending back discouraging and disparaging reports about the performance of American GIs to an increasingly disheartened, frustrated, and angry MacArthur.[13]

In an effort to retrieve the deteriorating situation in which the 32nd Division found itself, MacArthur dispatched to Buna his I Corps commander, Robert Eichelberger, with orders to take charge of the situation. To underscore his seriousness, MacArthur told Eichelberger to seize Buna or not return alive. Eichelberger arrived on 1 December and toured the lines with Harding. As far as Eichelberger could tell, the Red Arrow boys were in deplorable shape physically and psychologically, for which he blamed the division's leadership, starting at the top. Eichelberger concluded that Harding was not sufficiently ruthless in weeding out incompetent subordinates, so he relieved him. He also visited the front frequently, disentangled units, bolstered morale, and improved logistics. One Australian general remembered Eichelberger's arrival as "a very pure breath of fresh air [that] blew away a great deal of the impurities that were stopping us [from] getting on with the job."[14]

Unfortunately, Eichelberger's 5 December offensive met with limited success, though it gave him a more empathetic view of the 32nd Division's plight and obstacles. Despite the enormous pressure MacArthur was exerting on him to wrap up the operation, Eichelberger thereupon decided on a more methodical, albeit slower, approach to the battle. His new tactics were facilitated by the arrival of tanks, heavy artillery, and reinforcements in the form of the 32nd Division's 127th Regiment. In addition, the Japanese were growing weaker due to a dwindling supply of food, ammunition, and hope of rescue. Finally, the Red Arrow Division's GIs were learning through trial and error how to fight effectively. Coordination at all levels improved and officers settled into their roles. Although it took an additional month, the 32nd Division succeeded in grinding down and snuffing out the last Japanese defenders at Buna on 2 January 1943.

Although MacArthur's headquarters claimed otherwise, Buna's fall did not end the campaign. The Australians had seized Gona on 9 December, but Sanananda continued to hold out against their forces. Elements of the exhausted 32nd Division, as well as the 41st Division's 163rd Regiment, gradually joined the battle that shared all the characteristics of the fight at Buna, except that if anything the Japanese defenses at Sanananda were even more daunting. Here, too, superior Allied firepower and logistics carried the day. The last organized Japanese resistance ended in mid-January, though mopping up continued for another week.

Buna–Gona was celebrated as the first major Allied victory over the Japanese army. In addition to its symbolic value, Buna–Gona terminated Japanese offensive hopes in New Guinea and gave the Allies a base on the island's north coast from which to advance toward the big Japanese stronghold at

Rabaul. The cost of victory, though, was unexpectedly high. Defeating 6,500 Japanese troops required the Americans and Australians to commit more than two divisions. The 32nd Division lost almost 10,000 soldiers, of whom 2,620 were battle casualties and the remainder due to disease and accidents. The 41st Division's 163rd Regiment added 229 battle and 584 nonbattle casualties to the list. Australian losses in dead and wounded approximated 2,000 men. This was quite the butcher's bill for a piece of New Guinea real estate that no one had heard of six months previously and a sobering introduction to the sacrifices that the Japanese were willing to make to defend even the most remote parts of their newly acquired empire.

The 32nd Division may have won at Buna, but it did not look that way when it returned to Brisbane in January–February 1943 for rest and rehabilitation. The division had not only suffered heavy losses, but was also wounded psychologically and reputationally. Morale was shot and equipment in need of repair. Indeed, some observers wondered whether it was even possible to re-fit the outfit to return to combat. The new division commander, General William Gill, remembered:

> I began to rebuild but I didn't have much to go on. The men were there—it's an odd sort of a thing to say, I suppose, but actually—they were only part men. After Buna their morale was low, their equipment was low, many were sick with malaria, and they didn't know which way to turn. They didn't know who I was until I told them …. That was a very serious time, of course, but a very important one. The importance of preparations and plans and the execution of those plans in the reorganization of that broken-down [32nd] division can't be overstressed. It was very evident to me that a complete reorganization had to take place. By that, I mean not only the division as a whole had to be reorganized, but each of the smaller elements had to be tended to and made ready to go back into combat some day. That had to be done very carefully, because you were dealing with people: dealing with soldiers, dealing with officers, many of whom were sick and disheartened. It had to be definite; it had to be sympathetic; it had to be intelligently applied, this reorganization business. You could not do it over night; it took a long time to do it—a little bit at a time.[15]

Fortunately for the 32nd Division, it had plenty of time to recover from its Buna ordeal. Reconstituting the division was a gradual process that took a year, and was by no means an easy one. Recurrent malaria proved especially difficult to eradicate. Gill, however, was fortunate to have MacArthur's and Eichelberger's support, patience, and understanding. By July 1943, Eichelberger wrote the new Sixth Army commander, General Walter Krueger, that the 32nd was doing well.[16]

The reputational damage that the 32nd Division suffered at Buna was less susceptible to repair. Although the Red Arrow boys had won the battle, many focused on the difficulties they encountered in doing so. These included

MacArthur, who never understood the 32nd Division's Buna ordeal and never completely trusted it again. Indeed, he disparaged it on at least one occasion in front of other officers long after the division had proven itself in subsequent operations. In fact, the 32nd Division's woes at Buna were hardly uncommon for a National Guard outfit engaged in combat for the first time. The differences were that the 32nd faced a stronger enemy than usual without the typical logistical advantages available to American troops—at least not at first. Besides, it won the battle, though not on MacArthur's timetable. Years later, Eichelberger offered a nuanced tribute to the 32nd Division at Buna: "A great deal has been said and whispered about the 32nd Division, and much of it makes no sense. The 32nd which 'failed' at Buna was the same 32nd that won the victory there. No one else did …. There were men and officers who failed at Buna. But any historians will be hard put to discover in this war a division which earned, and deserved, so many citations and decorations for individual bravery."[17] It is regrettable and unfair that just about the only thing many World War II historians and aficionados remember about the 32nd Division is its Buna ordeal.[18]

The Americans assumed the offensive at both Guadalcanal and Buna to prevent the Japanese from consolidating their far-flung empire. Even before those campaigns had ended, though, MacArthur, Nimitz, and their staffs were hard at work formulating a coherent strategy for the South Pacific that would enable them to maintain the initiative with the limited resources at their disposal. To do so, they crafted what was eventually labeled Operation *Cartwheel*. *Cartwheel* called for a complicated and synchronized series of operations by MacArthur's SWPA and Halsey's SOPAC forces aimed at the big Japanese stronghold of Rabaul on New Britain Island. The Japanese had captured the strategically-located port the previous January and had since then turned it into a major naval and air base garrisoned by tens of thousands of troops. It was the wellspring of Japanese activity in the region. Under *Cartwheel*, Halsey would advance from Guadalcanal northwestward through the Solomon Islands chain while MacArthur pushed up along the New Guinea coast. Although MacArthur would exercise overall authority, Halsey had considerable autonomy to direct his part of the campaign as he saw fit. Implementing *Cartwheel* would consume the bulk of American and Australian attention in the Pacific for the next year.

Because the United States had prioritized the conflict against Germany, the army designated only a limited number of divisions for the Pacific War, not all of which were ready for overseas shipment. Moreover, those had to be divided between the POA and SWPA. This meant that MacArthur's divisional cupboard was bare in early 1943. He had at his disposal three American divisions: the 32nd, 41st, and 1st Marine. Unfortunately, the 32nd and 1st Marine were recovering from their ordeals at Buna and Guadalcanal, so they would not be ready for combat for months. As for the 41st Division, it was in the process of deploying to New Guinea, but it would not be enough to implement MacArthur's *Cartwheel* responsibilities. Happily for MacArthur, he had an ace in the hole: Australia. Australia had entered World War II as part of the British empire in September 1939. Since then Australian troops had fought extensively and courageously in the Middle East until brought back to defend Down Under and fend off the Japanese onslaught. Although the Australians possessed the experience that the Americans lacked, a chauvinistic MacArthur deliberately excluded them from his headquarters and his decision-making process. Australian units had suffered at Buna–Gona too, but enough divisions remained to fight in New Guinea. Indeed, the Australians bore the brunt of the ground war on the island throughout 1943.

MacArthur lacked the time to closely oversee SWPA's ground war. He needed a field army commander and staff to handle the day-to-day nuts-and-bolts of army operations in New Guinea. The obvious choice for this job was Eichelberger, who had led the I Corps to victory at Buna–Gona. MacArthur, though, was jealous of the publicity that Eichelberger had garnered, so he temporarily exiled him to Australia to train troops. Instead, MacArthur brought in General Walter Krueger. Krueger was an army anomaly in that he was neither native born nor a West Pointer. He was actually a German whose family emigrated to Ohio when he was a boy. He enlisted for the Spanish-American War, rose to sergeant, and then passed the qualifying exam to become an officer. Despite the absence of a West Point pedigree, Krueger ascended up the army's hierarchy through ruthless ambition, keen intellect, and iron self-discipline. He became an expert on small unit tactics and interservice cooperation. Unsmiling, hard-bitten, direct, and stubborn, Krueger fit the stereotype of a humorless Prussian officer. Although he wanted to be liked, he lacked the milk of human kindness. He was a carping and demanding officer, chary with praise and quick to criticize. This evoked bemused irritation in some, but hatred and resentment in others. MacArthur asked for Krueger because they were old friends and, undoubtedly, because Krueger would know enough to stay out of MacArthur's limelight. To keep American troops separate and independent from the Australians, MacArthur initially designated Krueger's command the "Alamo Force." However, he eventually redesignated it as the Sixth Army.

SWPA's next major objectives in New Guinea were the Japanese bases at Salamaua and Lae, more than 130 miles up the coast from Buna–Gona. Seizing them required nine months of effort. The Australians provided most of the ground forces involved, but elements of General Horace H. Fuller's 41st Division also participated. The 41st was another National Guard division, built around Guard units from Washington, Oregon, Idaho, Montana, and Wyoming. It was nicknamed the "Sunset Division" until its wartime experiences added another, more relevant, sobriquet—the "Jungleers." Mobilized in September 1940, the 41st escaped much of the personnel turnover that plagued other divisions and needed only 4,300 draftees to bring it up to strength. Even so, it suffered many of the same deficiencies in training, weapons, and equipment that afflicted the hard-luck 32nd Division. On the other hand, Eichelberger's I Corps headquarters made sure that the 41st had access to the lessons the Red Arrow troops learned at such high cost at Buna. This helped to explain why one of its regiments, the 163rd, fought credibly with the Australians at Sanananda. The rest of the division followed the 163rd to New Guinea. The 186th Regiment flew to Buna–Gona in late January, and the 162nd arrived by boat at Port Moresby and Oro Bay soon afterwards. This enabled the division to gradually acclimate itself to New Guinea's awful wartime environment.

Although the 163rd and 186th Regiments returned to Australia in July, the 162nd contributed to efforts to take Salamaua. It landed at Nassau Bay on 30 June and joined Australian units slugging it out with the Japanese at a height dubbed Roosevelt Ridge in an engagement that lasted from 21 July to 14 August. Most of the controversy generated at that battle revolved around the difficulties in working with the Australians, not with the regiment's performance. In the end, the Allies drove off the Japanese and compelled them to evacuate Salamaua on 12 September. Lae fell to Australian troops four days later. The 162nd Regiment lost 102 killed and 447 wounded in the operation. With that victory under its belt, the 162nd joined its divisional comrades back in Australia in October.[19]

The 41st Division emerged from its New Guinea baptism of fire with a better reputation than the unfortunate 32nd. Unlike the Red Arrow boys, the Jungleers were committed to action gradually and worked more closely with the experienced Australians. They were also better-trained. Unfortunately, the 41st had rehabilitation troubles after it returned to Australia. In its case, though, the difficulties were top down, not bottom up. The basic problem was a personality conflict between the division commander, Horace Fuller, and General Jens A. Doe, head of the division's 163rd Regiment. Doe was a hard-edged soldier who, according to Fuller, publicly disparaged the division's National Guard officers. His hypercritical attitude toward them undermined morale and generated considerable resentment. Fuller, for his part, was a brittle man whose inclination was to simply get rid of Doe. When Eichelberger learned of this interpersonal spat, he initially sided with Fuller and recommended transferring Doe to another unit. However, Eichelberger's threat to dispatch his inspector general to look into matters and create an official record of the dispute apparently scared both men into temporarily patching up their differences. In late November 1943, Eichelberger wrote to his boss, Sixth Army commander Walter Krueger, "I am watching the situation in the 41st Division very carefully but there is every indication of a new attitude throughout. Fuller has had a number of very friendly talks with Doe and it looks as though they are going to be able to cooperate in fine style."[20] He followed this up by assuring Krueger, "There will be no more trouble in the 41st. Conditions have been clarified a lot and I find a very friendly spirit on every hand."[21] This détente did not last, but for now the 41st Division was in a good position to spearhead MacArthur's lightning advance across New Guinea the following year before it faded into obscurity.[22]

New Georgia

While MacArthur's American and Australian troops were struggling toward Salamaua and Lae, Halsey's SOPAC forces had not been idle. Halsey's first major *Cartwheel* assignment was to seize the island of New Georgia in an operation tagged "Toenails." Located in the center of the Solomon Islands chain, New Georgia was, at 786 square miles, about two thirds the size of Rhode Island. It was a geographically complicated place. Reefs and barrier islands surrounded it, making any landing problematic. Its interior contained dense jungle and high mountains, but mangrove swamps dominated its coastline. New Georgia derived its strategic value from the airfield the Japanese had constructed during the Guadalcanal campaign at Munda on the island's northwestern tip. In American hands, New Georgia would enable SOPAC to project its power even closer to Rabaul, only 460 miles to the northwest. The Japanese had deployed 10,500 soldiers to defend the island, most of whom were concentrated at the all-important airfield.

Halsey's initial inclination was to use the Marines for *Toenails*. After all, the Marines were the amphibious warfare experts, and as part of the navy were more subject to Halsey's control. If any organization had the knowledge and motivation for such an operation, it was the Marine Corps. However, Marine strength in the region was deceptive. The 1st and 2nd Marine Divisions were still recovering from their Guadalcanal ordeal, and anyway Nimitz had traded the 1st Marine Division to SWPA for the 25th Division. On the other hand, the 3rd Marine Division was deploying to the area and available for use. Unfortunately for the Marines, their command structure was in too much turmoil to take advantage of the opportunity to demonstrate their relevance. The basic problem was that their I Amphibious Corps chief, General Clayton "Barney" Vogel, was simply not up to the job for a variety of reasons. Vogel claimed that attacking New Georgia would require a prohibitively large force. As it turned out, he was right, but this did not endear him to Halsey during the lead up to the operation. Halsey disliked Vogel's estimates about as much as he disliked Vogel, so he was happy to give the mission to the army when its SOPAC chief, Millard Harmon, offered to undertake it with fewer troops than Vogel recommended.

Harmon had at his disposal four divisions. Two of them, the Americal and the 25th, were refitting after their Guadalcanal adventure. The other two were untested National Guard outfits: the 37th and 43rd. Halsey decided to employ General John Hester's 43rd Division for the New Georgia operation, with the 37th in reserve. The 43rd had been created out of the Connecticut, Maine, Rhode Island, and Vermont National Guards in February 1941. Its patch was a black grapeleaf representing the four relevant New England states imposed over a red quatrefoil. The War Department dispatched it to the South Pacific in October 1942, first to New Zealand, then briefly to New Caledonia, and finally, in February 1943, to Guadalcanal. Like most other National Guard divisions at this time, the 43rd had some serious problems, especially among its officers, that became apparent only in retrospect. Although Nimitz had raised some concerns about the 43rd when it appeared in his theater, he did not follow up on them. To make things worse, the 43rd did not get sufficient jungle training before invading New Georgia, and what little that it did receive was based more on Guadalcanal's relatively open terrain, not the dense and impenetrable foliage that characterized New Georgia. Just like the 32nd Division at Buna, the 43rd was about to encounter a skilled and tenacious enemy in a hostile environment for which it was ill-prepared.[23]

Because of New Georgia's complicated geography, SOPAC staffers crafted a complex amphibious assault plan for *Toenails*. It called for a series of preliminary minor landings beginning on 30 June to secure artillery sites and anchorages before the main attack three days later. On 2 July, two regiments of the 43rd Division splashed ashore at Zanana beach, about five miles east of Munda. After consolidating the beachhead, on 6 July the 43rd Division's

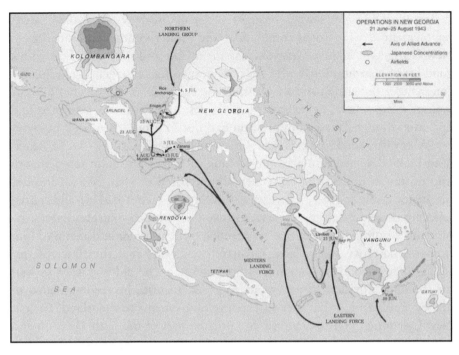

The New Georgia Operation, June–October 1943.

GIs advanced westward toward the Barike River, with the 172nd Regiment hugging the coast and the 169th Regiment moving inland. Just reaching the Barike River took everything the division had. Japanese opposition was not yet heavy, but the 169th Regiment's soldiers fell prey to something approaching mass hysteria. Units got lost because there were no usable landmarks in the dense jungle. The heat and humidity were overpowering. Troops became hungry when supplies hauled over muddy trails did not arrive in a timely manner. Japanese snipers seemed to lurk behind every tree. At night jittery and tired soldiers chucked hand grenades and shot blindly into the darkness at imaginary Japanese infiltrators who often turned out to be roving land crabs. Officers failed to set examples, control their men, demonstrate initiative, and execute orders. Rumors filled the void created by a lack of solid information and discipline suffered. Small wonder more and more GIs broke mentally under the strain. Indeed, by the end of the month more than 700 men in the 169th Regiment alone succumbed to combat fatigue and were unable to fight. By mid-July, the division had lost ninety killed, 636 wounded, and more than 1,000 cases of illness. One officer remembered, "[T]he 43rd Division had become really shot up—I mean by that, they were no good at all."[24]

The 43rd Division's woes brought General Oscar W. Griswold, Patch's replacement as XIV Corps commander and Hester's immediate superior, to New Georgia on 11 July. Griswold was an amiable and talented officer with a good bit of common sense who became, next to Eichelberger, the best corps commander the army produced during the Pacific War. He did not like the look of things. As far as he could tell, the 43rd Division was "about to fold up," even though Japanese opposition had not in his opinion been heavy so far. "Many wounded coming back," Griswold jotted in his diary. "Losses heavy. Men look all fagged out. Bewildered look of horror on many faces. Troops impress me as not having been mentally prepared or well trained. Impress me as not doing job very effectively."[25] Although Hester had already started relieving underperforming officers, Griswold concluded that Hester was too nice and accommodating to be an effective combat leader and removed him from his post two weeks later. Griswold was aware that the timetable for seizing New Georgia was rapidly slipping away, so he did not want to wait for the 43rd Division to get its act together. Instead, he recommended to Halsey and Harmon that they dispatch reinforcements to the island. Back at New Caledonia, Harmon agreed and ordered part of the 37th Division and a regiment of the 25th Division to New Georgia. He also put Griswold in charge of what now became a corps-sized operation.[26]

The 37th Division was the most effective National Guard division in the Pacific War. Nicknamed "Buckeye" because of its Ohio origins, its insignia was a red circle superimposed over a larger white circle. Like the 41st Division, the 37th escaped a lot of the personnel turnover that plagued other outfits, which undoubtedly promoted unit cohesion and morale. Much of its success, though, was due to its commander, General Robert Beightler. The prewar civil engineer was one of a bare handful of National Guardsmen who retained his high-level combat command when the war broke out. He owed his good fortune to his obvious competency and his willingness to relieve inefficient subordinates without any prodding from above. A couple of months before the Japanese attacked Pearl Harbor, the army's General Headquarters chief, General Lesley J. McNair, wrote Marshall that Beightler was "one of the best Nat. Gd. Commanders if he stays with the job."[27] The 37th Division had been slated to go to Northern Ireland at the conflict's start, but the War Department dispatched it to the Fiji Islands instead in June 1942 to protect them from the Japanese, from where it moved to Guadalcanal in April 1943.[28]

Although Griswold took control of the campaign on 15–16 July, he refrained from renewing the offensive against Munda until he got his military ducks in a row. He improved logistics by expanding the beachhead that the 172nd

Regiment had seized at Laiana and finished roads through the jungle to the front. He pulled the troubled 169th Regiment out of the line and replaced it with the 43rd Division's 103rd. He upgraded medical facilities and got a handle on the excessive number of combat fatigue cases. Finally, he acquired the reinforcements that Harmon had ordered to the island: two regiments from Beightler's 37th Division—the third regiment, the 129th, was busy garrisoning the New Hebrides—as well as the 25th Division's 161st Regiment.

On 25 July Griswold ordered an all-out attack on Munda. He directed the two 43rd Division regiments to push westward along the coast while Beightler provided the knockout blow by hitting the Japanese left flank. To give Beightler sufficient power, Griswold attached the 25th Division's 161st Regiment to his force. The result was a fierce and grinding battle of attrition that lasted for more than two weeks as the Americans methodically rooted out and pushed back the Japanese toward Munda. Artillery stripped the jungle of its foliage and churned up the ground. Cognizant of both his division's inexperience and Hester's fate, Beightler cautiously went about his part of the plan. This required more time, but less risk to his green outfit—and to his career. Even so, one of his regiments, the 148th, got too far ahead of the rest of the division and had to cut its way out to return to American lines. Although he had doubts about the 169th Regiment, the new 43rd Division commander, General John Hodge, committed it back to the fight to restore some of its confidence. Munda airfield fell on 5 August, giving the Americans New Georgia's big strategic prize.

Unfortunately, mopping up the island required considerable resources and continued for weeks afterwards. Some felt that this process was even more difficult than seizing Munda in the first place. "This clean-up," Griswold noted, "is almost as bad as the *big* battle."[29] Joe Collins later called the conditions under which these engagements were fought the most arduous of his combat-laden career. Taking the offshore island of Arundel, for instance, necessitated elements of four regiments, a month of fighting, and almost 300 American casualties. Collins and two of his hard-hitting 25th Division regiments undertook the bulk of this unglamorous and tedious work. By skillfully using tanks and flamethrowers to overcome severe Japanese opposition, the 25th Division demonstrated that its solid performance on Guadalcanal had not been a fluke.[30]

New Georgia may have been an American victory, but it was an unsatisfying one because of its duration and price. The campaign cost SOPAC 1,098 killed, 3,873 wounded, and twenty-three missing. Of these casualties, 694 were in the 25th Division, 1,114 in the 37th, and 2,497 in the 43rd. Moreover, these numbers do not count losses through illness and combat fatigue. The campaign consumed three American divisions whose rehabilitation required months. In return for this investment, the Americans gained one more island rung on the long Solomon Islands' ladder. The good news, though, was that the New Georgia operation got Halsey thinking about a faster and less expensive way of waging the war. Halsey decided to employ growing American naval and air power to bypass and isolate strongly held Japanese islands in favor of less well-defended ones. He proved the concept's worthiness by using a 25th Division regiment to occupy lightly held Vella Lavella on 11 August, which prompted the Japanese to evacuate their strong garrison on nearby Kolombangara Island.

Many contemporaries and future historians attributed most of the 43rd Division's problems at New Georgia to a lack of leadership. For example, George Marshall was undoubtedly alluding to Hester and his officers when, two months after the 43rd Division splashed ashore at New Georgia, he wrote to his POA army commander, General Robert C. Richardson, Jr., "[W]e have had too many instances of higher leaders without drive sufficient to carry them through the vicissitudes of climate and heavy fighting with the Japanese. They become demoralized or timid and exercise command largely by asking for reinforcements. They advance too slowly and take large casualties by attrition and malaria, rather than fewer casualties—except for the moment—by aggressive action."[31] Unfortunately for the 43rd Division, some conflated criticism of the outfit's leadership with condemnation of the division as a whole. New Georgia gave the 43rd Division a bad reputation in some circles that it never completely overcame, especially because of the large number of combat fatigue cases it sustained. The fact that many histories mention the 43rd Division only in connection with the New Georgia operation reinforces this mindset.

The 43rd Division undoubtedly had a difficult time in New Georgia, but it is important to place its woes in context. Most National Guard divisions struggled in their first actions, especially early in the war before training became more thorough and realistic. In this respect, the 43rd Division's trial was not that much different than that of the Americal and 32nd Divisions at Guadalcanal and Buna. Moreover, Halsey and Harmon certainly erred in sending one green division to fight about an equal number of tough, dug-in Japanese defenders in such a nightmarish environment. A more sensible view of the division's capabilities, leadership, and mission would have saved SOPAC considerable grief. Even when accounting for the 43rd Division's large number of combat fatigue cases, its overall ordeal on New Georgia was not an aberration, but rather the depressingly common experience of many National Guard outfits in their baptisms of fire during the Pacific War.[32]

On the other hand, the 37th Division did comparatively well on New Georgia in its first operation. Beightler fought his outfit in a systematic manner that did him credit. To be sure, the 37th made mistakes, most notably the narrowly averted destruction of the 148th Regiment, but there was little of the panic and mass confusion that characterized the 43rd Division's initial days of combat. The 37th Division, however, had some advantages unavailable to the 43rd—or to the equally put-upon 32nd Division at Buna late the previous year. By the time Griswold committed the 37th Division to action, he had gotten the XIV Corps' logistical system in order, so Beightler's soldiers did not go hungry or lack ammunition. The 37th was also fortunate to have a competent commander with a firm grip on his division and operations. Finally, by the time the 37th Division entered the battle, the 43rd had already worn down and battered the defending Japanese. As a result, both contemporaries and subsequent historians praised the 37th Division's performance on New Georgia. Griswold in particular became one of the outfit's biggest boosters. The 37th Division's experience proved that National Guard divisions could fight effectively in their combat debuts under the right circumstances. The trick was to identify those proper conditions into which to introduce these units.[33]

Lastly, the 25th Division emerged from the New Georgia operation with the good record it gained at Guadalcanal intact. Although only one of its regiments participated in the assault on Munda, Collins led two thirds of the division in helping to mop up the island. In this role the 25th Division saw plenty of danger and had another opportunity to demonstrate its combat prowess. Unfortunately, these actions so thoroughly degraded the division that it took months for it to recover. Even so, most observers concluded that it did a fine job, including Halsey. Perhaps the outfit's biggest advocate, though, was Marshall, who wrote to MacArthur a few months later, "Very few, if any, of our divisions have functioned from the start as well and aggressively as Collins' [25th] division."[34] Indeed, Marshall soon elevated Collins to corps command and transferred him to Europe, where he became one of the army's finest battle leaders and, eventually, the army chief of staff. The 25th Division's successful performance in two operations at this stage of the Pacific War put it in a league of its own, making it the army's most accomplished division so far in the conflict.[35]

Bougainville

Halsey's next major *Cartwheel* target was Bougainville, the northernmost and largest of the Solomon Islands. At 3,600 square miles, it was roughly twice the size of Delaware. Bougainville derived its strategic significance not so much from its proximity to Rabaul, 240 miles to the northwest, but rather from the airfields that the Japanese had constructed on its northern and southern ends at Buka and Buin. Bougainville contained the impenetrable jungles, swampy coastal plains, jagged mountains, and deadly tropical diseases that characterized so many of the islands in the Solomon's chain, making any operation there a logistical nightmare. To defend it, the Japanese deployed 37,500 troops, mostly around the airfields at the island's tips. This was three times as many soldiers as had brought SOPAC so much grief on New Georgia.

Happily for the American Pacific War effort, Halsey and his staff had learned from the frustrating New Georgia operation. Recognizing that growing American naval and air power in the region gave him a flexibility that the Japanese could not match, Halsey decided to avoid the well-defended Bougainville airfields and instead land troops at Empress Augusta Bay on the island's remote west coast. He figured that once the Americans were ashore, SOPAC's warships and warplanes could protect the beachhead from Japanese attack until engineers constructed airfields there and defenses to protect them. If the Japanese wanted to evict the Americans, they would have to march dozens of miles through trackless jungle to do so. By the time they arrived, exhausted and hungry, the Americans would have turned their beachhead into a veritable fortress that the weary Japanese would have to assault.

Halsey gave the job of assailing and securing Empress Augusta Bay to the 3rd Marine Division because the Marines were the amphibious warfare experts. However, the Marines lacked the logistical wherewithal to stay there indefinitely, so the army would have to relieve them at some point and assume the responsibility for fortifying and defending the place. To do so, Halsey had at his disposal four army divisions: the Americal, 25th, 37th, and 43rd. He originally slated the 25th Division to go, but its unplanned and exhausting commitment to New Georgia rendered it combat ineffective for the time being. Indeed, it did not get to New Zealand for refitting until December. Nor was the 43rd Division in any condition for another operation so soon after its difficult battlefield immersion on New Georgia. By process of elimination, Halsey decided to use the Americal and 37th Divisions. Both were battle-tested outfits, the former on Guadalcanal and the latter on New Georgia. The 37th Division had been training on Guadalcanal since September.

As for the Americal, it had not seen action since the previous February. Its new leader was General John Hodge, a hard-fighting two-fisted soldier transferred over from the 43rd Division after the New Georgia operation. Hodge was not happy with the division's state of discipline when he assumed command, so he trained it rigorously. By the time it left for Bougainville, Hodge was confident enough in the unit to write:

> This division worked hard during the past few months, preparing for tasks that lie ahead. We have made great progress under conditions that left much to be desired. Discipline, appearance and soldierly conduct have shown marked improvement. Wishful thinking has waned as more and more of us are showing a willingness to face squarely the hard facts about this war and our task therein. Intensive combat training has brought to all of us confidence in ourselves and in our ability to cope with the enemy under all conditions. The combined result is a great improvement in the mental and moral fiber of the command and the development of all important self control in individuals …[36]

On 1 November, two regiments of the 3rd Marine Division landed at Empress Augusta Bay. They met little opposition, and by the end of the day about 14,000 leathernecks were ashore. Japanese air strikes caused minimal damage, and American warships offshore beat back a Japanese naval force from Rabaul that attacked that night. In the ensuing days the Marines gradually expanded their foothold and brought in the supplies and equipment that engineers needed to construct the airfields that were the point of the whole operation. The first airfield was up and running on 10 December. Meanwhile, on 8 November, the 37th Division's 148th Regiment disembarked, followed by the 129th five days later and the 145th on 19 November. The 37th Division assumed responsibility for the left side of the American defense perimeter while the Marines watched the right. Halsey, however, decided to deploy the 3rd Marine Division for an assault on Kavieng on New Ireland Island that was eventually canceled, so he pulled the outfit out on 9 January 1944. To replace it, Halsey summoned the Americal Division, which arrived gradually from late December to early March. Halsey also directed Oscar Griswold and his XIV Corps headquarters to oversee all these troops. Griswold took over on 14 December and got to work bringing order out of the beachhead's logistical chaos. This included constructing an extensive road network for which Beightler's engineering abilities came in handy. By March there were 62,000 well-supplied, well-equipped, well-armed, and well-fortified American GIs in and around Empress Augusta Bay, a bit fewer than half of whom were battle-hardened combat soldiers in the Americal and 37th Divisions.

It took the Japanese army on Bougainville some time to respond to the American landing at Empress Augusta Bay because Japanese officers were

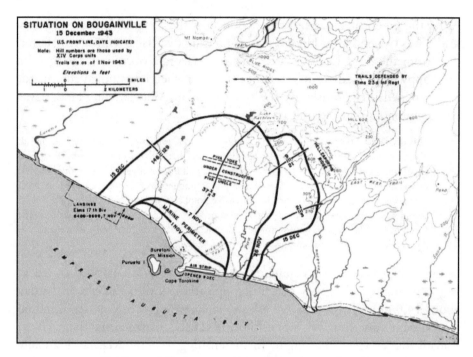

The Bougainville Operation, November 1943–March 1944.

unsure whether it constituted the main effort or a diversion. By the end of the year, though, it was obvious that Empress Augusta Bay was the focal point of American operations. That being the case, the Japanese decided to attack and eliminate the American lodgment. To do so, they mobilized 15,000 to 19,000 soldiers who had to cut their way through dozens of miles of dense jungle to reach their target, carrying or dragging all their supplies, weapons, and equipment with them. That was difficult enough, but the Japanese also severely underestimated local American strength. They calculated that there were about 30,000 Americans at Empress Augusta Bay, far short of the 62,000 actually there. These intelligence, numerical, and logistical shortcomings made any Japanese assault on the beachhead a long shot. Even so, Japanese troops started hacking through the jungle in mid-February, and by early March they were positioning themselves north and northeast of the American defensive perimeter.

The Japanese assault came as no surprise to the Americans, so they had had plenty of time to prepare their defenses. GIs had built bunkers, cleared fields of fire, preregistered artillery, strung barbed wire, planted mines, and positioned searchlights along their horseshoe-shaped perimeter. The Japanese launched their counteroffensive on 8 March and continued their efforts, on and off, for the next seventeen days. For all the disadvantages under which the Japanese labored, there was nothing wrong with their courage and determination. On the left, or western, side of the American line, Beightler's 37th Division successfully repelled all Japanese attacks after some hard fighting. It was a tighter contest—relatively speaking—for Hodge's Americal Division to the east. Confusion between Griswold and Hodge over whether to try to hold onto Hill 260 led to brutal back-and-forth combat that resulted in both sides withdrawing from the height. In the end, though, such close calls did not matter much; the Japanese never seriously threatened the integrity of the XIV Corps position. On 27 March, the defeated and exhausted Japanese melted back into the jungle, having lost an estimated 5,000 killed and 3,000 wounded in the battle. Griswold dispatched a couple battalions to see them off, but he was not interested in a vigorous pursuit into the Bougainville interior after a whipped foe who was no longer a serious threat. Protecting the airfields in his charge cost his XIV Corps 263 dead.

The Japanese assault on the American lodgment at Empress Augusta Bay was hardly a fair fight. To expect the outnumbered, outgunned, and destitute Japanese soldiers to overcome veteran American troops battling from prepared positions was outlandishly unrealistic. Even so, the Americal and 37th Divisions deserve credit for their actions. The 37th Division fought so well that the Japanese scarcely dented its lines. Beightler and his troops made no serious mistakes, certainly none that affected the engagement's outcome. The Americal Division, on the other hand, had a more difficult time. Its victory was messier because of the confusion over Hill 260, but it still fulfilled its mission and, in doing so, demonstrated a competency that it had not always displayed at Guadalcanal. Griswold saw it this way. From this point on he became a big Americal Division admirer. Whether it could fight as well in an offensive capacity, however, remained to be seen. The Bougainville operation gave the Americans two National Guard divisions that had largely overcome their growing pains and become veteran units.[37]

The Bougainville operation also had an impact on army race relations during the conflict. Like much of the rest of American society, the World War II army was racially segregated. Although there were several all-black prewar Regular Army regiments with good reputations, many high-ranking officers doubted the efficacy of raising and deploying black divisions in combat because they believed that such outfits had not performed well in World War I. As far as they were concerned, black soldiers should be limited to noncombat roles. However, black leaders successfully pressured the War Department to organize two black divisions, the 92nd and 93rd, which were activated at Fort Huachuca in Arizona in May 1942. Some of the lower-level officers were black, but whites populated the most responsible and senior positions. The divisions received the usual training, but none of the theater commanders wanted them. Finally, the War Department successfully strong-armed a reluctant Millard Harmon into accepting the more proficient of the two divisions, the 93rd, for SOPAC. Most of the division arrived at Guadalcanal in February–March 1944, where its GIs received jungle training and unloaded ships. From there, less than a month later, the division's 25th Regiment and a battalion from the 24th Regiment went to Bougainville and were attached to the Americal Division.

Because it was part of the first black division committed to an active military zone, there was considerable curiosity in the War Department and among the black press about how well these soldiers would fight. High-level officers were both skeptical and hopeful—skeptical because their ingrained racism led them to doubt that black officers in particular were up to the job of leading troops in combat, but hopeful that the army's training methods could overcome these problems. Fearful of bad publicity, Marshall cautioned Harmon to make sure that the 93rd Division did not see action until it was fully prepared. Thus forewarned, Harmon kept Marshall closely appraised of the division's activities. Unfortunately, on 6–7 April a 25th Regiment company on patrol panicked and retreated under fire in an otherwise inconsequential engagement.[38]

There was nothing unusual about American GIs performing poorly in their first actions. In fact, it had happened in almost every operation, from Buna to New Georgia. However, racist attitudes made it easy for white soldiers and civilians to extrapolate from this one incident on Bougainville that all black troops fought abysmally. As a result, black troops got a bad reputation in the Pacific. Because of the publicity this event generated, senior officials weighed in on it. In his 10 May report, Griswold blamed the 25th Regiment's difficulties on insufficient jungle training and unpreparedness. He went on to criticize black officers in particular for their lack of initiative. Harmon also identified leadership problems, but noted that most other divisions had had similar troubles and concluded that black soldiers should be given the chance to prove themselves in combat. Secretary of War Henry Stimson doubted that the 93rd Division could ever be brought up to snuff as long as it contained black officers. On the other hand, his assistant secretary, John McCloy, believed that trying to do so was worth the effort. Unfortunately, this was not important in SOPAC. Harmon instead scattered the division and assigned it noncombat duties such as loading and unloading ships, construction, and so forth. It also provided security for American bases. In this capacity the 93rd Division served well in the Solomons, New Guinea, and, eventually, in the Philippines. Although there may have been some validity to the criticisms leveled against the 93rd Division, most contemporaries failed to recognize that its unique woes did not stem from any inherent inferiority among its black GIs, but rather from a racist society that systematically segregated them, denied them full equality and opportunity, and treated them as second-class citizens.[39]

The 93rd Division's saga did not end there. Marshall continued to keep tabs on it, and in August 1944 asked MacArthur, in whose theater the 93rd now served, to find some combat employment for it, perhaps in mopping up bypassed Japanese troops in the Solomons and New Guinea. MacArthur responded, reasonably enough, that committing it to action just for the sake of fighting would waste resources and lives, but made no effort to use the division for its intended purpose. In February 1945, Walter White, the executive secretary for the National Association for the Advancement of Colored People and a *New York Post* reporter, complained to Franklin Roosevelt about the poor treatment of black soldiers in the Pacific. It was, said White, wrong to use the black GIs in a first-rate fighting unit such as the 93rd Division as laborers. Roosevelt passed White's criticisms to Marshall, who in turn relayed them to MacArthur. A defensive MacArthur responded that he had tried to keep the 93rd Division up to par and give it a variety of assignments, but low efficiency and poor leadership made it impossible for it to engage the Japanese successfully. Moreover, MacArthur continued, "The statement made by Mr. White that I do not favor use of Negro combat troops is pure fabrication. I have been especially anxious to develop this division into a reliable combat unit. The violent opinions and unfounded statements of Mr. White would seem to mark him as a troublemaker and menace to the war effort."[40] When MacArthur actually met with White, though, he turned on the charm and told White everything he wanted to hear, including that he was readying the 93rd Division for action. In fact, in April 1945, MacArthur brought most of the division together on Morotai Island in the Dutch East Indies. And most of it stayed in that area for the rest of the war, conducting patrols and providing labor details. MacArthur did not send it to the Philippines or make plans to deploy it in an invasion of Japan. When push came to shove, using the 93rd Division for combat operations simply was not a priority for him or anyone else with authority in the Pacific.[41]

In July 1945, Robert Eichelberger flew to Morotai from his Eighth Army headquarters in the Philippines to inspect the 93rd Division, which had recently come under his command. In a letter to his wife, Eichelberger reported enthusiastically:

> I have never seen so much snap in my life. They had every vehicle polished, the engineers were cleaned up fine and every colored boy saluted as far as he could see you. When the car stopped they would all jump out and salute. There were no disciplinary cases in the division and their kitchens are as clean and as neat as a pin. Johnson certainly has done a fine job .... It is apparent that he knows how to handle those colored boys and I must admit I was amazed although I had heard from my inspectors that the division is fine.[42]

It was only natural for Eichelberger to assign the bulk of the credit for the division's appearance to its commander, General Harry H. Johnson, but undoubtedly the black GIs deserve a good bit of praise as well for maintaining their morale and discipline in the face of discrimination and neglect. Eichelberger's discovery demonstrates that the army's use—or misuse—of the 93rd Division represented a missed opportunity. Although it is understandable that army leaders were unwilling to embark on large, risky, and unpopular social experiments such as integration in the middle of a global conflict, they could have undertaken other reforms that would have benefited the war effort. Most obviously, they could have kept the 93rd Division together and used it for its intended purpose. To be sure, the 93rd Division would have probably stumbled in its first operation, like many other divisions, but there is no reason to believe that patience, training, and experience would not have corrected whatever deficiencies its baptism of fire exposed. The army could have also done more to encourage unit pride by promoting deserving black officers, transferring out unenthusiastic or incompetent white ones, and publicizing the division's accomplishments. Simply holding the 93rd Division to the same standards and expectations as other divisions would have proved valuable. In not doing so, the army squandered a resource that might have made things easier for the other Pacific War divisions that had to take up the slack. Instead, the army ended up with a division that certainly contributed to victory by fulfilling other assigned and important duties, but one that was denied the opportunity to fulfill its potential.

Admiralties

For a year, seizing Rabaul dominated the American Pacific War effort. Operation *Cartwheel*, the plan to take the Japanese stronghold, had encompassed a dozen complicated and interrelated operations, the largest

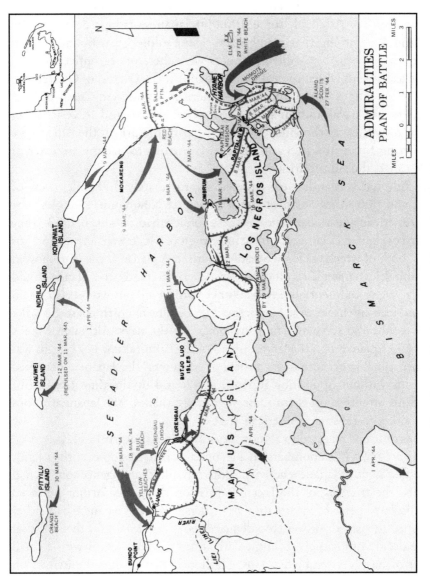

The Admiralty Islands Operation, February–March 1944.

of which were the assaults on New Georgia and Bougainville, but which also included minor landings involving units smaller than a division. As American air and naval forces inexorably degraded Japanese power and mobility in the region, Allied strategists reconsidered attacking the big Japanese fortress. After all, some 100,000 Japanese troops defended the place, and overcoming that many intransigent soldiers was bound to be a long and bloody process. Allied planners were therefore receptive to some other strategy with which to deal with Rabaul. At the Quadrant Conference in Quebec in August 1943, the Anglo-American Combined Chiefs of Staff decided to use naval and air power to isolate Rabaul and leave its hefty garrison to wither on the vine. As the last bar in the prison the Allies were constructing for it, the JCS authorized MacArthur to occupy a cluster of islands called the Admiralties.

The Admiralty Islands were situated approximately 360 miles west of Rabaul and 300 miles north of the fetid Papua New Guinea jungles over which American, Australian, and Japanese soldiers had fought in 1943. They consisted of eighteen islands, the most important of which were Manus and Los Negros, both of which enclosed Seeadler Harbor. A glance at the map showed the Admiralties' strategic significance. In American hands, the islands would not only isolate and neutralize Rabaul once and for all, but would also shield any American offensive westward across New Guinea's north coast. Seeadler Harbor could also serve as a fine anchorage for the navy. Although Manus was, at 633 square miles, the largest island in the Admiralties, Los Negros was the most valuable because of its airfield at Momote. The Japanese occupied the islands without opposition in April 1942, and by the time MacArthur focused his attention on them there were more than 4,500 Japanese troops there waiting to resist any American attack.

MacArthur had planned to assault the Admiralties in April 1944. However, on 23 February, SWPA bombers on a reconnaissance mission over the islands detected no signs of Japanese activity. Although other intelligence sources had identified the true size of the Japanese garrison there, MacArthur pounced on this isolated piece of information as evidence that the Japanese had either abandoned the islands or were too demoralized to fight hard for them. Either way, he decided to launch an immediate attack on Los Negros with a small number of hastily assembled troops. He hoped that seizing the islands on the fly would accelerate his offensive toward the Philippines and save time, resources, and lives. It was a dicey gambit because the Japanese, if still there in strength, might overwhelm the outnumbered detachment MacArthur planned to send before he could reinforce it. Even so, MacArthur thought it was worth the risk, explaining, "[It is] a gamble in which I have everything to win, little to lose. I bet ten to win a million, if I hit the jackpot."[43]

MacArthur's optimism was based at least to some extent on the confidence he had in the unit assigned to the mission. The 5th Cavalry Regiment was part of what many insisted was the best army division in the Pacific War: the 1st Cavalry Division. Despite its name, the 1st Cav was an infantry division. When the War Department chose to abandon its horses, it planned to assign the division a new title befitting its new branch. However, one of Marshall's staffers, General John Edward Hull, protested the decision to the chief of staff. Hull argued that renaming the division would strip it of its identity and lower morale. After all, the army would lose outfits with storied pasts such as George Custer's 7th Cavalry Regiment. Marshall was convinced and allowed the 1st Cavalry to retain its name, though it would still become an infantry division. Marshall also permitted it to keep its old square organization of two brigades containing two regiments apiece. Similarly, it would still have squadrons instead of battalions.[44]

The 1st Cav Division had a wonderful reputation. Because the cavalry branch was not expanding, the division contained a large proportion of Regular Army officers with Regular Army standards and expectations. Its commander was General Innis Palmer Swift, a tough, grim, heavyset older officer who eventually rose to lead a corps. Marshall lauded it before it even saw action. Although the War Department originally intended to deploy the division along the Mexican border, it decided to send it to SWPA after Krueger asked for it. Few things captured the crusty Krueger's attention like spit-and-polish, which the 1st Cavalry had in spades. Besides, Krueger and Swift were old friends. Swift once said, "If Krueger told me to cut off my left arm up to the elbow, I cut it off. He got me out here. I am sixty-two years of age and General Krueger got the 1st Cavalry Division and got me out here."[45] The division continued to impress after it reached Australia in July 1943, from where it shipped to Oro Bay, New Guinea, at the end of the year. To many, its troopers trained, marched, dressed, and carried themselves like soldiers were supposed to. Observers lauded their excellent morale, superb physical condition, and fantastic leadership at all levels. The only criticism leveled against it was the difficulty some of the former cavalrymen were having in transitioning to infantrymen. When someone worried that its 5th Cavalry Regiment was not up to the task of landing on Los Negros, MacArthur explained:

> I have known this 5th Cavalry for almost 60 years. When I was a little boy of four my father was a captain in the 13th Infantry at Fort Selden, in the Indian frontier country of New Mexico. Geronimo, the Apache scourge, was loose, and our small infantry garrison

was to guard the middle fords of the Rio Grande. A troop of this same 5th Cavalry ... rode through to help us. I can still remember how I felt when I watched them clatter into the little post, their tired horses gray with desert dust .... They'd fight then—and they'll fight now. Don't worry about them.[46]

On the morning of 29 February, a squadron from the 5th Cavalry Regiment landed at Hyane Harbor on Los Negros, just 200 yards from the airstrip there. Hyane Harbor was not really a harbor at all, but rather a gap in the surrounding coral reef. The Japanese had expected an attack through big Seeadler Harbor and deployed their forces accordingly, so they were caught by surprise and unable to seriously oppose the cavalrymen. The troopers swarmed ashore, seized most of the airstrip, and began construction of a defense perimeter. As they labored, MacArthur roamed the beach to take a look at the situation. From his elevated perspective, the operation was pretty much over now that the troopers possessed the airstrip. He departed confident that his gamble had paid off, but urged General William C. Chase, the brigade commander in overall charge of the Americans on Los Negros, to hold on tight. MacArthur's optimism seemed justified when the troopers repulsed an ad hoc assault that night. Over the next few days, Krueger funneled supplies, equipment and reinforcements to Los Negros, including the rest of the 5th Cav Regiment and engineers. Chase needed every man he could get because on the night of 3/4 March the Japanese launched an all-out counteroffensive against the beachhead with every soldier they could muster. Their charge was so ferocious that Chase had to commit his reserves to maintain his lines. Despite the valor of his green troopers, it was really fire support from two destroyers offshore that tipped the balance. The battle cost the Americans sixty-one killed and 244 wounded. As for the Japanese, they left behind 700 bodies in and around the airstrip. Having expended their reserves, from this point on the Japanese could only delay, not stop, the Americans from securing the remainder of the Admiralties.

Occupying Momote Airfield did not put an end to the operation. MacArthur and Krueger sought Seeadler Harbor not only to more easily supply the 1st Cav Division, but to develop into a major naval base as well. They also wanted to take the rudimentary airstrip at Lorengau on Manus Island. After he reached Los Negros on 5 March, Swift went about attaining these objectives with his increasingly proficient troopers. The division's 7th Cav Regiment arrived on 4 March, followed by the 12th Cav Regiment two days later. These reinforcements gave Swift the manpower he needed to gain a foothold on Seeadler Harbor at Salami. Before he could exploit his good fortune, though, he had to finish clearing the remainder of Los Negros of its Japanese defenders holed up on Hill 260 in the center of the island. The Japanese repelled an initial assault by the 5th Cav Regiment on 11 March, forcing Swift to commit elements of the 12th Cav Regiment to storm the hill three days later. With that flank secured, the next day, 15 March, Swift landed his last 1st Cav Division regiment, the 8th, just west of Lorengau's airstrip at Lugos on Manus Island. The 8th Cav Regiment took Lorengau on 17 March and, with the 7th Cav Regiment, pushed into the interior to eliminate the final organized Japanese opposition at Rossum on 25 March.

It took less than a month for the 1st Cav Division to seize the Admiralties. It did so at the relatively inexpensive price of 326 killed, 1,189 wounded, and four missing. Most of the Japanese garrison died through battle, hunger, or disease. By way of return on its collective investment, MacArthur's Admiralties coup put the last major nail in Rabaul's coffin and, once the engineers moved in, turned the islands into a base that SWPA could use to support an advance along New Guinea's northern coast. The operation marked the end of one long and bloody phase of the Pacific War and the beginning of another.

The 1st Cavalry Division garnered plenty of praise from contemporaries and future historians for its performance in the Admiralties. MacArthur, Krueger, and Eichelberger were among the former. The division fought remarkably well not only in a defensive role by repelling the initial Japanese assaults on the beachhead perimeter, but also in assuming the offensive to mop up the remaining enemy forces on the islands. It did so professionally, relentlessly, without excessive casualties, and in a timely manner. It suffered no major setbacks, and fulfilled its tasks without drama or fuss. Small wonder Krueger wrote Swift, "My hearty congratulations to you and to the officers and men of your command for a brilliant performance in the capture of Momote, Lorengau and Seeadler Harbor Area. The First Cavalry Division has added a glorious page to Cavalry Annals; the gallantry and indomitable spirit displayed by its members and those of the supporting Army and Navy units merit the highest praise."[47] Among the army divisions in the South Pacific, only the 25th had conducted itself so well in its first action. It was a fine debut for a green outfit fighting such a tenacious enemy in such a hostile environment. MacArthur's failure to use the division again until the following October was due to logistical constraints rather than any doubts about its abilities. When Ed Hull, the planner who had persuaded Marshall to keep the 1st Cav Division's name, later visited the Admiralties on an inspection tour, the division's officers gave him the royal treatment. They did so because they understood that the traditions he helped preserve were a vital ingredient to the recipe that made the division such a success.[48]

Conclusions

Operation *Cartwheel* required a year to complete and involved seven army divisions: the Americal, 1st Cav, 25th, 32nd, 37th, and 43rd. Of these, two—the 1st Cav and 25th—were Regular Army and the rest were National Guard. The army did not win the ground campaign alone. Three Marine Corps divisions were engaged there as well, participating in the occupations of Guadalcanal, Bougainville, and an all-Marine landing at Cape Gloucester in New Britain in December 1943. Also, a significant number of Australian units joined the campaign in New Guinea. The army divisions partook in six major operations at Guadalcanal, Buna, Papua New Guinea, New Georgia, Bougainville, and the Admiralties. The 32nd, 43rd, and 1st Cav Divisions each saw action once at, respectively, Buna, New Georgia, and the Admiralties. Another three divisions went through two operations apiece: the Americal on Guadalcanal and Bougainville, the 25th on Guadalcanal and New Georgia, and the 37th on New Georgia and Bougainville. Finally, the 41st was an anomaly in that although it sent regiments to fight at Sanananda and at Roosevelt Ridge, it never worked together as a whole in heavy combat. The army units ultimately won every major battle in *Cartwheel*, but some of these victories were messier and more problematic than others.

Cartwheel taught the army some important lessons. For one thing, Regular Army divisions performed better than their National Guard counterparts in their first actions. The 1st Cav Division fought splendidly in the Admiralties and the 25th did very well on Guadalcanal. On the other hand, the Americal, 32nd, and 43rd Divisions all struggled at, respectively, Guadalcanal, Buna, and New Georgia. These difficulties stemmed primarily from poor leadership among the line officers in the National Guard divisions. The army had attempted to purge the National Guard divisions of substandard and inefficient officers, but it had not gone far enough. Leading soldiers in combat was an extraordinarily challenging and stressful job that required enormous mental and physical stamina, as well as considerable cold-bloodedness. In too many instances, National Guard officers let prewar personal relationships interfere with achieving unit objectives. They became indecisive, complacent, and soft-hearted when a more aggressive approach, while costing heavier casualties in the short run, would save time and, ultimately, lives. Moreover, the army's early training had not been sufficiently rigorous to overcome this problem. Regular Army officers, though, developed professionally in a culture that prioritized the mission above all else, including personal feelings. This attitude might make these men unpleasant human beings, but they were more likely to be good soldiers—and that was the kind of men the army needed to lead its troops to victory.

Cartwheel demonstrated that American divisions performed better in a defensive role. This is hardly surprising. Although assuming the defensive meant surrendering the initiative, it also enabled the defenders to familiarize themselves with the battlefield's terrain, preregister artillery, prepare fortifications, establish fields of fire, and position reserves. The tactics for the defender often boiled down to remaining in place and shooting at anyone not doing likewise. Besides, the Japanese army did not shine on the offensive during *Cartwheel*. Under those circumstances, the Japanese consistently displayed little tactical finesse and underestimated American numbers, commitment, firepower, and logistics. The Japanese army's all-out attacks usually depleted their reserves, thus making it easier for the Americans to mop up the remaining Japanese troops. The Americal, 1st Cav, and 37th Divisions all repelled determined but unimaginative Japanese assaults on their positions at Henderson Airfield on Guadalcanal, Momote Airfield at Los Negros, and at Empress Augusta Bay on Bougainville. Unhappily for the army, it often did not have the time or opportunity to fight the Japanese this way.

On the other hand, army divisions undertaking offensive missions during *Cartwheel* struggled in achieving their objectives. Because assuming the offensive required more tactical skill, initiative, and sophistication than GIs initially possessed, it was not unusual for these divisions to become bogged down and fall behind schedule. Army planners exacerbated these difficulties by overrating the fighting prowess of American soldiers, especially inexperienced ones, and underestimating the tenacity of their opponents. As a result, they failed to deploy enough troops to overcome the Japanese on schedule. The Americal, 32nd, and 43rd Divisions all suffered initial setbacks trying to defeat the Japanese on Guadalcanal, Buna, and New Georgia. Although they all won their battles in the end through savage attrition, doing so was costly in casualties, morale, and time. The fact that other divisions, such as the 1st Cav, 25th, and 37th, succeeded offensively showed that these problems were not insurmountable, but were rather a matter of proper training and leadership.

In addition, *Cartwheel* demonstrated the tremendous toll that these battles took on the participating army divisions. Most of them suffered heavy casualties in a relatively short amount of time, especially among the infantrymen who did the vast majority of the actual fighting. GIs also fell prey to a host of tropical diseases that removed men from duty as effectively as Japanese bullets: scrub typhus, jungle rot, dengue fever, dysentery, and especially omnipresent malaria. These diseases became less of a problem as time went on and the army improved its prevention and treatment techniques, but it was always a work in progress. Finally, combat was as hard on weapons and equipment as on soldiers. As a result, even victorious divisions emerged from their operations in no condition to fight any time soon. They needed to be re-equipped, re-armed, and retrained, as well as infused with replacements to fill the gaps in their ranks.

Fortunately, the army had the luxury to refit these divisions in peace because of the nature of the Pacific War in its first three years. Logistical and geographic constraints limited the number of divisions the army could commit to battle at any given time and place. Until the last year of the conflict, army divisions spent most of their time preparing for or recovering from their last operations. The 32nd Division occupied Buna in January 1943, but did not see significant action again until July 1944. The 41st Division, for its part, did not fight a major engagement from the Battle of Roosevelt Ridge in July–August 1943 until the following April. Ten months elapsed between the Japanese evacuation of Guadalcanal in February 1943 and the Americal Division's commitment to Bougainville at the end of the year, and then another eleven months until it went to the Philippines. The 25th Division fought at Guadalcanal in early 1943 and on New Georgia in July–August. It then cooled its heels until summoned to take part in the invasion of Luzon in the Philippines in January 1945. The 37th and 43rd Divisions joined the 25th for its Luzon adventure. Before that, though, neither division had seen much fighting since Bougainville and New Georgia. Finally, after the 1st Cavalry Division stormed the Admiralties, it stayed there for nearly eight months until SWPA sent it to Leyte Island in the Philippines in October.

For all the problems the army had during Operation *Cartwheel*, the fact was that it emerged triumphant from the campaign. By the time it was over, Rabaul had been neutralized, and in the process the Allies had seriously degraded Japan's power on land, in the air, and at sea. Moreover, *Cartwheel* had given seven army divisions—the Americal, 1st Cavalry, 25th, 32nd, 37th, 41st, and 43rd—valuable combat experience that they could put to good use in future operations. By contrast, *Cartwheel* had gravely weakened the Japanese army. Very few of the soldiers who the Japanese committed to Rabaul's defense escaped to fight another day. Many had been killed in the Solomons and New Guinea, and even more were now isolated from the rest of the Japanese empire and living a squalid hand-to-mouth existence. They were therefore in no position to relay their hard-won experience to their comrades who had to face the American juggernaut next. In short, the American army was becoming more skilled and proficient than its Japanese counterpart as the conflict progressed.

CHAPTER TWO

The Central Pacific Offensive

Strange Battleground

As far as United States Navy officers were concerned, the Pacific War was *their* war. After all, the battlefield was an ocean upon which large fleets that only navies possessed could maneuver and fight. Because of its proprietary interest in such a hypothetical conflict, naval officers had for decades put considerable thought into waging war against Japan. The navy's design to do so, War Plan Orange, called for engaging the Japanese along the Central Pacific axis between Hawaii and the Philippines. There the navy would defeat its Japanese counterpart in a climactic naval battle, rescue the Philippines from the Japanese occupation that naval officers assumed the army would be unable to prevent, and, finally, go on to blockade the Japanese Home Islands into submission. From the perspective of naval planners, Rabaul and Operation *Cartwheel* were distractions from the main theater of war that forced the navy to divert warships, personnel, warplanes, and three Marine Corps divisions to the region. Of course, *Cartwheel* was not a pointless exercise because it cost the Japanese dearly and taught the navy a good deal about combat. Nevertheless, even before *Cartwheel* ended, naval strategists were already doing their best to refocus the conflict back to the Central Pacific where it belonged and from where the navy could more easily dominate it.

Unfortunately for the navy's planners, the broad geographic scope and scale of the initial Japanese offensive brought to the Pacific War's strategic table an unwelcome complication in the form of the egomaniacal General Douglas MacArthur. MacArthur had his own strongly held views about winning the conflict that did not necessarily include a Central Pacific campaign. By his logic, the best way to get to Japan was via the Southwest Pacific, starting from Australia and advancing through New Guinea and the Philippines. This route would enable him to take advantage of Australia's infrastructure, redeem his pledge to liberate the Philippines, and, not least, put him and the army in charge of the Pacific War. There was, however, little chance that the hard-bitten chief of naval operations, Ernest King, would permit MacArthur to exert any authority over significant naval assets. Reconciling MacArthur's and the navy's strategic visions required another of those JCS compromises that characterized the American war effort. The resulting Dual Drive offensive, finalized in March 1944, authorized concurrent campaigns by MacArthur's SWPA and the navy's POA, though the latter had priority. The goal of the Dual Drive offensive was the vaguely defined China–Formosa–Luzon region, at which point the JCS would have to decide whether to attack the Philippines or the navy's preferred target of Formosa. Although the Dual Drive offensive doubled the number of targets and diluted American power, it also dispersed Japanese resources and preserved the interservice harmony upon which the conflict's outcome depended.

Admiral Chester Nimitz commanded the POA. He was an intelligent, folksy, and low-key officer, skilled at avoiding drama and persuading different kinds of people to get along. Although Nimitz worked hard and effectively to wield his headquarters into a united military team, there was not much doubt that he prioritized the navy's personnel, doctrine, and agenda. From this perspective, his decision to place the navy's long-contemplated Central Pacific offensive in the Marines' hands made sense. The Marine Corps was organizationally part of the navy, making it the navy's own army. Their officers were therefore more familiar to Nimitz and subject to his control. Before the conflict, Marine officers had turned themselves into amphibious warfare experts to justify their existence and differentiate themselves from the army. Although Marine officers often attended army schools and were familiar with army doctrine, there were some important differences between the two entities. The Marine Corps was the smaller and more elite force, but the price for this exclusivity was that Marine officers could not specialize as much as their army counterparts. As a result, the Marines were not as tactically sophisticated and methodical, logistically advanced, and organizationally developed as the army. Marine officers knew a lot about landing on and securing a hostile beach—at least in theory—but, once ashore, they often relied on direct frontal assaults and élan to overcome the enemy. This enabled them to achieve their objectives in a timely manner, but also sometimes led to excessive casualties that the Marine Corps could not afford. Nimitz put the Marines in charge of attacking the islands in the Central Pacific by authorizing the establishment of the V Amphibious Corps under Marine general Holland M. Smith.

The Central Pacific's geography was unique and challenging. The vast majority of it was of course water, giving the navy plenty of room in which to maneuver its ships in its quest to engage its Japanese counterpart in a showdown battle. There were also a number of island groups over which to compete, including the Gilberts, Marshalls, Carolines, Marianas, and Palaus. There was nothing unusual about many of these islands, but others were actually atolls. An atoll consisted of chains of coral that formed a ring around an interior lagoon, all of which were surrounded by a fringing barrier reef. The coral islands that made up atolls were often low-lying, sandy, and contained little vegetation beyond coconut trees and scrub brush. No modern military had ever fought on atolls before, so the army and Marines—and of course the Japanese too—would have to learn about them as they went along.

Unfortunately for the navy and Marine Corps, they lacked sufficient resources to sustain an offensive across the Central Pacific on their own. Although the Marine Corps grew to almost 500,000 leathernecks during the war and deployed a half dozen divisions, it was simply not enough. Just as the navy sent a fleet to SWPA to help MacArthur wage his war, the army lent a hand in the POA. Marshall appointed General Robert Richardson to command the army's contribution to the theater, the so-called "Pineapple Army." Nicknamed "Nellie" for his finicky and pompous manner, Richardson assumed his duties in June 1943. On paper his job appeared a prestigious one. A closer look, though, revealed that there was much less to it than met the eye. Richardson had the authority to train, administer, and supply the army troops in the POA, but he could not actually lead them into battle. That was the Marines' prerogative. For Richardson, it was akin to a cuckold husband in an unconsummated marriage, and he never understood why Marshall permitted Marine officers to command army units. Richardson tried hard to get along with naval officers, but as the war progressed he grew increasingly frustrated with their high-handed and arbitrary ways and his limited power. As Robert Eichelberger explained to his wife, "He [Richardson] has been however a white slave under the navy, living in a fine house and driving a fine car and having a high title. However he was still the white slave and had little or no authority."[1]

Most of the army's initial contributions to the POA were siphoned away to participate in *Cartwheel*, from where they were eventually absorbed into MacArthur's SWPA for the remainder of the war. Ultimately, the army deployed and used four divisions in the Central Pacific: the 7th, 27th, 77th, and 81st. A last division, the 98th, arrived too late in the conflict to participate. These divisions saw some of the most savage and difficult fighting in the Pacific War. Along with their Marine counterparts, they provided Nimitz with the combat power he needed to seize the islands that the navy and Army Air Forces used to pummel Japan into submission.

Aleutians

By mid-1943 the Allies were slowly winning the war in both Europe and the Pacific. In Europe, American, British empire, and Free French troops had, in May, driven the Germans and Italians out of North Africa and captured a quarter million prisoners in Tunisia in the process. Sicily fell in July–August, prompting the Italians to overthrow Benito Mussolini's fascist regime. The new Italian government surrendered in September, just before an Anglo-American army invaded southern Italy at Salerno. The Americans and British had also turned the tide in the Atlantic campaign against U-boats and were intensifying their strategic bombing of Germany. Along the vast Eastern Front the Soviets had won the Battle of Kursk and were pushing the Germans out of Belarus and Ukraine in a series of engagements that extracted an enormous toll on the German army. Even so, the Germans still controlled Norway and Denmark, the Low Countries, France, northern Italy, the Balkans, much of central Europe, Poland, and the Baltics. Their military production was increasing, and they showed little inclination to give up.

On the other side of the world, the Americans and Australians were in the process of isolating Rabaul. The Japanese, though, still dominated their Home Islands, Manchuria, eastern China, Indochina, Burma, Malaya and Singapore, the Dutch East Indies, the Philippines, much of New Guinea, and the Palau, Caroline, Mariana, Marshall, and Gilbert island groups. The American submarine war had not yet reached its full potential and the strategic bombing of Japan from China had yielded few results so far. Although the Japanese navy had taken a beating in the Solomons, it remained extant and powerful. Clearly the Allies still had a long way to go to force Japan's capitulation.

While Nimitz was securing the POA's southern flank in Operation *Cartwheel*, he was also participating in efforts to protect its northern edge in the remote Aleutian Islands. The Aleutians were a 1,100-mile-long chain of more than sixty islands that looped from southwestern Alaska towards the Soviet Union and separated the Bering Sea from the Pacific Ocean. The Japanese had attacked them in June 1942 as the only successful component of their otherwise disastrous Midway campaign. They had bombed the American base at Dutch Harbor on 3–4 June and seized without opposition the westernmost islands of Attu and Kiska a few days later. The islands' strategic value was actually minimal. The Aleutians may have looked like a short and easy route between northern Japan and North America, but remoteness, dense fog, clammy cold, and inhospitable waters made operating there extraordinarily difficult. Even so, the Joint Chiefs of Staff wanted to expel the Japanese mostly for psychological reasons—to remove the only enemy foothold in North America. Moreover, the JCS expected it done sooner rather than later, before the Japanese could turn Attu and Kiska into impenetrable fortresses.

It took time for the Americans to assemble the necessary parts for their planned counterattack in the Aleutians. This task included constructing a logistical network almost from scratch on the islands from which to launch the assault. Merely supplying the growing number of troops in the region proved difficult. Moreover, concurrent fighting in the Solomons, New Guinea, and North Africa diverted limited army resources. Gradually, though, the pieces fell into place. Because of its harbor and airfield, Kiska was the more valuable of the two Japanese-held islands, but it also contained more Japanese defenders than Attu. Admiral Thomas C. Kinkaid, the overall American commander in the region, estimated that storming Kiska would require 25,000 troops, and there was not enough shipping available for that. He therefore recommended assailing Attu instead. American intelligence estimated that there were only 500 Japanese soldiers there, so seizing it would not be prohibitively expensive. Once Attu was in American hands, Kiska would be cut off from Japan and would hopefully wither on the vine. The JCS liked this logic and signed off on the idea on 1 April 1943.

Attu was unlike any other island over which Japanese and Americans fought in the Pacific War. Geographically there was nothing unusual about it. At thirty-five miles long and fifteen miles wide, for a total of 275 square miles, it was another mountainous speck in the Aleutians chain. Its frozen climate and gooey terrain, though, separated it from the hot and sticky battlefields of the Central and South Pacific. Dense fog frequently shrouded Attu, and the cold clammy dampness seeped into everything and everyone. Black bogs full of decaying vegetation and cold water called muskeg dotted the stark barren landscape, threatening to suck in and soak unwary GIs. Attu promised its own kind of frozen hell for the Japanese and American soldiers unfortunate enough to be deployed there.

General John L. DeWitt, the head of the Western Defense Command and the man responsible for the army's contribution to the Aleutians, originally wanted to attack Attu with the soldiers already stationed in Alaska. Unfortunately, these GIs lacked amphibious experience, were demoralized from their long tenure in such a hostile environment, and were scattered throughout the region. When he realized this, DeWitt recommended using the 35th Division. The War Department, though, concluded that the 35th Division was not yet prepared for action, so it gave DeWitt General Albert E. Brown's 7th Division instead. The 7th Division had been training to participate in the North African campaign, but the fact that it was readier to fight trumped the incongruity of assigning to the Arctic an outfit focused on

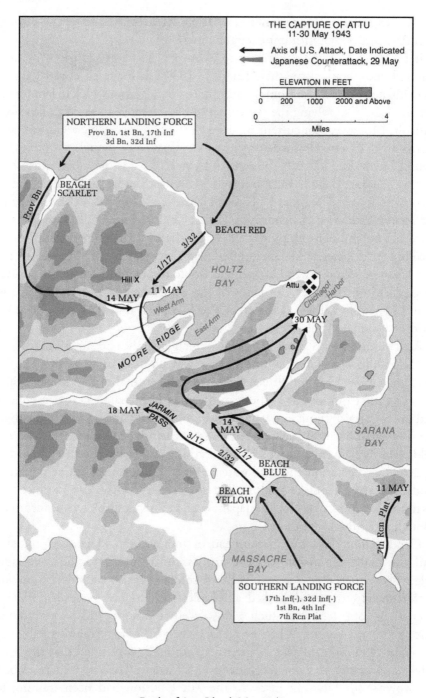

Battle of Attu Island, May 1943.

desert warfare. DeWitt worried, accurately enough, about Brown's fortitude and the War Department's inability to grasp the challenges of polar combat, but his concerns went unheeded.[2]

By the end of the Pacific War the 7th Division could plausibly claim to being one of the best army divisions of the conflict. Nicknamed the "Hourglass Division" because its patch was a black hourglass representing two "sevens" superimposed over a red circle, the 7th Division was activated in July 1940. Although it was a Regular Army outfit, one of its regiments, the 184th, was actually from the California National Guard. It also contained a disproportionate number of Mexican-Americans, American Indians from the Southwest, Texas cowboys, and Utah Mormons. It did all its training in California, which, along with the presence of the 184th, gave it something of a California flavor. Its commander, Albert Brown, was a good enough officer, but, as events demonstrated, he was not the kind of hard driver a combat unit needed. Unhappily, the 7th Division's amphibious training at Fort Ord was not accompanied by the equipment and preparation necessary to perform well in polar conditions. Moreover, the division departed from San Francisco for the Aleutians on 24 April 1943, giving its GIs precious little time to acclimate to the harsh environment they would soon face.

On 11 May, elements of two 7th Division regiments—the 17th and 32nd—splashed ashore on two Attu beaches, one north and the other south of the center of Japanese operations at Chichagof Harbor. There were actually 3,000 Japanese soldiers on Attu, more than the Americans expected, but considerably fewer than the 15,000 troops the Americans ultimately deployed there. The initial landings went as well as could be expected, but GIs advancing inland ran into stubborn Japanese opposition at Jarmin Pass that they were at first unable to overcome. Officers did not show much initiative and soldiers clumped together and did not maneuver. Two company commanders were killed, and two more broke mentally under the strain of combat responsibility, as did a battalion chief. Cold, inadequate boots, and a failure to change socks frequently led to trench foot and hypothermia among the GIs. Air support was practically nonexistent and artillery support spotty. After three days Brown called for reinforcements to help his beleaguered men. In response, on 16 May a dismayed Kinkaid removed him from his command and replaced him with General Eugene M. Landrum. That night the outnumbered and outgunned Japanese pulled back to Chichagof to make their last stand. Rooting them out required almost two weeks of brutal combat across the barren landscape and help from the independent 4th Regiment. Finally, on the night of 29/30 May, the remaining 1,000 or so Japanese launched an all-out banzai attack that broke in the face of American firepower. Organized Japanese opposition ended the next day when the Americans occupied Chichagof Harbor.

Retaking Attu had not been cheap. About 550 Americans died in the operation, with an additional 1,148 wounded and 2,100 succumbing to nonbattle injuries. The defending Japanese garrison was practically wiped out, except for twenty-eight men taken prisoner. By way of return, the Americans recovered Attu, for what that was worth, and learned important lessons about polar warfare that they could apply when the time came to storm equally valueless Kiska. To do that, the Americans deployed 34,400 troops, including 5,500 Canadians, and provided them with adequate clothing and footwear. However, when the Allies landed on Kiska on 15 August, they discovered that the Japanese were gone. They had evacuated the island three weeks earlier, on 28 July, right under the nose of the Allies. Even this "bloodless" victory cost more than eighty American and Canadian lives due to friendly fire incidents by soldiers roving across the island looking for a nonexistent foe.

Although the climate was drastically different, the 7th Division's baptism of fire on Attu mirrored that of some of its divisional counterparts in the Solomons and New Guinea in their first actions. On Attu many of the 7th Division's officers did not demonstrate good leadership. They failed to inspire their men, maintain discipline, take charge of the situation, show initiative, think on their feet, and subordinate all else to achieving their objectives. The 7th Division may have been a Regular Army unit, but in some respects, such as its activation date and composition, it was closer to a National Guard formation. It won at Attu not because it fought well, but simply through brutal attrition made possible by the navy's success in cutting the Japanese garrison off from outside help. The division's difficulties, though, did not reverberate throughout the army's Pacific high command like those of the 32nd and 43rd Divisions had. At Attu the 7th Division was not part of the POA or SWPA, but rather it belonged to the Western Defense Command. This limited the outfit's reputational damage. One of the few who did comment, albeit indirectly, on the division's record right after Attu was George Marshall. Marshall lamented the laxness, complacency, and helplessness that seemed to infect too many divisions under fire for the first time, such as the 7th. The question, of course, was whether the Hourglass boys would learn from their mistakes and perform better in their next outing.[3]

Gilberts

After some back-and-forth deliberations, Nimitz and his POA strategists decided to start their long-awaited Central Pacific offensive by assailing the

Gilbert Islands in an operation dubbed "Galvanic." Located about 2,400 miles southwest of Oahu, Hawaii, the Gilberts consisted of sixteen islands running 420 miles north to south with a total land area of only 100 square miles. The Japanese had seized them without opposition from the British several days after their attack on Pearl Harbor. Nimitz wanted them as a springboard for an assault on the neighboring Marshall Islands, and to provoke the Japanese fleet into a decisive battle with its American counterpart. The key to the Gilberts was Tarawa Atoll, which contained an airfield and was well-defended by around 4,500 Japanese troops. Nimitz assigned the 2nd Marine Division, veterans of Guadalcanal, the job of seizing it. POA planners also desired triangular-shaped Makin Atoll, 120 miles north of Tarawa, to construct an additional airfield. It was the northernmost of the Gilberts, but close enough to Tarawa for the navy to simultaneously support both invasions. The Marines did not have sufficient resources to storm both Tarawa and Makin, so the army agreed to take responsibility for the latter. To do so, it offered its 165th Regiment from what was undoubtedly the most controversial division of the Pacific War: the 27th.

The 27th Division had been built out of New York's National Guard. Indeed, its nickname was "New York" and its convoluted patch was a red-edged black circle containing in red the stars of Orion and the letters "N" and "Y" interwoven together. It was inducted into federal service in October 1940 and sent to protect Hawaii's Outer Islands in May 1942. Its commander was Ralph C. Smith, a good and intelligent man, but, like the 32nd Division's Forrest Harding and the 43rd Division's John Hester, not a driver. The 27th Division was one of two National Guard divisions that the War Department did not have the opportunity to extensively purge of its bad National Guard habits. As a result, critics stated that it possessed all the problems that afflicted other National Guard outfits, only worse. Its community ties were tighter and more intricate, its personal bonds between officers and enlisted men were stronger, its parochialism was more intense, and its officers were more indebted to patronage and popularity, rather than competency, for their positions than National Guard units reformed by the War Department. It was in this respect a throwback to a Civil War era militia outfit rather than a twentieth-century combat unit. Marshall suggested using it for the Makin operation because it was already in Hawaii, so there would be no need to further strain scarce Allied shipping by bringing in another division. Besides, *not* employing it would indicate a lack of confidence not only in the division itself, but in the army's entire training regime.[4]

Whatever its problems, the War Department believed that the 27th Division was a good outfit that could easily be readied for an amphibious assault on

Makin. Marshall stated that it was well-trained with excellent leaders, and MacArthur vouched for it after an inspection during a visit to Hawaii. When Marshall expressed concerns about the performance of other National Guard units, Robert Richardson, the POA's army chief, assured him that the 27th Division would not follow this unhappy pattern. "Some time ago," wrote Richardson to Marshall, "I discussed with General [Ralph] Smith the necessity of putting a lot of iron into his officers, and I think that he has been made quite aware of the necessity of doing so if he is to obtain success in battle."[5] Privately, though, Richardson had his doubts. After a couple of high-ranking officers expressed concerns about the division's readiness, Richardson wrote in his diary, "I don't feel that it is well commanded but I hope that is mistaken."[6] Even so, publicly he continued to express confidence in it.

Some Marine officers were also concerned about the 27th Division, though many of them articulated their doubts only after it was in their best interests to denigrate the outfit. Holland Smith, the V Amphibious Corps commander, later called the 27th Division a "gentleman's club" and claimed that he had to pressure Ralph Smith to conduct sufficient amphibious warfare training. The V Amphibious Corps' chief of staff, Colonel Graves Robert Erskine, echoed Holland Smith's reservations. He said that Ralph Smith confessed to him, "I have a hell of a time giving those people the right idea of discipline and relationships, but it's a problem I have to deal with."[7] Most Marine officers, though, were focused on Tarawa, and figured that whatever their misgivings about the 27th Division, its Makin assignment was so easy that it could not possibly fail.[8]

On 20 November, the army and Marine Corps assaulted their respective Gilbert Island targets. The 27th Division's 165th Regiment, along with a battalion from the 105th, landed on the main Makin island of Butaritari at two beaches dubbed "Red" and "Yellow." The soldiers at Red beach on the island's ocean side came ashore almost unopposed, but their Yellow beach comrades approaching from the lagoon had a more difficult time. Their amphibious vehicles ran aground on a coral reef, forcing the GIs to wade the last 250 yards to shore through rifle and machine gun fire. With some 6,500 troops at his disposal against 400 Japanese soldiers and an equal number of laborers, Ralph Smith could scarcely lose, but his men played it safe and advanced cautiously and hesitantly against Japanese bunkers, destroying them one by one. The Japanese helped the process along by launching an unsuccessful banzai attack with their remaining personnel on the night of 22/23 November. Next day Ralph Smith declared, "Makin taken." The 27th Division lost sixty-six killed and 152 wounded in the battle. Most of the Japanese garrison perished.

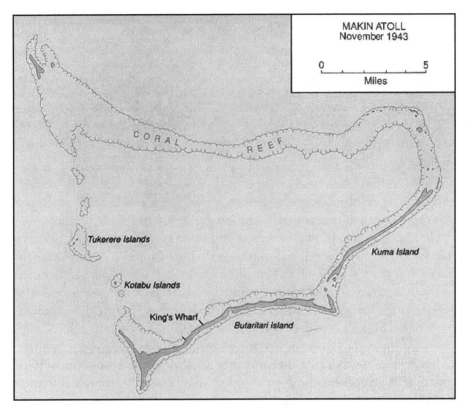

Battle of Makin Island, November 1943.

Makin was both a secondary and unfulfilling victory. Some accused the 27th Division of taking too long to achieve its objective. Although the Marines at Tarawa confronted 4,500 dug-in Japanese and sustained 3,400 casualties in eradicating them, they managed to secure their island in the same amount of time that it took the GIs to overcome far fewer of the enemy on Makin. And timeliness mattered. On 24 November, the last day of the operation, a Japanese submarine torpedoed and sank the escort carrier USS *Liscome Bay* off Makin, costing 644 sailors their lives. If the soldiers had taken Makin sooner, then *Liscome Bay* would not have been in the area when the Japanese submarine made its presence so dramatically known. Holland Smith certainly felt this way. He came ashore on Makin during the battle and was appalled with what he found. He called the 27th Division's advance "infuriatingly slow" and stated that a Marine regiment could have occupied Makin in a day. In particular, he complained that individual snipers held up large numbers of cowed GIs. He criticized indiscriminate and undisciplined firing, poor communications, and substandard leadership. He remembered:

> I was very dissatisfied with the [165th] regiment's lack of offensive spirit; it was preposterous that such a small Japanese force could delay the capture of Makin for three days. It probably was not the fault of the men. The 165th was not too well officered. When I returned to Pearl Harbor, I reported to Admiral Nimitz that had Ralph Smith been a Marine I would have relieved him of his command on the spot. His conduct of the operation did not measure up to my expectations at all.[9]

Holland Smith was not a reticent man, so he was quick to express his unhappiness to all hearers. Other Marines picked up on and echoed his refrain, undermining relations between the two services and sowing seeds of discord that eventually and unfortunately sprouted into interservice dissention.

On the other hand, some observers and historians took Holland Smith to task for his behavior and conclusions. Army historian S. L. A. Marshall, for instance, was on Makin too, saw Smith in action, and labeled him an ignorant and bullying grandstander. Others pointed out that the 27th Division did seize Makin on the schedule it had set and of which Holland Smith had approved. For him to condemn the division for fulfilling its mission on the agreed-upon timetable was unfair. Indeed, deviating from it might have led to confusion and increased casualties. At the same time, though, even those inclined to be sympathetic agreed that the 27th Division had shown considerable jitteriness and lethargy in its first action.[10]

At Makin yet another army division—or, more accurately, part of one—failed to live up to expectations in its baptism of fire. To be sure, the 27th Division did win the battle, and in a timelier fashion than the 32nd Division at Buna, the 43rd at New Georgia, and the 7th at Attu. It did so not because it was any better than those outfits, but rather because the odds were so overwhelmingly in its favor that it could hardly lose. Unfortunately for the 27th Division, several issues made its Makin debut problematic. For one thing, it occurred at the same time that the 2nd Marine Division assaulted Tarawa in a battle that became part of Marine Corps lore. It was only natural for many to make unfavorable comparisons between the 27th Division and the more experienced Marine unit. Moreover, only part of the 27th Division fought at Makin. This meant that the bulk of the division had still to see combat. When that happened, those expecting it to perform like a veteran division were likely to be disappointed. Finally, *Galvanic*—or, more accurately, Holland Smith's critical reaction to the 27th Division's actions there—set the stage for a dramatic confrontation between the army and Marine Corps eight months later on Saipan.

Marshalls

In mid-September 1943, GIs from the 7th Hourglass Division disembarked at Honolulu from the Aleutian Islands. It was a veteran outfit, having bested the Japanese at Attu and participated in the unopposed landing at Kiska. Its new commander was General Charles H. Corlett, a competent but high-strung man. Corlett had rather fixed ideas about training and discipline, so he got the division to work as soon as possible. His efforts paid off. One observer wrote, "I was so impressed with the 7th Division …. They'd been in combat, and when you came into their area, those guys snapped to attention and saluted. The area was clean; everything about them just looked great."[11] As things turned out, the 7th Division needed all the preparation it could get for the difficult operation that POA strategists had planned for it.[12]

The POA's next target was the Marshall Islands. The Marshalls were a group of twenty-nine islands divided into two north-to-south chains covering 750,000 square miles of ocean just north of the equator and west of the International Date Line. The Japanese had seized them from the Germans during World War I and saw them as the outer ring of their empire. For the Americans, the Marshalls were not important in and of themselves, but rather as stepping stones toward the more valuable Marianas and as bait to lure the Japanese navy into the climactic battle its American counterpart failed to get in the Gilberts but was still seeking. Nimitz opted to take advantage of growing American naval and air superiority in the region by striking at the very heart of the Marshalls at Kwajalein Atoll in Operation *Flintlock*.

Kwajalein was the largest atoll in the Marshalls. It was 540 miles northwest of recently seized Tarawa and 2,100 miles from Honolulu. Kwajalein was actually ninety small islands containing six square miles of soil that enclosed a huge lagoon of 655 square miles. The 7th Division's mission was to assail Kwajalein proper, at the southeastern end of the atoll, while the 4th Marine Division hit the connected islands of Roi and Namur at the atoll's northern apex. The Japanese had about 5,000 troops on Kwajalein proper, though less than 2,000 were really combat effective. Fortunately for the Americans, the Japanese had not fortified Kwajalein as heavily as they had Tarawa, but there were still plenty of pillboxes, machine gun nests, and artillery waiting for the GIs and leathernecks. It was not an easy mission.

The heavy Marine casualties at Tarawa revealed serious flaws in American amphibious doctrine that had to be addressed if the Kwajalein operation was to succeed with acceptable losses. POA officers took a hard look at

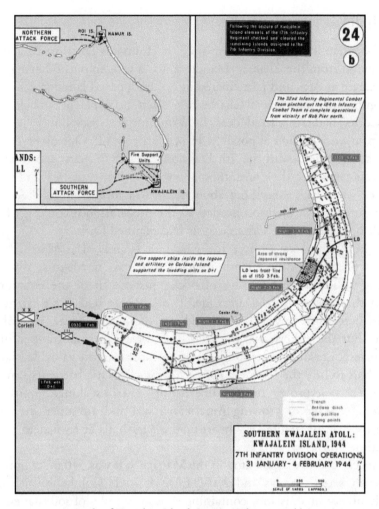

Battle of Kwajalein Island, January–February 1944.

the Tarawa battle and recommended innumerable changes. Their general conclusion was that they needed more of everything in future amphibious assaults: more troops, more landing craft, a longer and heavier and more accurate preliminary bombardment by more warships, more air support, more intelligence, and more effective interservice coordination. They also suggested seizing offshore islets prior to the main landing on which to establish artillery batteries to suppress enemy fire as the leathernecks and GIs came ashore. Holland Smith in particular lobbied for a clearer chain of command that would give him more authority. He got some of what he wanted, but Corlett thwarted his efforts to exert control over the 7th Division. When Smith suggested to Corlett that he accompany the 7th Division and, by implication, give orders to its men when it engaged the Japanese, Corlett emphatically refused. "I don't want you ashore until the fighting is done," exclaimed Corlett. "This is my battle. You may put some staff officers ashore as observers. If I find they have tried to issue any orders, I'll have them arrested."[13] Smith's protests that Corlett was insubordinate and rude merely provoked more of the same. Corlett clearly intended to fight the 7th Division his way on Kwajalein.

On 20–21 January 1944, the navy's enormous Fifth Fleet departed Hawaiian waters for the Marshalls. The portion devoted to conveying and supporting the troops, Admiral Richmond Kelly Turner's Fifth Amphibious Force, contained 297 vessels, including seven old battleships, eleven aircraft carriers of various sizes, twelve cruisers, seventy-five destroyers and destroyer escorts, forty-six transports, and twenty-seven cargo ships. Ten days later, elements from the 7th Division's 17th Regiment occupied a couple of lightly defended islets off of Kwajalein proper on which the Americans placed artillery to support the next day's main assault. After a prolonged and accurate preliminary bombardment that included 55,000 105 mm and 6,000 155 mm shells, on the morning of 1 February the 7th Division's 32nd and 184th Regiments splashed ashore on Kwajalein's western side at the same time as the 4th Marine Division stormed Roi-Namur. The army landings went smoothly, and from there Corlett directed his GIs in a methodical and deliberate advance across the island from phase line to phase line, destroying enemy bunkers, blockhouses, and pillboxes along the way. The Japanese fought doggedly and used infiltration tactics that kept the Americans on their toes, but there were no major surprises. Corlett declared Kwajalein proper secured on 4 February, though mopping up there and on nearby islands continued for days afterwards.

The Americans had every right to be pleased with Flintlock's outcome. Although there were approximately twice as many Japanese defending Kwajalein as there had been on Tarawa, American casualties had been lighter this time around. The army lost 142 killed, 845 wounded, and two missing taking Kwajalein proper. For their part, the Marines suffered 190 killed and 655 wounded in seizing Roi-Namur. The Japanese fleet did not challenge its American counterpart in the decisive battle naval officers wanted, but the offensive moved the Americans a giant step westward toward the strategically vital Marianas. In fact, Japanese opposition on Kwajalein was so ineffective that Nimitz ordered the Fifth Fleet to assail Eniwetok Atoll without returning to Pearl Harbor to refit. Eniwetok was about 420 miles northwest of Kwajalein and 2,725 miles from Honolulu. Nimitz wanted it for a forward anchorage and base for future operations westward. Leathernecks and elements from the 27th Division's 106th Regiment took the Eniwetok islands of Engebi and Parry and wiped out their Japanese garrisons in mid-February at the cost of 262 killed, 757 wounded, and seventy-seven missing.

Corlett and his 7th Division received considerable acclaim for their Kwajalein performance. Corlett was proud of his division and noted that the green 184th Regiment seemed determined to do as well as the more experienced 32nd Regiment. He later noted, "The 7th Division at this time was superbly trained. Its morale was high as a result of this training. It provided a pattern for future operations of this kind."[14] Corlett obviously had a proprietary interest in lauding the 7th Division, but others agreed with his assessment. Richardson, for example, voiced his approval in his report to Marshall, and later expounded in his memoirs: "The capture of Kwajalein was a classic of its kind. The careful preparation of every detail, the foresight displayed, the proper use of artillery, the tactics of the infantry, the excellence of the communications during the battle, and the leadership displayed by the officers and noncommissioned officers, all combined to ensure a very prompt victory with a minimum of casualties."[15] Naval officers were equally complimentary, including the irascible Fifth Amphibious Force commander, Kelly Turner. Subsequent historians were also quick to credit Corlett and the 7th Division for a job well done. In fact, the only criticism leveled against the division by these people was the GIs' tendency to bunch together and eschew maneuver. George Marshall probably best summed up the consensus opinion:

> Detailed reports of the 7th Division operation against Kwajalein Island in the Marshalls indicate that General Corlett's training of the division, cooperation with the Navy (Turner incidentally), plan of battle landing, artillery support, tank and infantry action, organization of beaches for supply, continuity of methodical effort and even details of burial of his dead, etc., approached perfection.[16]

This was high praise indeed from the staid chief of staff for Corlett that reflected equally well on his Hourglass Division. Small wonder that Marshall soon afterwards tapped Corlett for a corps command in Europe.[17]

On the other hand, some Marine officers adopted a more jaundiced view of the 7th Division's Kwajalein performance. They noted that it took the 7th Division's soldiers twice as long to secure Kwajalein proper as the 4th Marine Division needed to seize more heavily defended Roi-Namur. Not surprisingly, this was Holland Smith's opinion. Years later he wrote, "I fretted considerably at the slowness of the army advance. I could see no reason why this division, with ample forces ashore, well covered by land-based artillery and receiving tremendous naval and air support, could not take the island quicker. Every hour the transports and other ships of the fleet had to remain in the vicinity of the action the greater was the danger from enemy air and submarine attack."[18] His chief of staff, Bobby Erskine, was more philosophical: "The only thing is, I felt that the 7th Division could have gone faster, and I went ashore with their people several times there, and went around, and I didn't feel that they were aggressive enough in this operation. But in the end—I don't know whether that's a legitimate comment or not, because they did finally take the island, but it was pretty damn slow."[19] Whatever the truth of these sentiments, it demonstrated that Smith in particular neither understood nor appreciated army doctrine that emphasized a systematic approach to tactics, a defect that caused no end of trouble in the subsequent Marianas operation.

No matter how much critics nitpicked the 7th Division's Kwajalein performance, it was hard to overlook the fact that it won the battle on the timetable and in the manner Corlett planned. His methodical tactics may not have meshed with the realities of warfare in the Central Pacific from the Marine Corps' perspective, but they were certainly in sync with army doctrine. As usual, it took some time for the division to recover from its recent ordeal. It returned to Hawaii in mid-February, spent the next nine months refitting and training, and did not see action again until October 1944. Its victory at Kwajalein made it the premier army division in the Central Pacific. Indeed, by early 1944, only the 25th and 37th Divisions had secured two offensive victories, although the ones on New Georgia left something to be desired. The 7th Division was only halfway through its distinguished wartime saga that would include two of the bitterest campaigns in the conflict on Leyte and Okinawa.

Marianas: Saipan

In the big scheme of things, the Gilberts and Marshalls were not strategically that important to Japan. They were remote outposts on the fringes of Japan's empire, just stepping stones to more vital places. However, this was definitely not true of the Marianas. The Marianas were a group of fifteen islands running north to south for about 425 miles, located around 3,850 miles west of Hawaii and 1,400 miles from Japan. Except for Guam, the Japanese had seized them from Germany during World War I. Guam was an American possession, one of the spoils of the Spanish-American War, but it fell into Japanese hands shortly after the Pacific War began. The Marianas derived their significance from their location. In American hands, B-29 Superfortress bombers flying from the islands could raid Japanese cities, destroying infrastructure and showing the population rather dramatically that the war was not going well. American naval officers still seeking a decisive battle with their Japanese counterparts hoped that the Japanese would be willing to risk their fleet to protect the Marianas. Although the Joint Chiefs had originally slated an assault on the Marianas for November 1944, the increasingly successful Central Pacific offensive persuaded them to advance the attack to mid-June in an operation codenamed "Forager."

The POA targeted three Marianas islands: Saipan, Tinian, and Guam. Because they lacked sufficient resources to assail all three simultaneously, naval officers eventually decided to attack Saipan first, then Tinian, and finally Guam. Saipan was different from previous American objectives in the Central Pacific. At forty-five square miles, or twice the size of Manhattan, it dwarfed Tarawa and Kwajalein. It was not an atoll, but a single island with a mountainous spine, hills and rolling plateaus in the north and west, and flat coastal plains in the south and east. It possessed the offshore reefs with which POA soldiers and leathernecks were familiar, but numerous cliffs, jungles, and swamps too. Its infrastructure was also more developed than anything the Americans had so far encountered in the Central Pacific, with dense sugarcane fields, sugar refineries, small towns, two airfields, and even a railroad. The Japanese deployed 30,000 troops to defend Saipan, far more than the Americans had faced in the Gilberts or Marshalls.

Seizing a strongly defended island such as Saipan required a more powerful force than the POA had previously deployed in the Gilberts and Marshalls. To do so, POA planners assigned the job to two Marine divisions—the 2nd and 4th—as well as the army's 27th Division, and placed them all under the leadership of Holland Smith and his V Amphibious Corps. This meant that, for the first time in the war, a Marine general would directly command an entire army division. Although the 27th Division appeared to be an experienced outfit, that was not quite accurate. About two thirds of it had seen action at Makin and Eniwetok, but the remainder had not. More seriously, the division had never fought together as a unit. There was also a cloud over it because of its allegedly lackluster performances in its earlier battles. Holland Smith certainly viewed it this way. Smith had had doubts about the 27th Division before it even underwent its baptism of fire, and subsequent events had done nothing to dispel them. He later recalled, "After my experience with the Twenty-seventh [Division] at Makin and Eniwetok, I was reluctant to use

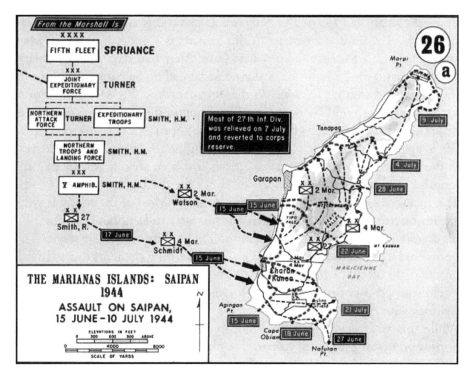

Battle of Saipan Island, June–July 1944.

them again in the Marianas, but when the operation was planned they were the only troops available in Hawaii and I had to take them."[20]

Unfortunately, Smith did little to encourage or understand the 27th Division. He instead recommended to Richardson that the army break it up, or at least give it a thorough housecleaning. Richardson refused. Whatever his earlier private doubts, he believed in the 27th Division, though he was probably blinded to its faults by his loyalty to the army and personal ties with some of the division's officers. He later wrote, "He [Holland Smith] seemed obsessed with venomous hatred of this Army unit [27th Division]."[21] To top it all off, 27th Division staffers were unsure where, when, or how Smith planned to utilize the unit after it reached Saipan, making it difficult to formulate the plans that promote smooth deployment. None of this boded well. Indeed, the fuse had been set for an explosion on Saipan that would roil interservice relations, ruin careers, generate controversy, and practically destroy the 27th Division as a useful organization.[22]

POA planners tasked Admiral Raymond A. Spruance's Fifth Fleet to convey and protect the approximately 70,000 soldiers and Marines slated to assail Saipan. It consisted of 800 vessels of various types, including 110 transports. The leading elements of this armada got under way on 25 May and gathered off Saipan nineteen days later. After two days of preliminary bombardment, on 15 June the leathernecks landed on Saipan's southwestern shore, the 2nd Marine Division to the north and the 4th Marine Division to the south. Both outfits encountered heavy opposition as they carved out a beachhead. Holland Smith's plans were upset by Spruance's 16 June news that the main Japanese fleet was on its way to engage its American counterpart in the decisive encounter that naval officers had been seeking for the past six months. Spruance wanted to clear the decks for the big battle shaping up. This included getting the transports out of range. Most of the Marines were already on Saipan, but the 27th Division's GIs were still shipbound. Whatever his doubts about the 27th Division, Smith did not want to lose its services, so he ordered it put ashore as soon as possible. Its leading elements disembarked on the night of 16/17 June.

Holland Smith's first assignment for the 27th Division was to help the Marines seize Aislito Airfield, which fell to the 165th Regiment on 18 June. While this was occurring, Smith prepared to redeploy his forces to drive northward across the rest of Saipan. He placed the 2nd Marine Division on the west coast and the 4th Marine Division on the east. He also dispatched the bulk of the 27th Division between the Marine outfits, and sent the remainder to clear the Japanese out of Nafutan Point to the island's south. He launched his offensive on 22 June. The Marines made good progress along the shorelines, but the 27th Division, jumping off in earnest the next day, got bogged down in aptly named Death Valley. Japanese troops ensconced in the overlooking mountains and ridges made it almost impossible for the GIs to advance across the barren terrain. Moreover, the rest of the division was unable to reduce Nafutan Point.

Not surprisingly, Holland Smith became increasingly frustrated with the 27th Division because he did not believe that there were that many Japanese in either Death Valley or Nafutan Point. As he saw things, the 27th Division's commander, Ralph Smith, and its senior leadership lacked sufficient aggressiveness and initiative. After all, Marine units were taking even heavier casualties, but they were gaining ground. On the afternoon of 23 June, Holland Smith consulted General Sanderford Jarman, the army officer slated to run Saipan once it was secured. After hearing Smith's concerns, Jarman volunteered to talk with Ralph Smith and try to light a fire under him. Ralph Smith admitted to Jarman that he too was unsatisfied with his division's performance and promised it would do better the next day. In fact, Jarman later stated that Ralph Smith said that he should be relieved if he could not deliver on his pledge. Unfortunately, the 27th Division did not meet Holland Smith's expectations on 24 June either. For Holland Smith, its failure was the last straw. That afternoon he and Erskine motored over to see Kelly Turner, still serving as head of the amphibious assault force, and stated that Ralph Smith needed to go. Turner took them to Spruance on his flagship, the heavy cruiser USS *Indianapolis*, who agreed and authorized Holland Smith to issue the necessary orders removing Ralph Smith from the 27th Division.[23]

Ralph Smith's departure did not immediately alter the tactical calculus on the ground. The 27th Division's attacks across Death Valley and into Nafutan Point remained unsuccessful. However, Japanese strength was finite and dwindling, and hard combat experience was improving the 27th Division's effectiveness. Nafutan Point fell on 27 June. Three days later, after repeated assaults, the 27th Division finally cleared Death Valley in an operation that won even Holland Smith's praise. It had taken eight days for the 27th Division to advance just 3,000 yards. Doing so broke the back of the Japanese army on Saipan, compelling its remnants to retreat northward. After more fighting around Tanapag, the Japanese fell back to the northern tip of the island. On the morning of 7 July, the remaining 3,000 or so Japanese soldiers launched an all-out charge against the 27th Division's 105th Regiment that overwhelmed its GIs. One officer remembered, "It was like the movie stampede staged in the old wild west movies. We were the cameraman. These Japs just kept coming and coming and didn't stop. It didn't make any difference if you shot one, five more would take his place. We would be in the foxholes looking up, as I said, just like those cameramen used to be. The Japs ran right over us."[24] Although it took a couple days for leathernecks and the 106th Regiment to regain the lost ground and clean up the last Japanese defenders, this failed go-for-broke Japanese effort marked the end of large-scale organized resistance on Saipan, though mopping up continued for months afterwards. It also generated more controversy about the 27th Division's effectiveness.

Seizing Saipan had not been cheap. Of the 71,000 ground troops committed to the invasion, about twenty percent became casualties: 3,674 soldiers and 10,437 Marines. The Japanese garrison was all but destroyed. By way of compensation, the Americans got the island. Unfortunately, Saipan's value was limited because its mountainous terrain restricted the number of airfields the Army Air Forces could construct for its B-29 Superfortress bombers. Saipan did, however, provide the Americans with a convenient jumping off point to assail nearby Tinian. At thirty-nine square miles, Tinian was flat enough to accommodate as many airfields as the Army Air Forces needed for its strategic bombing campaign against the Japanese Home Islands. Marines from Saipan landed there on 24 July and took the island in a short and sharp operation that ended in early August. Finally, attacking Saipan provoked the Japanese navy into a big engagement that American naval officers so fervently wanted. The resulting Battle of the Philippine Sea on 19–20 June was an American victory, but not a decisive one. Although the Japanese navy's air arm was destroyed, most of the warships escaped to fight another day.

Saipan was an important American victory, but it also damaged both interservice relations and the 27th Division. Many army officers were outraged that Holland Smith had relieved Ralph Smith and, in doing so, denigrated the army. Nellie Richardson certainly felt this way. When he got the news of Ralph Smith's relief, he concluded that Holland Smith was making Ralph Smith and the 27th Division scapegoats for his failure to take Saipan quickly. As soon as the fighting on Saipan ended, Richardson flew to the island for a firsthand look at the situation. Once there, he berated Holland Smith for his actions. He did not dwell on Ralph Smith's relief, probably because he saw it as more a symptom than a cause, but he instead focused on the Marine Corps' overall conduct during the operation. Holland Smith quoted Richardson as saying, "You and your Corps commanders aren't as well qualified to lead large bodies of troops as general officers in the army. We've had more experience in handling troops than you've had and yet you dare remove one of my generals. You marines are nothing but a bunch of beach runners anyway. What do you know about land warfare?"[25] Richardson later denied belittling the Marines, but he threatened to report everything he saw to George Marshall and promised a thorough investigation. Although Holland Smith managed to keep his temper, he defended the Marine Corps and welcomed an accounting of his conduct as long as he could cross-examine witnesses. Richardson kept his word and initiated an inquiry. The Buckner Board, named after its chairman, army General Simon B. Buckner, was hardly unbiased. It took testimony from army officers only, so navy and Marine officers did not get the opportunity to tell their side of the story. It concluded that although Holland Smith had the right to relieve Ralph Smith, his decision to do so was "not justified by the facts" because he was ignorant of the 27th Division's conditions and circumstances.[26]

Fortunately, the "Smith versus Smith" controversy did not get out of hand because high-ranking navy and army officers did not let it. They instead focused on winning the war. This included Nimitz. He wanted to keep any interservice disputes within the theater and was dismayed that Richardson seemed intent on fanning the flames of discord. His bland impartiality frustrated officers seeking their version of justice, but he knew that he needed both the army and Marine Corps to work together to successfully prosecute the war. Taking sides would only exacerbate the situation. As for the Joint Chiefs of Staff, King and Marshall came to a tacit agreement to put the hullabaloo behind them and get on with the war. Marshall did, however, inform King that it would probably be for the best for interservice relations if Holland Smith never again led army soldiers in battle. The Marine Corps subsequently kicked Smith upstairs to become the top Marine officer in the Pacific as Fleet Marine Force commander, a position that relegated him to the kind of administration and training duties that Nellie Richardson performed. Saipan was Smith's one and only time that he served as a combat commander.[27]

The Smith versus Smith controversy also had a big impact on the 27th Division. During the Saipan operation, some Marine officers took their cue from the outspoken Holland Smith and developed a vocal contempt for the outfit. They exaggerated its setbacks and denigrated its successes. One army officer remembered, "The Commanding General [Holland Smith] and Staff…held the units of the 27th Division in little esteem, actually a position bordering on scorn."[28] The 27th Division spent July and August mopping up Saipan while the Marines were busy storming Tinian. It then departed for Espiritu Santo Island in the New Hebrides. Conditions there were less than ideal. It was hot and humid, and there were not enough housing and recreational facilities. Moreover, by then about three quarters of the division's personnel had been overseas for two and a half years or more, leading to considerable homesickness and unhappiness. To top it all off, in September 1944, *Time* magazine published an article about the Smith versus Smith imbroglio that commented negatively on the 27th Division's performance on Saipan:

> Although terrific artillery barrages were laid down in front of them, Ralph Smith's men froze in their foxholes. For days these men, who lacked confidence in their officers, were held up by handfuls of Japs in caves. When it began to look as if what had been gained might be lost, Fourth Marine Division troops even moved in front of a sector of the 27th's line to save it. From the Marine point of view, General Ralph Smith's chief fault was that he had long ago failed to get tough enough to remove incompetent subordinate officers.[29]

This public humiliation was bad enough, but mail censorship prevented the division's GIs from providing their side of the story. Considering all these difficulties, it was small wonder that division morale suffered. A divisional historian later wrote, "To the men at Santo it appeared that they had been branded cowards and that unless something was done at once, cowards they would remain."[30]

There is an argument to be made for both sides of the controversy between Holland Smith and the 27th Division. Holland Smith's generalship on Saipan sometimes left something to be desired. It is important to remember that Saipan was the first time Smith had led troops into battle, so he was bound to make rookie mistakes. His orders were not always clear. He failed to recognize the seriousness of Japanese opposition at Nafutan Point and in Death Valley or visit both places for a firsthand look at the situation. He dissipated the 27th Division's combat power by ordering it to attack two unrelated objectives simultaneously. He undermined interservice relations by publicly criticizing the division and in doing so gave tacit permission for his staffers and subordinates to follow suit. Most seriously, though, was that he was predisposed against the 27th Division from the start, and made little effort to understand or accommodate its limitations and peculiarities. If he had been more patient and forbearing, he would have noticed that the division became more effective as the operation progressed and it learned from its mistakes. One Marine officer who spent time with the division singled out its regimental commanders as its weakest link, but added, "But I was with this division once it got started, and I will say they kept up with the marines, and sometimes did get a little ahead of them. And I so reported—they did a beautiful job when I was with them, but they were heading in the right direction, you see."[31] The fact that there were few difficulties between the Marines and army in subsequent interservice operations certainly indicates that Smith was the source of much of the tension and strife.[32]

Yet there were also reasons to criticize the 27th Division's performance on Saipan. The 27th was unlike almost all other National Guard divisions in that the War Department did not have the opportunity to reorganize it before it deployed overseas. As a result, the 27th Division still possessed the prewar community culture, personal ties, and patronage that enabled underqualified men to rise to the top. The high turnover rate among regimental commanders in particular confirms the unfortunate consequences of this arrangement. Moreover, it was not just Marines who noted the difficulties in getting the 27th Division's GIs to obey orders promptly, take the initiative, and prioritize attaining their objectives. The assistant chief of staff, General Thomas T. Handy, examined the division's record and concluded that its personnel had not been sufficiently aggressive in Death Valley. General Joseph T. McNarney, the deputy chief of staff, agreed with Handy and stated that Ralph Smith did not get as much out of the division as he should have. McNarney also remarked upon the GIs' poor march discipline, hesitancy, inability to perform proper reconnaissance, and willingness to give and accept excuses. The 27th Division, in short, was hardly blameless.[33]

Although elements of the 27th Division had seen action before its deployment to Saipan, it was not really a veteran outfit when it landed because it had never fought together as a unit. On Saipan it undoubtedly made all sorts of errors, but so did almost every other National Guard division in its baptism of fire in the Pacific War. Those other units, though, learned from their mistakes and became increasingly proficient and confident as the war progressed. The 27th Division's trajectory was different because of the public interservice rivalries the Saipan operation spawned. After Saipan, it was a division with a collective target on its back. As a result, some high-level officers saw it not as an asset, but rather as a potential liability, for the remainder of the conflict.

Marianas: Guam

Operation *Forager* called for the Americans to assault Guam three days after the Saipan landings. Guam was located 136 miles southwest of Saipan. At 212 square miles, it was the largest island in the Marianas' chain. Its northern half was a limestone plateau rimmed with formidable cliffs and covered with jungle, hardwood trees, and sword grass. The southern part was fertile and flat. A low mountain range filled the southwestern coast. To defend the island, the Japanese deployed 18,500 troops. POA planners had originally slated the 27th Division to participate in the Guam operation with the 3rd Marine Division and the 1st Provisional Marine Brigade as part of Marine General Roy S. Geiger's III Amphibious Corps. Fierce Japanese opposition on Saipan by land and sea, though, forced Holland Smith to commit it there. Nimitz therefore opted to postpone storming Guam until he could find enough shipping to transport another division to the Marianas. This took time, during which the navy thoroughly worked over Guam with a long, heavy, and systematic preliminary naval bombardment that did much to weaken its Japanese garrison.

Happily for the Americans, Nimitz had at his disposal the 77th Division, which was destined to become one of the army's finest Pacific War outfits. It was a draftee division activated in March 1942 and composed of a sizeable number of New Englanders and New Yorkers. Its patch was a gold Statue of Liberty superimposed over a truncated blue triangle. Some called it the "Statue of Liberty Division," but the 77th Division's GIs referred to themselves as "Old Buzzards" due to the advanced age of so many of them. Because it trained at Fort Jackson, South Carolina, it was something of a showcase unit for bigwigs passing through Washington D.C. In June 1942, for example, Chief of Staff General George Marshall and Secretary of War Henry Stimson brought Prime Minister Winston Churchill and a delegation of high-level British officials to watch a demonstration by three divisions that included the 77th. Field Marshal

Alan Brooke, Chief of the British Imperial General Staff, called them "fine hard looking men."[34] Another observer, Admiral Louis Mountbatten, wrote, "If the United States can go on turning out divisions like that, victory will be ours much sooner than I thought possible."[35]

There were a number of reasons for the 77th Division's successful transition into a well-prepared unit. The division's turnover rate was comparatively low, and its privileged status as a showcase outfit made it easier to transfer out substandard officers. Although its GIs were older than usual—the average age of the enlisted men was originally thirty-two—it contained a lot of specialists from civilian life such as mechanics, electricians, and stenographers who were intelligent and easy to train. It was also fortunate to have first-rate commanders such as Generals Robert Eichelberger and Roscoe Woodruff who ran the division until promoted to more responsible jobs. When it left for Hawaii in March 1944, General Andrew D. Bruce led the unit. Bruce was an intelligent, creative, and aggressive officer with a knack for thinking outside the box and a flair for the dramatic. He was also sometimes too ambitious for his own good. Upon taking over in May 1943, Bruce said, "This is a super outfit, but I'm going to make it a super duper outfit."[36] Even before it deployed overseas, many already considered the 77th one of the army's most promising divisions.[37]

Elements of the 77th Division began departing from Oahu for Eniwetok, the staging area for the Guam attack force, on 1 July. There they joined the thousands of Marines who had been marking time for weeks in their cramped and hot transports ever since Nimitz had postponed the invasion. The arrival of the soldiers swelled the number of troops in Eniwetok's lagoon to 55,000. The tedium was bad enough, but only the most gung-ho GI or leatherneck looked forward to imminent combat with any enthusiasm. On 21 July, the Marines landed on Guam's west coast on both sides of the Orote Peninsula, the 3rd Marine Division to the north around Asan and the 1st Provisional Marine Brigade five miles to the south at Agat. Despite heavy opposition, the Marines succeeded in establishing a beachhead.

Even before the sun went down, the 77th Division's 305th Regiment arrived to help, followed by the rest of the division over the course of the next few days. It took a week of hard fighting for the soldiers and Marines to consolidate their perimeter, after which the 1st Provisional Marine Brigade reduced the Orote Peninsula while the 77th Division fanned out eastward. After a short break, on 31 July Geiger ordered an offensive northward, with the 3rd Marine Division pushing up the west coast and the 77th Division advancing along the eastern shoreline. Both units made steady headway against moderate to severe Japanese resistance amidst the dense underbrush and craggy ridges.

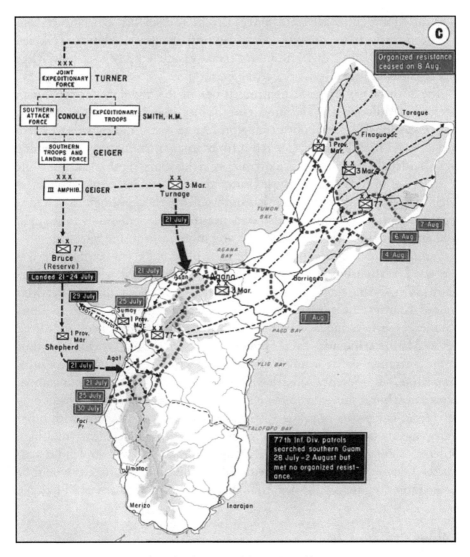

Battle of Guam, July–August 1944.

One tired Buzzard remembered, "The distance across the island is not far, as the crow flies, but unluckily we can't fly....After advancing a few yards you find that the handle of the machine gun on your shoulder, your pack and shovel, canteens, knife, and machete all stick out at right angles and are as tenacious in their grip on the surrounding underbrush as a dozen grappling hooks."[38] The troops reached Guam's northern tip on 10 August, at which point Geiger declared the island secured. Tedious and stressful mopping up, though, continued for months afterwards and caused more casualties. Liberating Guam had been costly. In twenty-one days of fighting, the Marines lost 6,716 killed and wounded. The 77th Division, for its part, suffered 839 casualties. Most of the Japanese garrison died one way or another.

The 77th Division's performance was one of the highlights of the Guam operation. Although it was in combat for the first time, it aggressively, skillfully, and professionally carried out its missions. Moreover, it did so with a certain panache and flair that differentiated it from other army divisions undergoing their battlefield initiations. The division may have made mistakes, but none so serious as to endanger the battle's outcome or timetable. It was a wonderful beginning for the division, one that both reflected and justified its status as a golden outfit. Its record was also evidence that draftee divisions could fight well and that army training was becoming more realistic and effective.

Perhaps most importantly of all, in light of recent events on Saipan, was the good relationship that Bruce and his soldiers forged with the Marine Corps. On Guam there was almost no friction between the two services. Indeed, Marine officers went out of their way to commend the 77th Division's abilities, even referring to it as the "77th Marine Division," because it lived up to Marine standards. Even Holland Smith, not a man inclined to dole out unwarranted praise to any organization except his beloved Marine Corps, later wrote, "The Seventy-seventh was a raw division, with no previous combat experience, but it showed combat efficiency to a degree one could expect only of veteran troops. Its aggressive patrolling, its close coordination with other units, and its superior conduct of assigned missions gave evidence of a high order of training, fine leadership and high morale."[39] It was a splendid start for the Old Buzzards of the Statue of Liberty division, but its GIs would be tested more strenuously the next time they saw action just a few months later.

Palaus

The last major geographic obstacle between the POA and the China–Formosa–Luzon region was the Palaus. Located about 500 miles north of New Guinea and east of the Philippine island of Mindanao, the Palaus were a collection of islands that ran northeast to southwest for approximately 100 miles. In American hands, the Palaus would project the navy's power northward and provide airfields and anchorages to protect MacArthur's right flank when he assailed the Philippines. The POA's original plan called for a major offensive against them, but Nimitz scaled it back because of perceived Japanese weakness in the vicinity. Nimitz decided to use Roy Geiger's III Amphibious Corps to seize three objectives in the Palaus—Angaur, Peleliu and Ulithi—in a revised operation ominously dubbed "Stalemate II."

POA planners assigned the job of seizing well-defended Peleliu to the battle-hardened 1st Marine Division, veterans of Guadalcanal and Cape Gloucester. Angaur and Ulithi, for their part, became the responsibility of General Paul J. Mueller's untested 81st "Wildcat" Division. The 81st was a draftee division activated in June 1942. It had served in World War I, and had then adopted what was supposedly the army's first divisional patch: a black wildcat superimposed over a black-bordered olive disc. It had trained for two years before it went overseas, during which time it avoided the kind of heavy turnover that handicapped other divisions. It was a fine-looking outfit with enough unit loyalty for its GIs to adopt their own song and to go out of their way to acquire a large and mean caged wildcat as the divisional mascot. As for Mueller, he was a colorless, dour, abrupt, and unengaging man who one officer described as a "cold fish." Mueller's immediate superior, XXIV Corps chief General John Hodge, questioned Mueller's competency. Hodge complained that Mueller misused his staff by making them justify everything they did, which led to unnecessary arguments. Richardson, for his part, doubted Mueller's forcefulness. Whatever his shortcomings, Mueller had enormous pride in his division. There was really nothing out of the ordinary about the 81st; it gave every indication of becoming another one of those solid draftee formations that the army was so good at creating during World War II.[40]

To the extent that *Stalemate II* is remembered at all, it is for the unnecessary ordeal that the Marines underwent on Peleliu. However, history has largely forgotten the army's role in the operation. Angaur was a crescent-shaped island of three square miles situated ten miles south of Peleliu with a Japanese garrison of about 1,400 men. Its northwest was full of forested coral ridges, but the remainder consisted of dense scrub brush. It derived its military value from its flat landscape that made airfield construction possible. On 17 September, two regiments from the 81st Division came ashore at two beaches on Angaur's northeast coast, the 322nd to the north and the 321st to the south. Moderate Japanese resistance, rough terrain, some unfortunate friendly fire incidents with warplanes, and, above all else, inexperience delayed the GIs' advance inland. Even so, the southern part of the island fell easily, prompting a naïve Mueller to declare Angaur secured on 20 September. In actuality, the Japanese had withdrawn their surviving troops to the deep and broken crevices, fissures, and caves that dotted Angaur's northwestern quadrant. It took more than a month of hammer and tongs combat for the 322nd Regiment to eradicate these stubborn Japanese hold-outs, during which its commander was wounded.

By the time the 81st Division had finished the job on 23 October, it had suffered 264 killed, 1,355 wounded, and 696 nonbattle casualties. It was a stiff price to pay for an island that, as things turned out, had little worth. On the other hand, the 81st Division's 323rd Regiment occupied Ulithi without opposition on 22 September, providing the navy with a vital forward deepwater anchorage in the region that it used to refit and refuel hundreds of its vessels for the remainder of the conflict.

The 1st Marine Division's commander, General William H. Rupertus, predicted that his leathernecks would seize Peleliu in a violent and brief operation that would last just a few days. He did not know that the Japanese, like the Americans, were learning from their battlefield mistakes and adapting accordingly. The Japanese recognized that the banzai charges that they had previously employed not only invariably failed in the face of American firepower, but also accelerated their defeat by squandering their remaining reserves. They therefore decided to forego such assaults and instead ordered their troops to dig in, hunker down, mount only small, limited counterattacks, and make the Americans come after them. Doing so would not win the engagement because the Japanese troops would still be outnumbered, outgunned, and cut off from reinforcements and resupply. Even so, these new tactics would hopefully inflict heavy losses on the Americans, delay their victory, and give Japanese soldiers on the Home Islands time to build up their defenses for the American invasion that seemed increasingly likely. The Marine proclivity for head-on drives played into Japanese hands on Peleliu. Although the Marines successfully landed on the island on 15 September and conquered about half of it within a few days, they suffered heavy casualties in the process and soon became bogged down. Rupertus did not know how to break the stalemate and mentally unraveled under the strain of battle. One obvious solution was to call upon the army for help. However, Rupertus neither trusted the army nor liked the idea of it rescuing the Marine Corps. Fortunately, Geiger took a broader view of the situation. He visited Peleliu on 21 September and was shocked to learn of the high losses the Marines were sustaining. Because Mueller had mistakenly declared Angaur secured a few days earlier, Geiger figured that the army had surplus soldiers who could help the beleaguered leathernecks. He ordered Mueller to ready his 321st Regiment for deployment to Peleliu immediately, and it arrived two days later.

Although the 321st Regiment had seen some action on Angaur, it was still a relatively green outfit with much to learn. It also had to serve at first under the direction of the jaded Marines, who were unlikely to gracefully tolerate the shortcomings of their interservice cousins. In fact, some Marines criticized the

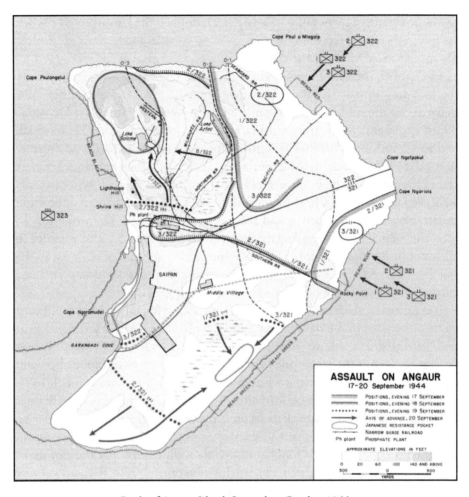

Battle of Angaur Island, September–October 1944.

321st for its caution, methodical tactics, and overreliance on fire support. This included an obviously bitter Rupertus, who said after the 321st mishandled an assault on a knoll: "That's the Wildcat Division of pussycats all the way. Now I can tell Geiger, 'I told you so.' That's why I didn't want the Army involved in this in the first place."[41] Other Marines, though, were more charitable in their evaluation of the 81st Division and worked well with it. One remembered, "In retrospect, that was a very good division."[42] Indeed, the Wildcats demonstrated considerable ingenuity in their use of armored bulldozers, napalm, improvised flamethrowers, makeshift spotlights, and impromptu conveyor systems. Once deployed, the 321st Regiment's GIs and the leathernecks cooperated to push the Japanese into a corner in northern Peleliu dubbed the Umurbrogol Pocket. Its forested caves, deep fissures, and invisible crevices made it an ideal place for the Japanese to make their last stand.

In October, the 81st Division gradually assumed the primary responsibility for mopping up the remaining Japanese, and the last Marine combat units departed by the middle of the month. About a week later, the 81st Division's 323rd Regiment arrived from Ulithi to take over from the blown 321st, which had lost 146 killed and 469 wounded since it reached Peleliu. Bad weather delayed the final assault on the Umurbrogol Pocket, and then ferocious Japanese resistance extended the battle even longer. The 323rd, though, systematically went about its business and finally snuffed out the last Japanese opposition in late November. By then it had suffered 118 killed and 420 wounded. In fact, the 81st Division on Angaur and Peleliu sustained 3,275 casualties in all, a not insignificant number. The Marines added another 6,525 men to the butcher's bill. As so often occurred in the Pacific War, the defending Japanese garrison was practically obliterated.[43]

It is easy to lambast *Stalemate II*. Although occupying Ulithi paid significant strategic benefits to the navy, it is in retrospect hard to see how seizing Angaur and Peleliu did much to advance the American war effort, certainly not enough to justify the steep price the POA paid for them in blood shed and time expended. Whatever the wisdom of the operation, there is much to be said for the 81st Division's performance. To be sure, it is possible to criticize it for the amount of time it took to secure Angaur and Peleliu, but, considering the inexperience of the division's GIs, the viciousness of Japanese opposition, and the horrible terrain, it fought reasonably well. It certainly did not make any mistakes that jeopardized the battle's outcome. Nellie Richardson saw it this way. After visiting the Palaus and inspecting the division, he wrote Marshall, "The 81st Division deserves high commendation for its work on these two islands. I have never seen such difficult terrain."[44] In addition, although some Marines clearly resented the appearance of the army rescuing the 1st Marine Division, there were no serious interservice disputes such as those that caused trouble on Saipan. Angaur and Peleliu demonstrated that the 81st Division was a quality outfit on its way to becoming a valuable part of the army's Pacific War divisional stable, even though its regiments had not fought together. Unfortunately for the division's reputation and record— though not, of course, for the soldiers who put their lives on the line in every engagement—*Stalemate II* was the Wildcats' only major operation. It remained in the Palaus until after the new year, when it left for New Caledonia to rest and refit. In May–June MacArthur summoned it to Leyte in the Philippines. It stayed there, training and patrolling, until the end of the war.

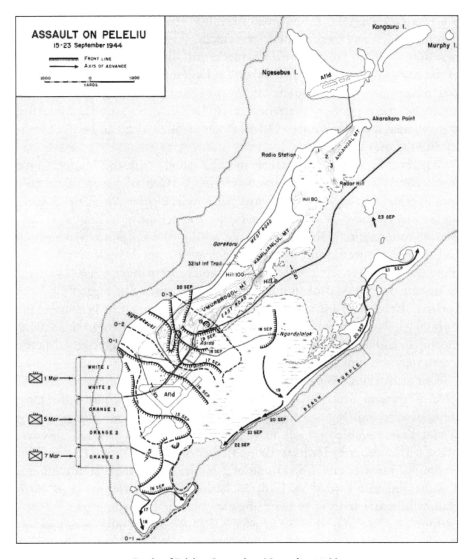

Battle of Peleliu, September–November 1944.

Conclusions

Because the Marine Corps specialized in amphibious warfare and was organizationally part of the navy, Nimitz made it the star of the Central Pacific offensive's ground fighting and relegated the army to a supporting role. In the Gilberts, the 2nd Marine Division tackled formidable Tarawa while a regiment from the 27th Division assailed lightly garrisoned Makin. In the Marshalls, the 7th Division's attack against Kwajalein proper was not as daunting as the

4th Marine Division's assault on Roi-Namur. The Marines did most of the fighting on Saipan and all of it on Tinian. Although the 77th Division performed well on Guam, the leathernecks still did a disproportionate share of the heavy lifting there. Finally, the 81st Division's mission against Angaur was in no way comparable to the 1st Marine Division's Peleliu nightmare. The one seeming exception to this trend, the 7th Division's operation against Attu, was conducted by the Western Defense Command, which had no Marines at its disposal, not the POA.

Whatever its role, the army had to work closely with the Marine Corps to effectively prosecute the ground war in the Central Pacific. Generally speaking, the two services cooperated fairly well. Neither the 77th Division on Guam nor the 81st Division on Peleliu had serious problems with their Marine counterparts. On Kwajalein, the 4th Marine and 7th Divisions each had their own specific and separate objectives that made tight coordination unnecessary. And in any case the 7th Division's commander, Charles Corlett, made sure that the Marines minded their own business. The biggest difficulty between the Marines and army was not institutional, but rather personal in the form of Holland Smith. It was Smith who poisoned army–Marine relations on Saipan through his tactlessness and heavy-handedness. Once the Marine Corps removed him from the scene, collegiality prevailed.

Four army divisions participated in the Central Pacific offensive: the 7th, 27th, 77th, and 81st. Of these four, the 7th Division acquired the most impressive record. It fought and won two battles in an offensive capacity. It may have stumbled its way to victory on Attu, but it received universal praise within the army for its textbook victory on Kwajalein proper. The latter accomplishment became something of a model for subsequent amphibious assaults and also earned its leader, Charles Corlett, promotion to corps command and a transfer to the European theater. The Hourglass Division's performance not only showed of what a Regular Army outfit was capable, but, because one of its regiments was composed of National Guardsmen, it also demonstrated that those units could fight well. By the time the Central Pacific offensive ended, the 7th Division was perhaps the most accomplished army division in the Pacific.

In addition, the 77th and 81st Divisions performed well in their first outings at, respectively, Guam and Angaur/Peleliu. Of the two, the 77th Division's record was the more impressive because it lived up to the high expectations placed on it, fought skillfully as a unit, kept up with the always demanding leathernecks, and finished its operation in a timely manner. The 81st Division's debut was notable too, but its three regiments did not serve together in combat and it took longer than expected for it to overrun Angaur and Peleliu. Even so, both units were off to fine starts, and their records showed that draftee divisions could pull their weight.

Lastly, the 27th Division's record was problematic. It was different from the other army divisions sent to the Central Pacific because it was a National Guard outfit deployed early in the conflict. Moreover, unlike almost all the other National Guard divisions, the War Department had never reformed it. As a result, it possessed all the problems that infected other Guard units, but in spades. It was therefore hardly surprising that it struggled on Makin and Saipan. To make things worse, Holland Smith's unsympathetic, chauvinistic, tactless, and outspoken attitude simply exacerbated the 27th Division's difficulties. However, it had shown improvement by the end of the Saipan operation. Whether it could put to rest the bad reputation it had acquired, fairly or not, remained to be seen.

CHAPTER THREE

MacArthur's New Guinea Road

"A Military Nightmare"

While the navy steamrollered its way across the Central Pacific through the Gilberts, Marshalls, and Marianas, Douglas MacArthur was undertaking his own campaign in the Southwest Pacific across New Guinea's northern coast. That he could do so resulted from the JCS strategic compromise authorizing the Dual Drive offensive in both the navy's POA and the army's SWPA theaters toward the amorphous China–Formosa–Luzon region. The JCS envisioned SWPA operations as secondary to the navy's, but MacArthur certainly did not see it that way. As far as he was concerned, the Dual Drive offensive was a race, with him running hard along the New Guinea littoral toward the China–Formosa–Luzon finish line. If he got there first, he hoped that his prize would be the right to undertake a campaign to liberate the Philippines. The Japanese had driven MacArthur out of that archipelago in 1941–42, but he had pledged to return. Redeeming the islands was to him only slightly less important than defeating Japan. Because his ambitions were contingent upon reaching the China–Formosa–Luzon area before the navy, he was a man in a hurry, and such men were rarely tolerant of excuses or delays.

The track upon which MacArthur intended to run his race was among the most remote, inhospitable, and primitive places on earth. New Guinea, the world's second largest island at 303,000 square miles, was larger than Texas. Indeed, if superimposed over the continental United States, with Port Moresby located at Miami, the Japanese strongholds along New Guinea's northern littoral would stretch from St. Augustine, Florida, to the Texas panhandle. The island's terrain ran the gamut from towering mountains in the interior to swampy jungle and uncharted coral reefs along the shoreline where most of the fighting took place. Frequent tropical downpours, even

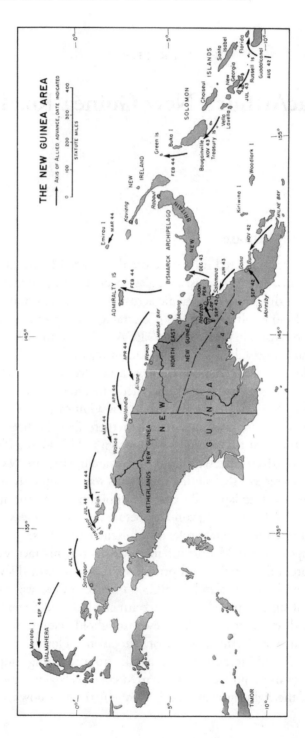

New Guinea.

during the so-called May to October dry season, rotted everything from uniforms to tents and turned camps and battlefields into flooded saunas. The jungles were filled with dangerous and creepy animals, including man-eating crocodiles, three-feet-long lizards, big black flightless cassowaries, huge bats, tree kangaroos, parrots, snakes, wasps, scorpions, centipedes, cockroaches, flies, ants, chiggers, fleas, and mosquitoes. The animals rarely killed anyone, but microorganisms did. Soldiers succumbed to dengue and blackwater fevers, dysentery, tropical ulcers, scrub typhus, yaws, and especially malaria. New Guinea's nonexistent road system made the various Japanese positions along the coast in effect fortified islands of military civilization surrounded by a sea of jungle. New Guinea was just as inhospitable as most Pacific islands in the region, but on a grander scale. Small wonder that one participant called it a "military nightmare."[1]

To undertake his campaign, MacArthur possessed, on paper, plenty of army divisions. At the end of 1943 he had the 1st Cav, 32nd, and 41st Divisions, as well as the recently arrived 24th Division. Moreover, the JCS had decided to give SWPA all of SOPAC's army ground units once *Cartwheel* was done. This would put the American, 25th, 37th, 40th, 43rd, and 93rd Divisions under his control. In addition, the 6th, 11th Airborne, 31st, 33rd, and 38th Divisions were on the way. When put together, these units would provide MacArthur with fifteen divisions to throw against the Japanese. However, these numbers were deceptive. Some of the divisions in SOPAC were tied up in operations against the Japanese or otherwise employed. The American and 37th divisions, for example, were still combatting the Japanese at Bougainville, and the army refused to use the 93rd Division for its intended purpose. Others, such as the 25th and 43rd Divisions, were recovering from recent ordeals and could not be committed to action anytime soon. As for those divisions reaching New Guinea, they were not necessarily ready for immediate action. The biggest obstacle to the employment of all these outfits, though, was logistical. Moving them to and supplying them in the combat zone in a timely manner required shipping that was not readily available. MacArthur instead committed a few divisions to his New Guinea campaign rather than waste time and shipping bringing up fresh ones. This kept his operations moving, but, as events proved, was hard on those outfits repeatedly sent into battle.

Hollandia

MacArthur had spent 1943 advancing slowly and painfully up the New Guinea coast with his Australian and American forces. He had only gained

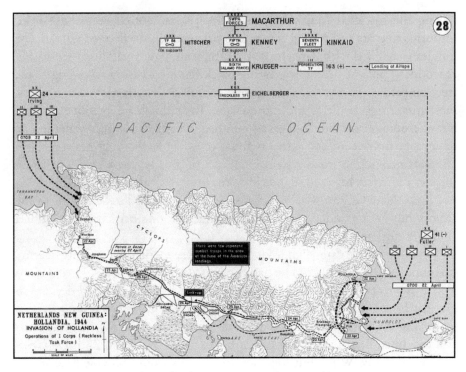

The Hollandia Operation, April–June 1944.

a few hundred miles, so he needed to pick up the pace if he hoped to beat the navy to the China–Formosa–Luzon region. He was therefore open to creative ideas to do so. The next SWPA target was Hansa Bay, about 120 miles northwest of Allied-held Saidor. Unfortunately, there were three battered but viable Japanese divisions nearby, supported by warplanes from Wewak, that would undoubtedly put up a good fight if attacked. Rather than assail such a strongly defended position, MacArthur borrowed a page from Halsey's Solomons playbook. He opted to use growing American air and naval power in the region to go around Hansa Bay and instead strike the Japanese position at Hollandia, situated in the middle of the New Guinea northern littoral. Hollandia possessed two big harbors—Tanahmerah and Humboldt—separated by the Cyclops Mountains, as well as three airfields. In American hands, Hollandia would cut off the Japanese around Hansa Bay–Wewak and serve as a base for further advances westward. The Joint Chiefs not only approved the plan in their March 1944 directive authorizing the Dual Drive offensive, but directed Nimitz to provide carrier-based air support for it as well. As added insurance, MacArthur also decided to seize Aitape at the same time as Hollandia. Aitape was located between Hollandia and Wewak, so airfields constructed there would supply additional air coverage. MacArthur scheduled the operation, codenamed "Reckless," for 22 April 1944.

MacArthur assigned Walter Krueger's Sixth Army the job of overseeing *Reckless*. Krueger, in turn, operated through Robert Eichelberger's I Corps. Krueger gave Eichelberger two Australia-based divisions with which to seize Hollandia, General Horace Fuller's 41st and General Frederick A. Irving's 24th. By early 1944, the 41st Jungleers had been in SWPA for nearly two years, longer than any other American division. It had served in New Guinea the previous year, where its regiments had fought well at Sananada and as part of the Australian effort to take Salamaua. It had returned to Rockhampton for refitting and retraining by October 1943, and a few months later its GIs were buoyed by a new War Department rotation policy that authorized a frustratingly small number of men who had been overseas for eighteen months or more to return to the States for reassignment. In March, the Jungleers moved back to New Guinea, to Finschhafen, to undertake the final preparations for *Reckless*.

Although the 41st was not necessarily the best American division in SWPA, it was certainly the most experienced. Both Krueger and Eichelberger had been pleased with its progress and were confident that it would do well in its next mission. There were, however, a couple of issues with the Jungleers that might have given them pause. For one thing, the division had never fought together as a unit, and was therefore bound to have coordination problems when it did. In fact, only two of its regiments—the 162nd and 186th—were slated to participate in the Hollandia landing. Krueger directed the third one, the 163rd, to storm Aitape. In addition, the conflict between Fuller and the 163rd Regiment commander, Jens Doe, still festered despite Eichelberger's superficially successful effort to mend the fences between the two men. The continuing personality clash between them did not bode well. Even so, MacArthur's decision to employ the 41st Division made perfect sense. The 1st Cavalry Division was the better outfit, but it was busy participating in and recovering from the Admiralties invasion. The 32nd Division was under a cloud for its Buna performance, and anyhow part of it had recently been used in minor operations around Saidor. The Jungleers were fresh, battleworthy, and ready for a new mission.[2]

The other division allotted to *Reckless*, Irving's 24th, had not yet seen action, but it had deep Pacific roots. Along with the 25th Division, it had been created out of the old Hawaii Division in October 1941. Nicknamed "Victory," its patch was a yellow-bordered green taro leaf on a black-edged red circle to mark its tropical origins. In fact, some of its personnel had seen action when the Japanese raided Pearl Harbor. The division remained on garrison duty in Hawaii until mid-1943, during which it earned Richardson's respect. It arrived in Australia in August 1943 and continued training at Rockhampton. It impressed everyone with the high morale, physical condition, and orderliness of its GIs. These included Krueger and Eichelberger. Although Eichelberger worried about the division's lack of small unit skills and was somewhat nonplussed by seeing officers walking around with parrots on their shoulders that they had captured and trained, he wrote to Krueger, "These men looked hard and tough. If there were any criticism on my part it would have been that I seemed to notice a bit of tenseness on the part of the men." He added, tongue in cheek, "This might have been the result of looking at my homely face."[3] Krueger, for his part, rated it among the best divisions in the theater. In January 1944, the division shipped to Goodenough Island to train for a planned assault on Hansa Bay. When MacArthur switched the target to Hollandia, it was a simple and commonsensical matter to transfer the 24th Division's assignment as well.[4]

On 22 April, elements from the 24th and 41st Divisions landed at Hollandia, the 24th at Tanahmerah Bay and the 41st at Humboldt Bay. Although SWPA intelligence estimated that there might be 15,000 Japanese soldiers in the area, the GIs encountered little opposition as they struggled ashore. Indeed, the Japanese had expected an attack on Hansa Bay–Wewak, so they were caught completely by surprise. There were only 10,000 Japanese at Hollandia, and few of them were combat troops. As a result, the Americans got off the beach and moved inland without meeting serious resistance. Their biggest problems were logistical. The beaches were thin and soon became packed full of piles of supplies and equipment. That night a Japanese bomber dropped a stick of bombs on the Humboldt Bay beach, one of which landed on an ammunition dump. The explosion and resulting fires destroyed considerable materiel and killed or wounded 125 Americans. The subsequent shortages put a crimp in operations, but did little to stop the American advance. The airfields fell on 26 April, at which point the remaining Japanese retreated into the surrounding jungle to survive as best as they could. To the east, the 163rd Regiment easily seized Aitape, and within two days Australian engineers had carved out an airfield so that American warplanes could fly over the region.

Operation *Reckless* was a major American victory. At the cost of only 152 killed and 1,057 wounded, the Americans advanced halfway up the New Guinea coast in one fell swoop, putting MacArthur that much closer to the China–Formosa–Luzon region and his dream of liberating the Philippines.

Although Hollandia never became as big a base as SWPA intended, it did eventually house the airfields, port facilities, warehouses, powerplants, and so forth that MacArthur needed to project American power further westward. Finally, seizing Hollandia cut off 55,000 Japanese soldiers around Hansa Bay–Wewak, making them as irrelevant to the Japanese war effort as their comrades stuck in Rabaul. It was a fine start to MacArthur's New Guinea campaign.

The Hollandia operation also reflected well on the 24th and 41st Divisions. Indeed, two days after the landing, MacArthur messaged Krueger:

> My sincere congratulations on the splendid way in which the forces under your command prepared for and carried out their part in the Reckless Operation. Organization and execution were equally excellent. My special thanks are due you, Eichelberger, Fuller, Irving and Doe. Please convey my appreciation to these officers and to the commanders, officers and enlisted personnel of all units involved. Their devotion to duty, courage and determination have contributed greatly to this great advance into enemy-held territory.[5]

The Jungleers had had a good reputation even before Hollandia in large part because they had avoided the mistakes that afflicted so many National Guardsmen in their baptisms of fire. Although *Reckless* was certainly one of the less intense battles of the Pacific War, the 41st Division fought it competently. MacArthur, Krueger, and Eichelberger were all happy with its performance. In fact, MacArthur was so impressed with Fuller's actions that he made a mental note to elevate Fuller to corps command at the first opportunity. Hollandia gave the 41st the best divisional record in SWPA, and made it a logical choice for subsequent operations along the New Guinea coast.[6]

Nor did Irving's 24th Division have anything of which to be ashamed for its performance in its first operation. There is no doubt that its baptism of fire was far less horrific than, say, the 32nd Division's at Buna or the 43rd's at New Georgia in part because Japanese opposition at Hollandia was so scattered and unorganized. However, the 24th Division's good training and leadership undoubtedly contributed to its ability to overcome in a timely manner what Japanese resistance it did encounter. MacArthur, Krueger, and Eichelberger were all impressed with its skills. The 24th Division had become a SWPA favorite even before it saw action, and its record at Hollandia demonstrated that it had the potential to develop into a premier outfit in the theater.[7]

Wakde–Sarmi

MacArthur, Krueger, and Eichelberger were all present to witness the Hollandia landings. After visiting the Tanahmerah Bay beachhead, the three generals huddled onboard the light cruiser USS *Nashville*. There an elated MacArthur noted the lack of significant Japanese opposition and suggested sending the expedition's reserves up the New Guinea coast immediately to assault the next SWPA target: Wakde Island, a speck of land off New Guinea at Maffin Bay about 125 miles from Hollandia. Wakde possessed an airfield that, in American hands, would give SWPA air supremacy in the area. Eichelberger dissuaded MacArthur by pointing out that the reserve forces were not combat loaded, and anyway there was no guarantee that *Reckless* would continue to go smoothly. MacArthur reluctantly agreed, but he remained focused on the next step in his campaign. SWPA planners initially wanted not only Wakde, but also two uncompleted Japanese airfields on the mainland at nearby Sarmi. A closer look, though, revealed that Sarmi was strongly defended and the terrain too soggy to permit the timely completion of those airfields. Improvising, SWPA planners decided to retain the Wakde part of the operation, but to substitute for Sarmi the Geelvink Bay island of Biak, which contained three airfields.

MacArthur authorized Krueger to employ the 24th, 32nd, or 41st Division in the attacks on Wakde and Biak. Krueger's initial inclination was to use the 32nd. The Red Arrow boys had not seen serious action since their Buna bloodletting more than a year earlier. They were currently at Saidor, about 450 miles southeast of Hollandia, after conducting minor operations there. Discussions with his staff and naval officers, though, showed that SWPA lacked enough shipping to get the 32nd Division to the target on MacArthur's demanding schedule. That left either the 24th or 41st Divisions. Krueger opted to deploy the more experienced Jungleers and leave the dangerous but predictable mopping up at Hollandia to the 24th Division. He assigned Jens Doe's 163rd Regiment, still at Aitape, the job of assailing Wakde and ordered Horace Fuller and the other two 41st Division regiments, the 162nd and 186th, to storm Biak ten days later.

Because Wakde was not big enough to hold all the materiel the Americans needed to operate, Doe's 163rd Regiment landed on the New Guinea mainland opposite of the tiny island and set up shop at Toem. The next day, 18 May, a battalion from the regiment stormed Wakde in an amphibious assault and seized the island after three days of bitter fighting. The battle cost the battalion forty killed and 107 wounded. Of the 738 defending Japanese soldiers, all but four perished. It was a fine demonstration of the battalion's combat prowess, one that reflected well on the 41st Division as a whole.

Occupying Wakde, though, did not end the operation. Krueger concluded that the Toem beachhead would never be safe as long as it was within artillery range of the Japanese holed up in the hills to the west. He therefore ordered an independent regiment, General Edwin D. Patrick's 158th, to Toem with

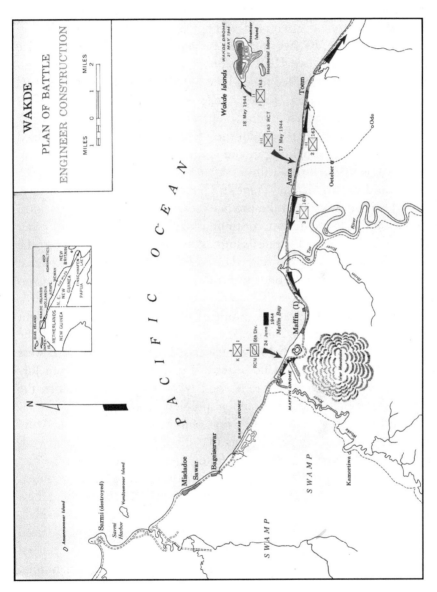

The Wakde–Sarmi Operation, May–July 1944.

instructions to pry the Japanese out of those hills while Doe's 163rd watched the beachhead. The Americans labeled the heart of the Japanese position Lone Tree Hill. Despite its name, Lone Tree Hill was actually a 175 feet high maze of dense jungle, coral outcroppings, ravines, and crevices. From 26–28 May the 158th Regiment attempted without luck to take the area. Before Patrick could try again, Krueger recalled the outfit back to Toem to replace the 163rd Regiment. The two 41st Division regiments attacking Biak had run into trouble, so Krueger decided to send the 163rd there to help its divisional comrades. Then, on 22 June, Krueger relieved the 158th Regiment of its responsibilities around Toem so it could prepare for an invasion of the Geelvink Bay island of Noemfoor. By that point the 158th had lost seventy-four killed and 257 wounded in the fighting in and around Lone Tree Hill. To pick up where the 158th Regiment had unsuccessfully left off, Krueger deployed a new American division, General Franklin C. Sibert's 6th.

The 6th Division was one of the Pacific War's most tenacious, pugnacious, and durable outfits. It spent more continuous days in combat than any other army division in the Pacific. Despite its impressive record, it was also among the army's least well-known and appreciated units. Its patch was a simple six-sided red star, from which it derived one of its nicknames: "Red Star." Another was "Sightseers," due to its innumerable marches around France in World War I. The War Department reactivated the 6th Division in October 1939, right after World War II began in Europe. It originally trained to operate in the North African desert, but the fighting there ended before the Sightseers were ready, so it ended up in the Pacific instead. It garrisoned Hawaii from July to December 1943 and then went to Milne Bay, New Guinea, right after the new year, where it practiced jungle and amphibious warfare.

After the Sightseers deployed to New Guinea, Krueger's Sixth Army headquarters received disturbing reports that the division was plagued with irregular punishments, misappropriated funds, and demoralization. The fact that the unit became so proficient at "moonlight requisitioning" that it acquired a new sobriquet, "Sibert and His Ten Thousand Thieves," lent credence to these charges. Krueger ordered his XI Corps commander, General Charles P. Hall, to investigate. Hall in turn gave the job to his inspector general, who traced complaints to a couple of disgruntled officers. As far as the inspector general could tell, there was nothing seriously wrong with the 6th. Hall agreed, noting, "The present state of morale of the Division is considered to be high; this is evidenced by my Inspector General's report as well as my personal observation and investigation."[8] As it turned out, a more serious problem was its leader, Franklin Sibert. Sibert usually made a good first impression, but prolonged exposure caused some to question his intelligence and ability, though this might have been due to declining health. However, he was still in his prime when he led the 6th Division. Both Krueger and Eichelberger lauded him. When Krueger needed more ground units to prosecute the growing number of operations up the New Guinea coast, the 6th Division was an obvious candidate because it was well-trained and nearby. The Sightseers got their first opportunity to prove themselves in action when Krueger dispatched them to Wakde–Sarmi in early June 1944.[9]

Although Sibert hoped to give his troops time to familiarize themselves with their new surroundings, lest they repeat the mistakes that had brought the 158th Regiment to grief, an impatient Krueger said no. Krueger had already slated the 6th Division for another operation in late July, so he wanted the Japanese threat to Wakde–Sarmi eliminated as soon as possible. This being the case, Sibert eschewed all tactical finesse and ordered his 20th Regiment to directly attack Lone Tree Hill. This resulted in a nightmarish battle that caused some of the highest American casualties in the entire New Guinea campaign. The Japanese lured one of the 20th Regiment's battalions into a trap on Lone Tree Hill's summit. Rescuing it required considerable fire support, a small-scale amphibious landing behind Japanese lines, and copious amounts of gasoline, grenades, and demolition charges. In the process, the GIs broke the back of Japanese opposition, so Lone Tree Hill fell on 25 June. Unfortunately, Lone Tree Hill was merely one of several Japanese-held positions in the area. Sibert brought up his 1st and 63rd Regiments to relieve the blown 20th, and then went about demolishing each strongpoint one by one until Japanese resistance collapsed on 12 July. By that time, the 6th Division had lost 114 killed, 284 wounded, and around 400 nonbattle injuries.

Occupying Wakde–Sarmi cost SWPA about 630 killed, 1,742 wounded, and forty-one missing. Seizing Wakde made sense because the airfield there enabled SWPA to achieve local air superiority and undertake additional invasions up the New Guinea coast. On the other hand, it is debatable whether the Sarmi battles were worth the casualties the Americans sustained. Whatever the wisdom of the operation, it is hard to denigrate the 6th Division's overall performance. Although it made mistakes in securing Lone Tree Hill and its neighbors, the division's GIs fought aggressively, persistently, and with bulldog determination. Sibert certainly thought so. So did Krueger. He wrote to MacArthur, "During a visit to the Wakde-Maffin Bay area a few days ago, I was impressed with Sibert's skilful [sic] handling of his troops. He is cool and very aggressive and his [6th Division] troops reflect that spirit."[10] Indeed, Krueger was so impressed with Sibert that he recommended his elevation to corps command. As for the 6th Division, when someone informed Krueger that the outfit had sustained many officer casualties, he said, "Well, I know you've got a fighting unit now."[11] In winning at Lone Tree Hill, the Sightseers demonstrated that they were every bit as proficient after their baptism of fire as SWPA stalwarts such as the 1st Cavalry and 24th Divisions. And there was no reason to doubt that the 6th Division would continue to function efficiently in the big battles yet to come.

Biak

While the Sightseers were struggling to overcome the Japanese on Lone Tree Hill, the 41st Division was undergoing its own wretched ordeal on Biak. Biak was an island in Geelvink Bay off New Guinea's north coast around 385 miles from Hollandia. At 948 square miles, it was about two thirds the size of Long Island. It derived its value from the three airfields that the Japanese had constructed there in 1943 that the Americans could easily upgrade to accommodate bombers. These bombers could then support the navy's Central Pacific offensive as it approached the Palaus. MacArthur, though, was mostly thinking about his own future. As he saw it, Biak was the last significant *military* obstacle between him and his dream of liberating the Philippines. He therefore wanted the island taken as soon as possible. On the morning of 27 May, after the Army Air Forces dropped 317 tons of bombs on and the navy threw 6,100 shells at the target, two regiments from Horace Fuller's 41st Division—the 162nd and 186th—landed unopposed on Biak's southern shore at Bosnek, east of the airfields. As the GIs sorted themselves out, some wondered whether this lack of Japanese resistance might indicate that this operation would mimic their Hollandia experience a month earlier. Indeed, some speculated that the Japanese might have evacuated the island.

They were wrong. There were actually 10,700 Japanese soldiers on Biak who took full advantage of the island's awful landscape to turn it into a fortress. Jungle-covered coral ridges, deep caves, hidden fissures and crevasses, and huge sinkholes honeycombed the island, all of which provided Japanese troops with ample cover from which to fight the Americans. In addition, there were almost no streams or wells on Biak, which, combined with the heat and humidity, guaranteed a lot of parched GIs. The men of the 162nd Regiment discovered these unpleasant facts within hours of landing on Biak. When they advanced westward down the coast toward the airfields, they ran into such tenacious opposition that they retreated back to the Bosnek beachhead

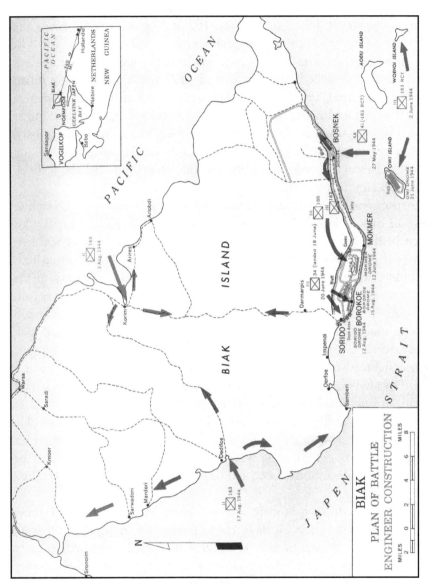

Battle of Biak, May–August 1944.

on 29 May. Indeed, one of the battalions was evacuated by sea because it got cut off from the rest of the regiment. Fuller was sufficiently concerned to ask Krueger for his last regiment—Doe's 163rd, then defending Toem at Wakde–Sarmi—and to take a couple of days to await its arrival and prepare his next move. On 1 June, he sent the 162nd Regiment back down the coast, but also dispatched the 186th Regiment overland toward the airfields. Despite horrible terrain, unbearable heat, inadequate supply lines, and a lack of water, the 186th reached Mokmer Airfield on 7 June. Unfortunately, it had marched into a trap. Once the Americans were on the airfield, the Japanese dug into the surrounding ridges opened fire with everything they had. Fuller responded by directing his men to assail the ridges. For six days, from 9–14 June, the Americans tried unsuccessfully to clear the Japanese overlooking the airfield. The upshot was that although the Americans had the airfield, they were no closer to victory.

MacArthur and Krueger were as frustrated and dismayed with the lack of progress on Biak as Fuller. MacArthur's unhappiness was exacerbated by his mistaken belief that the 41st Division's objectives were as good as achieved as soon as it got safely ashore. He wanted those airfields open for business so he could claim victory, or at least a tie, in his race with the navy to the China–Formosa–Luzon region. On 5 June, ten days after the operation began, he complained to Krueger about Fuller's sluggishness. Krueger responded by sending some of his Sixth Army staffers to the island for a firsthand look at the situation and by pressuring Fuller to hurry up. From their reports, Krueger concluded that the basic problems were Biak's horrible terrain and the 41st Division's lack of aggressiveness and skill. He referenced the 162nd Regiment's unsuccessful and unsupported 27–29 May drive up the coast as his chief evidence. Fuller did not respond well to Krueger's admonitions. He was a brittle man to begin with, and his poor health merely exacerbated his less admirable traits. As far as he was concerned, he was doing the best he could under difficult circumstances, and he neither welcomed nor appreciated Krueger's badgering.

Finally, after another hectoring message from MacArthur on 14 June, Krueger took decisive action. He dispatched a regiment from the 24th Division to Biak and ordered Robert Eichelberger and some of his I Corps staffers there to oversee what now became a corps-directed operation. When Eichelberger arrived on 15 June, he was surprised to learn that Fuller had quit as 41st Division commander out of anger toward Krueger. Eichelberger and others tried to persuade Fuller to withdraw his resignation, but he was adamant. Indeed, he threatened to resubmit it every hour until Krueger accepted it.

Krueger did so and blandly noted to MacArthur, "He states that my numerous messages to him with reference to his failure to secure the airdromes quickly and his relief as Task Force Commander have evidenced that his services have been unsatisfactory to the high command."[12] One officer remembered Fuller's forlorn departure:

> He left the tent, mounted a jeep, and rode away from the Division he'd brought to Australia more than two years before, trained to razor edge at Rockhampton, commanded brilliantly from Buna to Hollandia, and landed at hot, cave-infested, waterless, stubborn Biak—with a smaller force than the mission required. I watched his [Fuller's] jeep go down the muddy road. A GI turned and gazed curiously after it. That was the [41st] Division's farewell to Fuller, a brave, seasoned, jungle fighter lost to the Southwest Pacific.[13]

Although Eichelberger had his doubts about Jens Doe, he opted to give him the division, at least temporarily. Doe may or may not have known that Fuller had recently commenced another campaign to get rid of him, but that no longer mattered. Now, in an unforeseen twist of fate, Fuller's discomfiture had redounded to Doe's advantage. With this new arrangement in order, Eichelberger and Doe got down to the business of securing Biak.[14]

Eichelberger's initial cursory inspections of the 41st Division's dispositions dismayed him. He was, in fact, deeply disappointed with the Jungleers' performance, all the more so because he had helped train it back in Australia the previous year. He concluded that divisional staffers spent so much time in headquarters that they had lost touch with the situation on the ground. Line officers did not seem well-informed either. The resulting confusion meant, among other things, that the Japanese still held positions that were supposed to be in American hands. Eichelberger later wrote, "There was too much sitting around in offices instead of having everyone get out and find what the true situation was."[15] Although the GIs were not as tired as Eichelberger expected, they were starting to feel sorry for themselves, which was always a bad sign. Eichelberger quickly decided to call off most attacks to give the troops a day of rest while he figured out a more effective way to wage the battle.[16]

Mulling things over, Eichelberger concluded that, in addition to his other sins, Fuller had relied too much on nibbling attacks that were unlikely to achieve decisive results any time soon. Eichelberger preferred simpler tactics that would yield bigger and better operational dividends. He opted to assault the Japanese defenses with all four regiments at his disposal—the 41st Division's three, as well as the 24th Division's recently arrived 34th—to turn their right flank. Doe objected that moving these units into place would expose the 186th Regiment to Japanese mortar fire, but Eichelberger overruled him. He kicked off his offensive on 19 June. The 186th Regiment managed to clear the ridge overlooking Mokmer Airfield while the 34th Regiment seized Biak's other two airstrips. On 21 June, the 162nd and 186th Regiments converged on the heart of the Japanese defenses at the West Caves. Its core was the Sump, an eighty-feet deep cave that took days for the Americans to even locate, let alone reduce. The GIs overcame the West Caves and the Sump by sealing off the underground entrances, pumping gasoline into them, and setting them aflame. Although it took three days to clear the West Caves, doing so finally shattered the Japanese line. Eichelberger returned to Hollandia on 29 June and left Doe to finish mopping up. Doing so consumed much of July and required hard fighting to subdue the Teardrop, East Caves, and, finally, the last organized Japanese opposition at Ibdi Pocket. By then the airfields were getting up and running. Mokmer was ready for fighter planes on 21 June and bombers on 2 August.[17]

Taking Biak cost the Americans more than 400 killed and 2,000 wounded. There were also 6,800 nonbattle casualties, many resulting from a scrub typhus outbreak. In return for these losses, MacArthur got the airfields he wanted to wrap up his campaign. Planes flying from them assisted subsequent SWPA operations in the region, but did not do much to help the Central Pacific offensive. Biak also became an important SWPA base. As for the 41st Division, there were plenty of reasons for which to criticize its performance on Biak. Poor reconnaissance, inadequate intelligence, substandard leadership, overconfidence, and carelessness all contributed to its woes. For these reasons the 162nd Regiment was fortunate to escape destruction during its initial advance along the coast toward the airfields. Similarly, these flaws played a role in the 186th Regiment walking into the Japanese ambush at Mokmer Airfield. Fuller did not always appear to have a good grip on the tactical situation, and his Jungleers frequently did not respond effectively to his orders.

However, the 41st Division also operated under some difficulties not of its own creation. The two regiments that MacArthur initially sent to Biak simply were not enough to overcome on his schedule the 10,700 tough Japanese soldiers ensconced there in some of the worst terrain in the Southwest Pacific. Moreover, the Jungleers were not as experienced as they seemed. The 162nd Regiment had fought at Roosevelt Ridge, but the 186th Regiment's biggest previous fight had been at Hollandia a month earlier. Seizing Hollandia had not been a walkover, but it was not the kind of operation that really tested a unit's mettle. The division's best regiment, Doe's 163rd, veterans of Sanananda and Aitape and Wakde, was not initially deployed on Biak. As for Fuller, he had never led two or more of his regiments into a major engagement before. Eichelberger undoubtedly deserved credit for ruthlessly executing a simple plan, but he also had four regiments at his disposal with which to do so. And, finally, the Jungleers did prevail through some of the hardest combat of the Pacific War. Their mistake was not winning on MacArthur's timetable.

The 41st Division entered the New Guinea campaign as SWPA's most experienced division. For that reason it spearheaded MacArthur's drive up the New Guinea coast at Hollandia, Aitape, Wakde, and Biak. Interestingly, the Biak operation was the first time all three of the division's regiments fought together. After Biak, though, the division's star faded. MacArthur continued to praise the division publicly, but never expressed much affection for the outfit behind closed doors. Krueger did not like National Guard units much to begin with, and the Jungleers' woes on Biak did nothing to change his opinion. The 41st Division eventually came under Eichelberger's umbrella when he took over the Eighth Army. Eichelberger gave it credit for its successes in the low-stakes operations in the central Philippines in which it participated, but he almost always qualified his affirmations. Biak, in short, marked a sad ending to the Jungleers' leading role in the Pacific War.[18]

Driniumor River

One of the Hollandia operation's strategic benefits was that it isolated the three Japanese divisions around Hansa Bay–Wewak, some 55,000 troops, from outside assistance. However, their commander, General Hatazo Adachi, was a pugnacious man disinclined to sit back and do nothing while MacArthur's juggernaut rolled on toward Japan. Mulling things over, Adachi instead decided to assault American-held Aitape, about 220 miles east of Hollandia and 100 miles west of Wewak. Doing so might slow down MacArthur's offensive by forcing him to divert resources to deal with this threat to his rear, thus buying time for the Japanese to bolster their defenses closer to the Home Islands. Although marching to Aitape required hand-carrying all the supplies, weapons, and equipment that they needed for the operation through the trackless jungle, the tough Japanese persisted. As May turned into June, some 20,000 Japanese soldiers gradually closed in on Aitape.

The 41st Division's 163rd Regiment had seized Aitape on 22 April as part of Operation *Reckless*. The next day the 32nd Division's 127th Regiment arrived to reinforce it. The 163rd Regiment departed for Wakde and other adventures up the New Guinea coast on 15 May, leaving the 127th to keep an eye on Aitape. As evidence of an imminent Japanese assault on Aitape accumulated, a worried Krueger responded by dispatching the remainder of the 32nd Division there. The Red Arrow Division was, like the 41st, an old SWPA outfit, built out of the Michigan and Wisconsin National Guards, that arrived in Australia in June 1942. Unlike the Jungleers, though, the 32nd had a tarnished reputation because of its actions at Buna in late 1942. Although the 32nd won that brutal battle—a not-so-insignificant tidbit of information that its critics sometimes forgot—it initially fought so poorly and sustained such heavy casualties that it may as well have been a defeat in terms of its image. Indeed, its losses were so substantial in men and materiel that some doubted that it would be possible to rehabilitate the unit. Its new commander after Buna, General William Gill, sometimes privately wondered too, but he worked hard with Eichelberger and others to bring it back up to snuff. The 32nd received new weapons, equipment, and replacements, as well as plenty of training. By June 1943 Eichelberger was increasingly optimistic that the division was ready to go. A SWPA report stated:

> When this division returned from New Guinea its combat efficiency was practically nil. Practically all officers felt that they had received too much adverse criticism on account of the Buna campaign. During the past seven months' training period this division has very greatly improved. The morale is excellent, physical condition good and the malaria has been controlled. The command, from battalion commanders upward, is excellent and there is a large percentage of company commanders who have had previous combat experience. It is believed that this division is anxious to give an excellent account of itself in its next combat action. I have talked to a number of officers who have been intimately connected with the division and it is our opinion that at present this is an excellent division ready for combat.[19]

Defending Aitape would provide the Red Arrow boys with their first major opportunity to prove themselves after their Buna ordeal.[20]

In May and June, the Japanese progressively pushed elements of the 127th Regiment westward to the Driniumor River, about twenty miles from Aitape, in a series of skirmishes. Gill did not like the look of things, so he asked Krueger for reinforcements. Although the 43rd Division was on its way from New Zealand, its first elements would not arrive until mid-July. To fill the gap, Krueger ordered the independent 112th Cavalry Regiment and the 31st Division's 124th Regiment to Aitape. The former disembarked on 27 June and the latter on 2 July. Moving these units required scarce shipping resources that SWPA could ill afford. By compelling Krueger to divert resources from SWPA's westward offensive, Adachi achieved one of his objectives before he even commenced his attack.

American efforts to defend Aitape were complicated by a dispute over tactics between Gill and Krueger. Gill felt that the best course of action was to dig in and permit the Japanese to assail American positions in front of Aitape. This

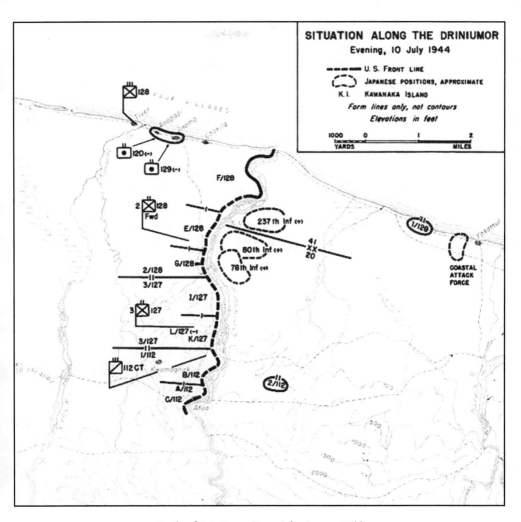

Battle of Driniumor River, July–August 1944

would enable the Americans to deploy their superior firepower and logistics to decimate the attacking Japanese at little risk to themselves. Oscar Griswold's XIV Corps had successfully used such an approach on Bougainville a few months earlier in defeating the Japanese assault on Empress Augusta Bay. Krueger, however, had other ideas. He wanted to end this looming battle at Aitape as quickly as possible to free up resources that SWPA needed to continue operations up the New Guinea coast on MacArthur's rigorous schedule. Krueger believed that Gill's passive methods would require too much time and too many resources. When Gill proved recalcitrant, Krueger ordered General Charles Hall and his XI Corps headquarters to assume command of American troops defending Aitape. Hall was a quiet, deferential, and somewhat remote man willing to bend orders when necessary. He was thoroughly competent, but had no experience in jungle warfare or at the corps level.

Hall arrived on 27 June and got to work. Unfortunately, he unwisely decided to divide his forces in two. He ordered one defensive line established along the Driniumor River under General Clarence A. Martin, the 32nd Division's assistant commander, and sent the 112th Cavalry, 127th, and 128th Regiments there. He saw these GIs as a tripwire that would delay any Japanese assault while he prepared a counterattack with forces from a second defensive line around Aitape. There he deployed the 124th and 126th Regiments, as well as disembarking elements of the 43rd Division. Although there was a logic to Hall's dispositions, splitting his soldiers in the face of the enemy would not make it easy for the 32nd Division to fight well.

It was bad enough that Hall had, over Gill's objections, divided his forces between the Driniumor River and Aitape, but there was also confusion over when or whether the Japanese would attack. As a result, the Japanese assault on the night of 10/11 July caught some units by surprise. The Driniumor was around 100 yards wide and shallow enough to walk across. It was also just about the only identifiable landmark in the surrounding ocean of jungle. Although American firepower bloodied the river in a gruesome manner, the Japanese succeeded in breaking through the 128th Regiment's lines and establishing a bridgehead on the western shore. As far as Clarence Martin was concerned, his troops had done their job by sounding the alarm. He wanted to fall back and join up with the rest of the XI Corps in front of Aitape. Hall agreed and directed Martin's men to retreat behind the X-Ray River, about 4,000 yards west of the Driniumor.

Krueger was unsurprisingly unhappy when he arrived at Aitape the day after the big Japanese offensive for a firsthand look at the situation. He ordered the Japanese threat eliminated at once. Hall placated him with a plan for an immediate counterattack that would hopefully bring the Americans back to the Driniumor. Hall ordered the 124th and 128th Regiments to push along the coast while the 112th Cav and 127th Regiments advanced inland to the south. By 15 July, the Americans were back on the Driniumor, but this did not end the operation. In fact, heavy fighting continued along the Driniumor through early August. At one point the Japanese split the 124th Regiment in two and almost surrounded the 112th Cav Regiment. In the end, superior American firepower and logistics carried the day and forced the Japanese back across the river for good. The Japanese began retreating around 4 August, and Hall helped them along by ordering the 124th Regiment to sweep down the east side of the river in a march that did the new outfit credit.

After the Driniumor River battle ended, MacArthur wrote Krueger, "The operations were planned with great skill, were executed with great determination and courage and were crowned with great success."[21] Here MacArthur was either ignorant or disingenuous. Although the Americans won the engagement, they did not demonstrate much operational ability. Driving the Japanese from the Driniumor cost the Americans nearly 600 killed, 1,700 wounded, and eighty-five missing. Japanese losses approximated 8,800 men. With all the firepower, logistical support, and intelligence available to them, American victory in front of Aitape should have been a foregone conclusion regardless of the undeniable courage Japanese soldiers exhibited. If Hall had heeded Gill's advice and dug in before Aitape with all of his troops, the Japanese assault would have crumbled as easily as their attack on the XIV Corps on Bougainville a few months earlier. Hall instead split his forces between Aitape and the Driniumor. He did so because Krueger was more interested in saving time for MacArthur than in saving lives, though he could of course argue that ending the war as quickly as possible would keep total American casualties down. However, it is quite likely that the more conservative approach would not have appreciably slowed down MacArthur's dash up the New Guinea coast. This tactical mismanagement enabled the Japanese to have more success than they had a right to expect.

Although elements of the 31st and 43rd Divisions, as well as the 112th Cav Regiment, also participated in the Driniumor River fighting, the 32nd Division did most of the heavy lifting. Its performance was uneven in part because it was mishandled by Hall and Krueger. Most obviously, it was unable to maintain the Driniumor River line in the face of the 10–11 July Japanese assault. General Julian Cunningham, who ably led the 112th Cav Regiment throughout the operation, later complained that the 32nd Division was too timid, careless, and clique-ridden. He remembered: "There were cliques and pressure groups within that Division which led to lack of aggressiveness on part of some of the officers. A lot of them were too far from the front to know what was going on."[22] Hall agreed, complaining that it required great effort to get the 32nd Division to take aggressive action, though he credited Gill for instilling some offensive spirit in his men. On the other hand, Sixth Army staffers praised the division's actions. Krueger was more inclined to blame Gill than his men for the division's woes, and made sure that Gill never rose to become a corps commander. Krueger's and Hall's decisions helped turn an easy victory into a slugging match that the 32nd did win, but one which, like Buna, was hard to appreciate.[23]

Conclusions

The Biak and Driniumor River operations did not quite end the New Guinea campaign. Now that SWPA had air and naval supremacy in the region, MacArthur used these assets to avoid concentrations of Japanese troops. Instead, the Americans resorted to building airfields from scratch in undefended areas rather than battle Japanese soldiers for pre-existing ones. New Guinea's Vogelkop Peninsula was MacArthur's next geographic obstacle. Rather than assault the big Japanese bases at Manokwari or Sorong, MacArthur ordered a landing between the two. On 30 July, elements of the 6th Division, fresh from their recent no-holds-barred victory at Lone Tree Hill, splashed ashore at remote Sansapor–Mar. There was no opposition, and on 17 August fighter planes could use the airfield aviation engineers constructed on nearby Middelburg Island. The Sightseers' biggest challenge was disease. Scrub typhus and a mysterious fever afflicted 805 soldiers, some of whom did not recover sufficiently to return to duty.

About six weeks later, on 15 September, the 31st Division landed on lightly defended little Morotai Island, halfway between New Guinea and the Philippines. Doing so enabled SWPA to avoid nearby Halmahera Island and its 30,000 Japanese defenders. Planes were operating out of the airfield constructed there on 4 October. The Morotai operation signified the end of the New Guinea campaign. MacArthur was there to mark the occasion, wading through the surf for a firsthand look a few hours after the GIs came ashore. Before he left the island, he reportedly gazed northward toward the Philippines and murmured to an aide, "They are waiting for me there. It has been a long time."[24]

MacArthur's New Guinea campaign was tremendously successful. In five short months his forces streaked across the big island's northern coast and reached the China–Formosa–Luzon region at about the same time as the navy. MacArthur conducted his campaign with only four divisions that saw significant action—the 6th, 24th, 32nd, and 41st—as well as a number of independent regiments. He had more units available, but refrained from using them because doing so would have consumed scarce shipping and slowed the pace of his operations. Of the four divisions, two experienced their baptisms of fire during the New Guinea campaign, the 6th at Lone Tree Hill and the 24th at Hollandia. Although both emerged victorious, the 6th Division's performance was more impressive, albeit imperfect, because of the ferocity of Japanese opposition. Both units, though, demonstrated considerable tactical fortitude, if not necessarily skill, and showed every indication of becoming valuable additions to MacArthur's growing stable of combat divisions.

Both the 32nd and 41st Divisions were experienced outfits at the start of the New Guinea campaign. Neither unit, though, significantly enhanced its reputation. The Jungleers had the better record because of their successes at Sanananda and Roosevelt Ridge. As a result, MacArthur used them to spearhead SWPA's offensive across the northern New Guinea coast. The 41st won at Hollandia and Wakde, but had more trouble overcoming determined Japanese opposition at Biak. In fact, the Biak battle demonstrated that the Jungleers were not as proficient as advertised. As for the 32nd Division, it had more to prove than the 41st because of its Buna ordeal. Unfortunately, it did not get the opportunity to do so at Driniumor River in part because Krueger, Hall, and Gill mishandled it, but also because of an inherent sluggishness that plagued the outfit.

MacArthur emerged from the New Guinea campaign with a roster of mostly battle-hardened divisions at his disposal. The 1st Cav, 6th, and 24th Divisions all had one victory under their belts and had proven themselves capable outfits ready for future operations. The 32nd and 41st Divisions were certainly veteran units with good records, but some of their New Guinea experiences raised questions about their effectiveness. Even so, they remained potent weapons in MacArthur's arsenal. MacArthur had also inherited several divisions from SOPAC—the American, 25th, 37th, 43rd, and 93rd—which were available for upcoming campaigns. With the exception of the hard-luck 93rd Division, all were experienced and ready for action. Finally, MacArthur had a handful of new divisions that had yet to see significant combat: the 11th Airborne, 31st, 33rd, 38th, and 40th. It was a formidable force, led by increasingly skillful generals, buoyed by growing naval and air assets, and employing an amazing amount of logistical support and firepower.

CHAPTER FOUR

Liberation of the Philippines

Redeeming MacArthur's Pledge

By October 1944, World War II had clearly turned in the Allies' favor. In Europe, the American, British, and Canadian navies had overcome the German U-boat threat, enabling Allied troops and war material to flow unhindered throughout the globe. The Anglo-American strategic bombing campaign against Germany's vulnerable oil industry was slowly paralyzing the German war machine and turning German cities to rubble. Rome had fallen and Allied armies were advancing steadily northward through Italy. In France, the Allies had broken out of Normandy after their D-Day landing in June, seized Paris, and were approaching the German border. The German military situation to the east was equally dire. The Soviet Red Army had inflicted enormous losses on the Wehrmacht and was advancing into Poland toward the gates of Warsaw. Bulgaria, Finland, and Romania had all abandoned Germany and surrendered to the Soviets, compelling the Germans to evacuate Greece. German-controlled territory was limited to Germany itself, Norway and Denmark, northern Netherlands, central Europe, chunks of the Balkans and Baltics, and western Poland. By any objective assessment, time was rapidly running out on Adolf Hitler's Third Reich.

On the surface, the Japanese situation did not seem quite so dreadful. Even after nearly three years of war with the United States, Japan still retained its Home Islands, Manchuria, eastern China, Burma, Malaya and Singapore, Indochina, the Dutch East Indies, Hong Kong, the Philippines, Formosa, and innumerable island strongholds. A closer look, though, indicated that the Japanese empire's sun was rapidly setting. The Japanese army had suffered 55,000 casualties in an unsuccessful foray into India at the Battle of Imphal in March–July 1944, ending its threat to the subcontinent. The American navy had crippled its Japanese counterpart at the Battle of the Philippine Sea, and its submarine fleet was rapidly sinking the Japanese merchant marine. Although the American strategic bombing campaign against the Home Islands had yet to yield significant results, there was no guarantee that it would remain that way. Increasingly experienced and proficient American armies had neutralized Rabaul and steamrollered their way across the Central Pacific and Southwest Pacific to the China–Formosa–Luzon region. At the Teheran Conference in November–December 1943, Soviet dictator Joseph Stalin pledged to declare war on Japan within three months of Germany's defeat. Japan's situation, in short, was increasingly desperate.

The Philippines was a geopolitical oddity. It was one of the world's largest archipelagos, consisting of more than 7,100 islands of various sizes and shapes upon which sixteen million people lived. Most of these islands possessed mountainous interiors and humid tropical climates with wet and dry seasons. Its total land mass was 115,800 square miles, about the size of Arizona. Its two largest islands, Luzon and Mindanao, accounted for two thirds of that. If superimposed over the continental United States, with its capital of Manila at Chicago, the Philippines would stretch north to south from Michigan's Upper Peninsula to central Mississippi and Alabama, and east to west from South Carolina to Arkansas. Manila was one of the Pacific's great cities, with a prewar population of 623,000. The United States had seized the archipelago from Spain during the Spanish-American War and then waged a bitter three-year conflict to subjugate its population. American rule since then had been relatively mild, and in fact the United States was preparing the islands for independence when World War II began. Unfortunately, its American-trained army, backed by a small number of American troops, proved unable to stave off the Japanese invasion that began in earnest about two weeks after the Japanese raid on Pearl Harbor. The Japanese drove the Filipino and American soldiers into the Bataan Peninsula soon after the new year and, after a prolonged siege, compelled the 78,000 survivors to surrender in April 1942. Harsh Japanese rule sparked Filipino resistance of varying effectiveness. By the time the Americans reached the China–Formosa–Luzon region, there were approximately 430,000 Japanese troops garrisoning the islands, mostly on Luzon.

As commander of American and Filipino forces in the Philippines, MacArthur was the man most responsible for the defeat there. He had planned to remain in the archipelago and share his soldiers' fate, but President Roosevelt, conscious of the propaganda value that the Japanese would derive from such a high-level prisoner—or corpse—ordered him out. No sooner had MacArthur reached Australia than he began advocating a campaign to liberate

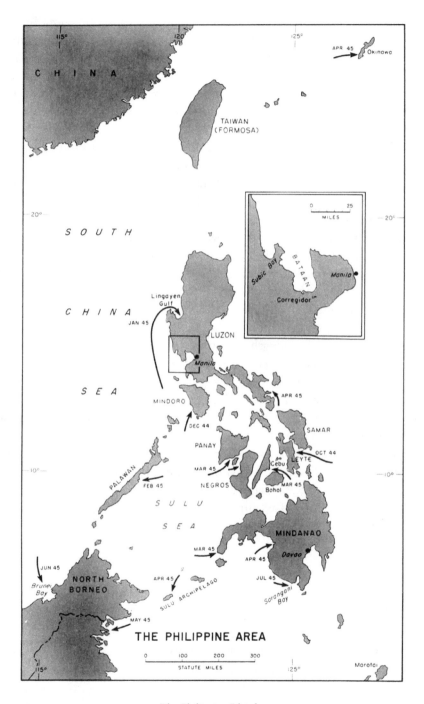

The Philippine Islands.

the Philippines, starting with his famous "I shall return" speech at Terowie. He was motivated partly by pride, but also by a sincere if paternalistic concern for the Filipino population. MacArthur, however, did not speak for the Joint Chiefs of Staff. Ernest King and many naval officers thought that the best way to prosecute the Pacific War was by seizing Formosa, not Luzon. This, they believed, would most effectively cut Japan off from its all-important oil supplies in the Dutch East Indies. By way of compromise, in March 1944 the JCS authorized the Dual Drive offensive by SWPA and POA toward the vaguely defined China–Formosa–Luzon region and placed in abeyance any final decision as to which island to ultimately target. MacArthur continued to lobby for a Philippines liberation campaign as both his and Nimitz's forces pushed westward. Although he effectively pleaded his case with Roosevelt during a late July meeting at Pearl Harbor to review strategy, the president was content to leave the details of the Pacific War's prosecution in the Joint Chiefs' hands.

In the end, it was a combination of logistics, opportunism, and misinterpretation that got MacArthur what he so desperately wanted. In mid-September, Admiral William Halsey's Third Fleet conducted a series of almost unopposed air raids against Japanese positions in the central Philippines. The Japanese were actually hoarding their strength for future battles, but Halsey misconstrued his success as evidence of enemy weakness in the area. He suggested taking advantage of this lack of Japanese activity by striking at the Philippines island of Leyte immediately. The Joint Chiefs were receptive to the idea because assailing Formosa was logistically unfeasible until early 1945. Rather than let the Pacific War stagnate until then, the JCS opted to seize the opportunity before it to accelerate operations. After hurried consultations with MacArthur and Nimitz, on 3 October the JCS ordered SWPA and the POA to cancel most of their various intermediate and now unnecessary operations and occupy Leyte as a preliminary to an assault on Luzon. The Joint Chiefs believed that by cooperating MacArthur and Nimitz would have sufficient resources for the job.

Leyte

Leyte was a rectangular-shaped island in the central Philippines, 110 miles long and fifteen to fifty miles wide. At 2,845 square miles, it was a bit more than twice as big as Rhode Island. Like so many Filipino islands, it possessed an interior mountainous spine with peaks up to 4,400 feet high. The Leyte Valley was on the eastern side of the mountains and the Ormoc Valley on the west. About 900,000 Filipinos lived there, and its Japanese garrison consisted of around 20,000 soldiers. MacArthur's planners zeroed in on Leyte because its

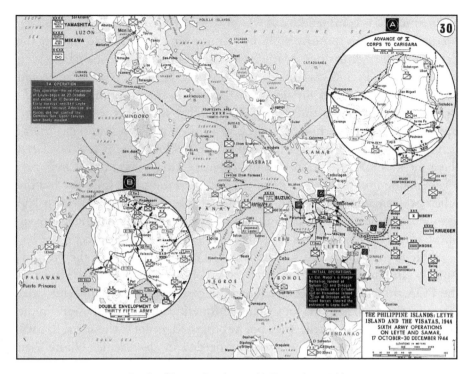

Battle of Leyte, October 1944–December 1944.

exposed eastern shore would make disembarking, supporting, and supplying troops there easier. Once in American hands, Leyte would provide a base from which to strike Luzon, the Philippines' political, economic, and social heart. MacArthur gave the job of seizing Leyte to Krueger's Sixth Army. Krueger planned to land General Franklin Sibert's X Corps along a three mile stretch of beach near Tacloban airfield and General John Hodge's XXIV Corps, borrowed from the POA, fifteen miles to the south in between the San José and Daguitan rivers.

Sibert's newly arrived X Corps consisted of two stalwart SWPA divisions, the 1st Cav and 24th Infantry. Many high-level officers considered the 1st Cav Division MacArthur's finest unit. Almost everyone praised it for its stellar appearance and professional demeanor. Moreover, during the Admiralties operation the previous February–March it proved that there was more to it than mere spit-and-polish. In the Admiralties the 1st Cav had broken the back of Japanese resistance in a timely and systematic manner that did the new outfit credit. Now, after months of resting, refitting, and retraining, it was up to strength and ready to go. Its former chief, Palmer Swift, had been elevated to corps command, so it was now led by General Verne D. Mudge. Mudge had won his spurs by skillfully helming his 1st Cav brigade during the fighting in the Admiralties. Many later claimed that he was one of the best, if not the best, Pacific War division commander. In short, MacArthur could not have chosen a better division to participate in the upcoming invasion.[1]

As for Fred Irving's 24th Infantry Division, it was another respected outfit, but its reputation was not as impressive as the 1st Cav's. Although it had performed well enough in its baptism of fire at Hollandia, it had not faced there the kind of opposition that the Japanese usually mounted. One of its regiments went on to participate in the Biak operation, but the record of the other two remained limited to Hollandia. Even so, the 24th Division had given every indication of becoming a first-rate unit that would fight effectively in the future, so committing it to the Leyte invasion made perfect sense.[2]

Nellie Richardson had organized the XXIV Corps in Hawaii the previous April in an effort to give the army more control over its combat units in the POA. Its chief was General John Hodge, a tough, forceful, and strict disciplinarian who had previously led the Americal and 43rd Divisions in the Solomons. He was no intellectual, but he possessed plenty of the aggressiveness and common sense that good soldiers needed in the Pacific. Nimitz had agreed to lend the XXIV Corps to MacArthur for the Leyte operation after he had scaled back POA plans to attack the Palaus Islands. Hodge deployed two divisions to invade Leyte. The first was General Archibald V. Arnold's 7th Hourglass Division. It was an excellent outfit commanded by an officer who one person, apparently unfamiliar with Verne Mudge, later wrote, "There was no finer division commander in the war."[3] The 7th Division had plenty of combat experience, having fought at Attu and Kwajalein. Although its record in the former battle left much to be desired, many knowledgeable officers considered its performance in the latter a model for army amphibious assaults. Richardson was among its biggest boosters. After President Roosevelt's July 1944 Pearl Harbor visit, Richardson reported to George Marshall, "After the luncheon a review of the 7th Division was held on Stanley Field. It was magnificent. The [7th] division has participated in two battles and shows in its general character the maturity gained by those experiences. The President was much impressed."[4] The 7th Division was in fact the POA's most proficient army outfit in discipline, training, and sanitation. It was also well-rested, having not seen action in nine months. Its selection for Leyte was logical, but, having fought solo in its first two outings in cramped and close quarter engagements, it was unaccustomed to the maneuvering and coordination with other units that the operation would demand.[5]

The 96th "Deadeyes" Division was the last division committed to the Leyte landings. It was a draftee outfit, like the 77th and 81st Divisions. It was not exactly new, having been activated in August 1942, but it had yet to see battle. Its patch consisted of interlocking blue and white diamonds superimposed over a khaki hexagon. Its commander, the only one it had during the war, was General James L. Bradley, who Robert Eichelberger described to his wife as "… the homely and fat little fellow that used to be G-3 in the Fourth Army. He is just as scintillating now as he was then."[6] Whatever his personality shortcomings, Bradley ran the division ably enough. The War Department had sent the Deadeyes to Hawaii in July 1944, and it had been training there ever since. MacArthur would have preferred to use the battle-hardened 77th Division for the Leyte invasion, but the Statue of Liberty boys were still recovering from the Guam operation, so he took the 96th instead. Although observers praised the 96th Division's training, discipline, and orderliness, there was really nothing intrinsically distinguished about the unit. It became one of the army's unglamorous workhorse divisions: reliable and durable, but not notable.[7]

On 20 October, an invasion force of 738 vessels of all shapes and sizes, from aircraft carriers to tugboats, carrying 160,000 GIs from Hollandia and the Admiralties, gathered off Leyte's eastern coast. After the usual preliminary bombardment, troops from the 1st Cav, 24th, 7th, and 96th Divisions splashed ashore near Tacloban and Dulag. They met only light and scattered enemy resistance, so they quickly sorted themselves out and plunged inland while beachmasters began organizing the beachhead for the follow-up waves of supplies, equipment, and reinforcements. In the early afternoon, MacArthur, Philippines president Sergio Osmeña, and a gaggle of staffers, journalists, and various hangers-on boarded a landing craft that took them to the 24th Division's beachhead south of Tacloban. The landing craft drew too much water to reach the beach, so MacArthur and his party had to walk the last yards to the shore through surf up to their waists while photographers and newsreel camera operators recorded the event for posterity. Although Japanese sniper and mortar fire still peppered the area, MacArthur insisted on visiting the troops. When he returned to the beach, a microphone had been set up for him. He strode over to it and intoned, "People of the Philippines, I have returned! By the grace of Almighty God, our forces stand again on Philippine soil." After he finished his speech, he turned the microphone over to Osmeña to say a few words, and then returned to his flagship, the light cruiser *Nashville*. He had every right to be satisfied with the day's accomplishments which had placed some 60,000 GIs on Leyte at the cost of only 157 casualties.

The Sixth Army made good progress in the ensuing days against the outnumbered and outgunned Japanese. To the north, in the X Corps sector, the 1st Cav Division seized Tacloban airfield soon after it came ashore and then went on to occupy Tacloban itself the next day, with Mudge riding through the town on a tank. From there the troopers cleared the San Juanico Strait between Leyte and Samar, landed on southern Samar, and finally, on 2 November, took the port town of Carigara. As for Fred Irving's neighboring 24th Division, he was handicapped because one of his regiments, the 21st, was busy patrolling the Panaon Strait. Nevertheless, the Victory Division's two remaining regiments overcame stiff opposition and grabbed the high ground overlooking the Leyte Valley.

MacArthur wanted to use the Leyte Valley to establish a logistical network for subsequent operations in the Philippines. To that end, Krueger ordered the XXIV Corps into the area. The untested 96th Division performed well in seizing the Japanese supply hub at Tabontabon after a three-day fight. The 7th Division did even better. It took Dulag airfield the day after the landing and on 24 October stormed additional airfields around Burauen. Other elements of the division entered the coastal village of Abuyog and, more impressively, crossed the mountains to within sight of Ormoc Bay. By early November it appeared that the Sixth Army would liberate Leyte in plenty of time for MacArthur to invade Luzon on schedule.

Unhappily for the Americans, their good fortune soon turned bad. First of all, the Japanese decided to dramatically augment their army on Leyte and fight for the island. Although General Tomoyuki Yamashita, the new commander of Japanese forces in the Philippines, wanted to husband his strength for Luzon, his superior, Field Marshal Hisaichi Terauchi, insisted on making a decisive stand on Leyte because he mistakenly believed that the Japanese had inflicted far heavier losses on the American navy in recent engagements than was actually true. That being the case, he concluded that the Sixth Army on Leyte was now exposed and vulnerable. Despite his doubts, Yamashita obeyed orders and started sending reinforcements to Leyte through the port of Ormoc. By 11 December, there were more than 50,000 Japanese soldiers on Leyte, more than enough to contest the place. Meanwhile, although the American navy was not nearly as damaged as the Japanese thought, it had still sustained losses during the Battle of Leyte Gulf. Aircrews in particular were exhausted and needed refitting. Doing so limited air support for the GIs on Leyte. The Army Air Forces should have taken up the slack, but it could not. Heavy rains hindered airfield construction, obscured enemy troop movements by land and sea, and washed out roads. Indeed, it poured thirty-five inches in the first forty days of the operation. This made it difficult for GIs to acquire supplies and air support at the same time that Japanese resistance was increasing.

The Sixth Army was initially unaware that the Japanese were so heavily reinforcing Leyte. In fact, Krueger was more intent on finishing the operation so that MacArthur could move on to Luzon than in digging in for a prolonged fight. To that end, he planned to seize Ormoc with a giant pincer movement, with the X Corps advancing down the Ormoc Valley from the north and XXIV Corps driving up from the south. When the 24th Division, now up to three regiments, moved toward Ormoc, it ran into heavy Japanese opposition on 7 November at a place dubbed Breakneck Ridge, though it was actually a series of fortified knobs. For five days the Victory Division battered at the Japanese positions without luck, followed by equally unsuccessful flanking maneuvers. Heavy rains impeded American efforts by flooding roads, miring vehicles, and interfering with air support. One soldier melodramatically remembered:

> From the angry immensity of the heavens floods raced in almost horizontal sheets. Palms bent low under the storm, their fronts flattened like streamers of wet silk. Trees crashed to earth. In the expanse of … [cogon] grass the howling of the wind was like a thousand-fold plaint of the unburied dead. The trickle of supplies was at a standstill. On Carigara Bay the obscured headlands moaned under the onslaught of the … seas. Planes were grounded and ships became haunted things looking for refuge. Massed artillery … barrages to the summit of Breakneck Ridge sounded dim and hollow in the tempest. Trails were obliterated by the rain. The sky was black.[8]

Finally, a frustrated Krueger not only pulled the 24th Division out of the line, but also relieved Fred Irving as its commander.

Irving's relief and his division's performance generated controversy. Neither Krueger nor Sibert told Irving why they had fired him. The obvious reason was the 24th Division's failure to seize Breakneck Ridge, but this could have been symptomatic of deeper problems they detected within the unit. MacArthur later grumbled that although Irving was a good general, he was unwilling to relieve incompetent staff officers. Others added that the division's staffers seemed mentally and physically tired. Krueger also disliked Irving's use of frontal assaults at Breakneck Ridge. Sibert, for his part, criticized Irving for spending too much time at the front—a rather odd accusation to level against a combat leader, and one that Eichelberger, after listening to Sibert's reasoning, found thoroughly unconvincing. There were also charges of excessive malaria and dysentery cases, as well as complaints of coordination difficulties with the neighboring 1st Cav Division. The fact that the division's regiments had never fought together, or against such determined opposition, might have contributed to its woes as well. The initial consensus, though, was that Irving's inability to effectively manage the 24th Division, more than anything else, caused its defeat at Breakneck Ridge.[9]

Subsequent events, however, vindicated Irving and, to a lesser extent, the 24th Division. Eichelberger respected Irving and the Victory boys, so he had a difficult time believing that they were as ineffectual as Krueger and Sibert believed. He offered Irving a job in his new Eighth Army as its informal deputy commander and lobbied MacArthur to reconsider his decision. Because Irving remained in the theater, he was in a position to air his grievances and plead his case. Early the following year, Irving wrote to MacArthur's chief of staff, General Richard K. Sutherland, to defend himself and his division. Among other things, he noted that the XXIV Corps commander, John Hodge, had praised the 24th Division's actions. He ended by stating, "Summarizing, the [24th] Division drove farther, against stiffer opposition, with fewer troops, inflicted more casualties on the enemy and incurred more casualties during the period in question than any other division and successfully accomplished its original mission. I feel that if a complete investigation is made, it will show that the Division performed exceptionally well and that there was not a single unsound move made."[10]

These efforts had an impact. However, battlefield reality did more than anything else to rehabilitate Irving and his men. The division that replaced the Victory boys before Breakneck Ridge, Bill Gill's 32nd, initially did no better against continuing bitter Japanese opposition. As Eichelberger explained to his wife:

> It is in comparison with the work of Bill Gill after he took over that makes everyone realize that Fred [Irving] was doing a grand job. In fact most people who were with him at the time including all the newspaper men thought so. Fred's outfit was strung out for quite a long time and bumped up against the 1st Japanese Infantry Division which was fresh out of Manchuria and one of their very best outfits. He was lucky to do as well as he did.[11]

Months later, in a rare display of humility, MacArthur not only acknowledged that relieving Irving had been a mistake, but also secured him another division, though the war ended before Irving could lead it into battle. As for the 24th Division, Krueger appears to have soured on it and made no effort to keep it in his army. On the other hand, Eichelberger was happy to acquire it and used it extensively and profitably in his operations in the southern Philippines.[12]

The Japanese were not the only ones sending reinforcements to Leyte. So was MacArthur. The first elements of Gill's 32nd Red Arrow Division arrived on 14 November from Hollandia and Morotai. It was a veteran outfit in fine shape, with two rather tarnished victories to its credit at Buna and

Driniumor River, but by no means prepared for the ordeal it soon faced. Krueger quickly committed it to Breakneck Ridge in place of the beleaguered 24th Division. Unfortunately, those expecting significant progress now that a fresh battle-hardened unit was in place were disappointed. The Red Arrow boys were soon afflicted by the same climatic, terrain, and supply problems that brought the 24th Division so much grief. Japanese soldiers continued to fight tenaciously and skillfully, taking full advantage of the opportunities the thick tropical rain forest offered to an army on the defensive. The 32nd Division suffered heavy losses and gained little ground over the course of the next two weeks. This grinding stalemate certainly proved Irving's point, but it did not bring the Sixth Army any closer to victory. To make things worse, Gill suffered some sort of emotional breakdown. He complained that his superiors did not understand the harsh conditions that his division confronted, and apparently physically abused some of his officers and enlisted men. Finally, on 18 December, Sibert ordered Mudge's 1st Cavalry Division to add its weight to the stalled 32nd Division drive toward Ormoc. This extra heft did the trick, and three days later the X Corps and XXIV Corps linked up.[13]

The XXIV Corps' drive northward did not go according to schedule either. Although the corps commander, John Hodge, complained that Archibald Arnold's 7th Hourglass Division did not maneuver skillfully, the outfit performed very well at the operation's start. Most obviously, elements of it snaked their way across Leyte's central mountain range within sight of Ormoc Bay before the Japanese even knew they were there. MacArthur was among those impressed with the division's initial actions. However, Arnold got only one regiment, the 32nd, to Leyte's west coast because the other two were tied up in the Burauen area until relieved by the newly arrived 11th Airborne Division. While Arnold was redeploying his regiments, the Japanese struck the isolated 32nd Regiment on the night of 22/23 November at a place about ten miles north of Baybay that the GIs dubbed "Shoestring Ridge" because of the paucity of supplies available to them. The soldiers fought off the Japanese attack in a vicious battle, but it was a near thing. Arnold thereupon relieved the exhausted 32nd with his 17th and 184th Regiments and sent them northward to Ormoc accompanied by amphibious tanks. Unfortunately, they got hung up by obstinate Japanese defenders at a series of ridges overlooking the coastal road. By 12 December, the Hourglass boys were still about ten miles south of Ormoc.[14]

Japanese aggressiveness was not limited to assailing Krueger's pincers converging on Ormoc. The Japanese also attacked across Leyte's central mountain range. Their goal was to seize the airfields around Burauen that the 7th Division had occupied early in the operation in the mistaken belief that the Americans were using them. The Japanese attacks, which began on the night of 6/7 December and included a parachute drop by about 350 Japanese soldiers, were uncoordinated. Even so, it took five days of fighting for the Americans to repel the assault. This unsuccessful effort marked the last major Japanese offensive on Leyte.

The paratroopers of the recently arrived 11th Airborne Division were among those defending the airfields around Burauen. The 11th, nicknamed "Angels," was the only airborne division that the army deployed in the Pacific during World War II. Its patch was a white numerical "eleven" on a white-rimmed red circle superimposed over a blue shield with "Airborne" written over the top. Airborne divisions were elite, containing as they did volunteers, so the 11th Airborne unsurprisingly showed great promise from its February 1943 creation. In fact, the army ground forces commander, General Lesley McNair, later credited the 11th Airborne with saving large airborne units. He had been considering limiting airborne outfits to battalion size because of their uncertain performances in North Africa and Sicily. After watching the 11th Airborne Division train, though, he changed his mind. Moreover, the division went from activation to deployment faster than any other in the army, a good sign of an efficient organization. It reached New Guinea in May 1944 and practiced in amphibious and jungle warfare. MacArthur had not intended to use it on Leyte, but the demands of the operation compelled Krueger to ask for it. It arrived on Leyte on 18 November, landing at a beach about forty miles south of Tacloban. Like all paratrooper divisions, it was small, containing only around 8,000 men, and lacked heavy weapons and equipment. However, from the start it had impressed almost everyone in the know. Its commander, the hard-nosed and intense General Joseph M. Swing, was one of the Pacific War's best division chiefs. Eichelberger was a big booster and frequently lauded it. Krueger was also impressed, though less effusive than the gregarious Eichelberger. MacArthur, for his part, eventually rated it second only to the 1st Cav Division.[15]

In addition to the 32nd and 11th Airborne Divisions, Krueger also received Andrew Bruce's 77th Division for use on Leyte. It was a veteran outfit led by a skilled if overambitious officer that had earned kudos even from the Marines during the liberation of Guam. Krueger had wanted the Old Buzzards for the Leyte invasion instead of the untested 96th Division, but, unbeknownst to him, MacArthur had ordered them to New Caledonia for rest and refitting. Krueger got MacArthur to divert them to Leyte, and they arrived on 23 November. The division was so short of supplies, weapons, and equipment that Krueger had to secure the materiel from other units. Both

MacArthur and Krueger deemed the 77th Division exemplary after looking it over. What made it so important was not its numbers, but rather how Krueger intended to use it. Krueger had toyed with the idea of launching an amphibious assault on Ormoc as early as mid-November. He figured that seizing the only major port on Leyte still available to the Japanese would win the operation in one fell swoop by cutting off the Japanese troops on the island from outside assistance. Krueger had lacked sufficient shipping for the operation until MacArthur ordered the postponement of a planned landing on Mindoro Island. This freed up enough shipping to turn Krueger's plan into reality. He opted to use the 77th Division for a shore-to-shore amphibious attack on Ormoc.[16]

On 7 December, Bruce's 77th Division landed unopposed on a beach three and a half miles southeast of Ormoc. Bruce got his GIs moving as quickly as possible, but it still took him three days to seize the port. Doing so isolated the Japanese soldiers on Leyte from outside support, making Japanese defeat on the island inevitable. Before Krueger could begin mopping up those remaining enemy troops, though, he had to tie his disparate army together. The 7th Division linked up with the Old Buzzards the day after Ormoc fell. Connecting the X and XXIV corps took longer. The 77th Division encountered significant enemy opposition as it pushed northward to meet the 1st Cav and 32nd Divisions still bulling their way down the Ormoc Valley. Bruce went about his job methodically and creatively. Maintaining his supply and communication lines with Ormoc required too many men, so he did not even try. He instead brought his rear with him, so to speak, by daily moving his entire division, from artillery batteries to medical tents, as it advanced northward and buttoning up tight every night. Armed convoys within his peripatetic perimeter brought food and ammunition to his men, and Filipino guerrillas screened his flanks. Even so, the 77th Division did not finally contact the X Corps until 21 December, near Kananga. MacArthur and Krueger remained frustrated with the overall pace of operations on Leyte, but they admired the 77th Division's performance. On the other hand, Robert Eichelberger, who was waiting in the wings to take command of American forces on Leyte when Krueger moved on to the Luzon invasion, was disappointed with the Old Buzzards. He wrote his wife, "You have doubtless watched in the papers the progress of my old boys [77th Division]. They failed to go fast when they had nothing much against them. Now they seem to be going slowly because there is something against them. I do not agree that the Japanese are in any great force. They haven't shown much power."[17] Eichelberger's uncharacteristic criticism was probably directed as much against Krueger, with whom he had an increasingly vehement and one-sided vendetta, as against his old division. Indeed, once his Eighth Army assumed control of the island, he reverted to type and gave the 77th Division most of the credit for finally winning the operation.[18]

Stitching the Sixth Army together did not end the Leyte operation. Many hungry and desperate Japanese soldiers remained on the island who had to be dealt with. The unpleasant job of hunting them down went to Eichelberger's Eighth Army, which assumed responsibility for Leyte on 26 December. Although Sixth Army staffers estimated that only 6,000 Japanese troops were still on the island, Eichelberger later claimed that his Eighth Army killed 27,000 of them by the war's end. The truth was undoubtedly somewhere in between. Mopping up the remaining Japanese was an unglamorous, exhausting, and tedious chore. Platoon- and company-sized patrols spent days hiking through the difficult terrain in search of contact with the enemy. It involved long periods of boredom punctuated by minutes of terror. In the end, seven divisions—1st Cav, 7th, 32nd, 77th, 81st, 96th, and the Americal—participated in this thankless task that sometimes saw entire battalions engaged in heavy combat. The Americal Division, for example, had been stationed on Bougainville for almost a year before MacArthur summoned it to Leyte. It was a veteran outfit with an undistinguished record, having seen action at Guadalcanal and Bougainville. Eichelberger had not intended to commit it to combat on Leyte, but clearing the island required so many resources that he felt obligated to use it. The Americal subsequently sustained 700 casualties in a place which, as far as most people were concerned, had long ago been secured. Small wonder the division's historian later wrote, "General Eichelberger would now have fresh troops, seasoned in combat on Bougainville, with which to continue the thankless, forgotten mission of locating and destroying elements of the once-potent Japanese forces on Leyte."[19]

The Leyte operation was a miserable one for everyone involved. Winning it required more time and resources than MacArthur intended, delaying his long-awaited invasion of Luzon. Two corps containing eight divisions—the 1st Cav, 7th, 11th Airborne, 24th, 32nd, 77th, 96th, and Americal—played important roles in it. These units comprised forty percent of all the divisions the army committed to the Pacific War, more than it had used in any previous operation up to that point. Securing Leyte took over two months. GIs dealt with inclement weather, harsh terrain, inadequate supplies, unreliable and even nonexistent air support, and expert and obstinate defenders. More than 15,500 Americans were killed or wounded in the campaign, enough to fill an entire division. By way of return in their investment, the Americans gained a foothold in the Philippines that they used three months later for an assault on all-important Luzon. Assailing Leyte also provoked the Japanese navy into a disastrous engagement with its American counterpart at the Battle of Leyte Gulf that so decimated the Japanese fleet that it ceased to be a serious threat. On land, the Japanese army's decision to make its stand on Leyte cost it perhaps 50,000 of its best troops, not counting those still wandering around the island at the war's close.

On 12 December, Eichelberger wrote in his diary about a conversation he had with MacArthur. In it, MacArthur expressed frustration with the Sixth Army's inability to wrap up the Leyte operation on his schedule. For this he did not blame the rainy weather, difficult terrain, or skillful Japanese defenders, but rather the low quality of some of the participating American units. He worried that if these outfits could not win on Leyte, then they were unlikely to fight better in future engagements. "The Big Chief," Eichelberger noted, "stated [that the] 32nd [Division] never had been any good and that he was very disappointed over [the] slow progress of 77th and 7th [divisions]."[20] MacArthur repeated his sentiments to others. According to one account, when MacArthur articulated his unhappiness to Krueger, the crusty Sixth Army commander barked back that all his men were fine soldiers. However, the very fact that even the chauvinistic MacArthur doubted the quality of some of his divisions on Leyte raises questions about their effectiveness.[21]

The number of casualties a division sustained is not an indication of its combat prowess. A good unit can attain its objectives without incurring heavy losses and a poor one can lose many men through simple incompetence. Casualty figures, however, often indicate the severity of combat, and that can serve as a starting point for evaluating a division's effectiveness in an operation. On Leyte, the 7th Hourglass Division suffered more casualties than any other. Its 2,764 killed, wounded, and missing was followed by 2,342 for the 24th Division, 2,266 for the 77th, and 1,949 for the 32nd Division. Further down the list, the 1st Cav Division accumulated 931 casualties, the Americal Division 731, and the 11th Airborne Division 532. At the corps level, the X Corps' casualties came to 7,126 and the XXIV Corps' amounted to 7,093. Generally speaking, these numbers seem in line with the level of combat each division witnessed, although the Americal Division's rates were high for a unit engaged in mopping up duties.[22]

Although the 7th Hourglass Division sustained heavy casualties on Leyte, it was probably the most effective division, if not the flashiest, on the island. It was a veteran outfit, having seen action on Attu and Kwajalein, and that undoubtedly contributed to its success. On Leyte, it got ashore without serious difficulties, seized the airfields around Burauen, crossed the central mountain range before any other American unit, fought off a fierce Japanese attack at Shoestring Ridge, spearheaded the drive northward to Ormoc, and supported the 77th Division's advance to link up with the X Corps. It did so despite tenuous supply lines and in the face of heavy Japanese opposition. MacArthur may have grumbled about its supposed lethargy, but he also praised the Hourglass boys. Their XXIV Corps commander, John Hodge, agreed that the division did a fine job. He called it a "smooth operating team" and added that Arnold was a "grand commander." To be sure, he noted that the division still needed to learn how to maneuver more effectively and cooperate better with others.[23] Such criticisms, though, reinforce the objectiveness and validity of Hodge's overall positive assessment. After a January 1945 inspection, Nellie Richardson agreed with Hodge. He rated the 7th Division as the XXIV Corps' best, and added that only the 77th Division's Andrew Bruce was Arnold's equal as a divisional leader. Krueger was also complimentary, if less ebullient, in his endorsement, and attributed whatever problems the division had on Leyte more to the terrible terrain than anything else. On Leyte the Hourglass Division proved that it was one of the most accomplished, tough, and expert outfits in the Pacific War.[24]

The 77th Division also performed well on Leyte by building on the good reputation it had acquired on Guam. It was certainly a more flamboyant outfit than the 7th Division, in part because its commander, Andrew Bruce, was something of a showman. Its amphibious assault on Ormoc and subsequent drive northward to link up with the X Corps broke the back of Japanese opposition on the island. Moreover, Bruce used unconventional and innovative tactics to achieve his objectives. On the negative side of the ledger, the 77th Division was not in action as long as some other divisions on Leyte, and should have seized Ormoc sooner. MacArthur and Eichelberger initially criticized the Old Buzzards' sluggishness, but both appreciated the division by the time the army had secured Leyte. Indeed, Eichelberger rated it as highly as the elite 1st Cav Division. Neither Krueger nor Richardson expressed reservations about the 77th, but instead praised it for its splendid morale and discipline. Some officers were more inclined to question Bruce than his men. Hodge, for instance, wrote:

> I am a bit disappointed in Bruce. He is brilliant as a tactician but is a top line egotist, a publicity hound and is not as stable as he should be. He has a fine division and deserves all the credit in the world for it. They all deserve all credit but Bruce forgets that the stage was all set and the combined efforts of all elements of the XXIV Corps was behind the [Ormoc] attack.[25]

Whatever doubts some may have harbored about Bruce, his division emerged from the Leyte operation as a talented, creative, professional, and sophisticated outfit.[26]

The 96th Division did not play a decisive role on Leyte. With a few exceptions, Krueger and Hodge restricted its missions to grappling with Japanese forces in the central mountain range, an important job, but not one that would singlehandedly turn the battle's tide. Considering the Deadeyes' inexperience, this made perfect sense. There it made many of the mistakes common to a green division, but none so serious as to jeopardize the operation's outcome. Both MacArthur and Krueger concluded that it did a good job in its limited role. Richardson thought so too. He called the 96th Division a top unit, but added that it was not as good as the 7th and 77th. As for Hodge, he wrote, "The 96th Division turned in a very credible performance for first combat. They did not have any inhibitions about free maneuver and they were willing to mix it up with the Japs. Administratively, the division has caused me considerable trouble though nothing really serious."[27] Many rookie divisions had horrific experiences in their Pacific War baptisms of fire, so the Deadeyes' acceptable performance was nothing of which to be ashamed.[28]

Like the Deadeyes, the new 11th Airborne Division contributed less to American victory on Leyte than other units. It spent most of the operation securing the central mountain range, an important job to be sure, but not one that brought decisive results. Even so, its marginal involvement did little to shake the consensus that the Angels possessed great potential and were a cut above the ordinary. Krueger for one felt this way, as did its commander, Joseph Swing. He believed that his paratroopers fought harder than any other division on the island. However, for all its determination, the 11th Airborne was still a rookie outfit in its first action, as Swing himself acknowledged in a comment Eichelberger related to his wife:

> Joe [Swing] tells some very interesting stories. In one case he sent his assistant G-3 to accompany a unit that was making an attack. This officer was with the assault units all day and only saw two dead Japs. The next day the reports indicated 240 dead ones. In another case he saw a hospital reported to have a thousand dead Japs in it. He said he could only count between 50 and 60. However there may have been some dead ones which nobody counted.[29]

Fortunately for the army, the 11th Airborne's performance on Leyte and in subsequent operations demonstrated that the division was not all talk.[30]

Verne Mudge's 1st Cavalry Division emerged from the Leyte operation with its grand reputation intact. However, the division spent much of its time on Leyte battling on the left, or eastern, flank of first the 24th Division, and then the 32nd Division, during their attacks down the Ormoc Valley. It was also responsible for secondary operations on Samar and western Leyte that diluted its strength. The troopers achieved no major breakthroughs, but instead fought in the same slogging and grinding manner as the rest of the X Corps. The division's historian later noted histrionically, "Every bit of the division's great fighting prowess had been needed to down the Sons of Heaven who had decided that this campaign was the pay-off."[31] Irving complained that his 24th Division faced more ferocious opposition than Mudge's GIs. It is likely that the respect that high-ranking officers had for the 1st Cav Division helped insulate it from the kind of criticism leveled at the 24th and 32nd Divisions. Although the 1st Cav Division made no serious mistakes on Leyte, it did not do anything to enhance its status either.[32]

The performances of the 24th and 32nd Divisions generated the most controversy on Leyte, the former for failing to quickly overcome Japanese defenses at Breakneck Ridge and the latter for its slow advance down the Ormoc Valley. Horrible terrain, terrible weather, severe logistical problems, inaccurate maps, and stout Japanese resistance handicapped both units. In the 24th Division's case, Krueger and Sibert responded by relieving its commander and yanking the outfit out of the line. Although high-ranking officers, including MacArthur, later reconsidered their harsh criticism and concluded that the division had done about as well as could be expected under the circumstances, this does not mean that that 24th Division's record was flawless. Leyte was the first time that Irving had led all three of his regiments in a major battle, so he unsurprisingly had coordination difficulties. In addition, his successor, Roscoe Woodruff, concluded that the divisional staff was not up to snuff. The upshot was that the 24th Division failed to augment the good reputation it had acquired on New Guinea.[33]

As for the 32nd Division, its drive through the Ormoc Valley was hardly the acme of tactical sophistication. Indeed, Krueger probably had the division in mind when he complained that on Leyte Sixth Army units relied too much on frontal assaults and not enough on envelopments, that infantry failed to demonstrate sufficient initiative and were too road-bound, and that officers did not look after their men as well as they should. Moreover, the division's tarnished reputation undoubtedly colored MacArthur's negative opinion of it. For all its problems, though, the 32nd Division remained in the line until the end of the operation and its commander, Bill Gill, stayed in charge, mostly because he and Sibert were friends. The Red Arrow boys succeeded in linking up with the 77th Division, but their victory was, like their previous ones at Buna and Driniumor River, tainted.[34]

Leyte challenged the army in all sorts of ways, especially in terms of scale. During the New Guinea campaign, SWPA operations rarely involved more than a division and were relatively brief. Generally speaking, American control of the seas around and skies over the battlefield meant that success was assured once the GIs were safely ashore, though mopping up was sometimes a long and difficult process. The outcome was usually a question of time and casualties—how much time it would take to win and how many casualties the army would suffer in the process. On Leyte, though, victory was in doubt for two months. Moreover, triumphing required the Sixth Army to commit two corps and eight divisions. For the first time, Krueger and his corps commanders had to maneuver large numbers of men over a big area. For some divisional leaders, it was their first opportunity to use all their regiments in combat. The performances of the eight divisions that fought on Leyte varied; some did well and added to their reputations, but others, while not losing, raised concerns about their effectiveness. Such questions were not academic because all these divisions would be tested again on Luzon, the central and southern Philippines, and Okinawa.

Luzon: Lingayen Bay to Manila

Leyte was really not that much different from all the other larger islands that comprised the Philippines. Luzon, though, was another story. At 42,458 square miles, or about the size of Virginia, it was the archipelago's largest island by far. More importantly, it was also the Philippines' social, economic, and political center. It contained the capital, Manila, along with the splendid harbor that serviced the city. Luzon was rectangular-shaped, except for two dangling peninsulas to the south and southeast, Batangas and Bicol. It also possessed three major mountain ranges: the Cordillera Central in the north, Sierra Madre on the eastern coast, and the Zambales on the central western shore. Finally, a large agricultural plain extended northward for about 100 miles from Manila. If the Americans wanted to control the Philippines, they needed to take Luzon.

General Tomoyuki Yamashita, the commander of Japanese forces in the Philippines, had about 260,000 soldiers with which to defend Luzon. Yamashita understood that his army lacked the supplies and equipment it needed to defeat an invading American force. That being the case, he decided instead to use his troops to delay, not prevent, an American victory. Doing so would hopefully give his compatriots in the Home Islands additional time with which to prepare for an increasingly imminent American assault. He chose not to defend Manila and the Luzon plain, but rather to take advantage of Luzon's geography to deploy his soldiers in the easily defended and well-placed mountain strongholds throughout the island. He put 152,000 men in the Cordillera Central Mountains surrounding the fertile Cagayan Valley in central Luzon (the Shobu Group), another 30,000 soldiers in the Zambales Mountains overlooking Clark Airbase between Manila and Lingayen Bay (the Kembu Group), and 80,000 troops in the Sierra Madre Mountains east of Manila to control the city's water supplies (the Shimbu Group). Yamashita gambled that the Americans would expend considerable time, resources, and energy pounding on these tough defenses.

MacArthur's plan to invade Luzon was simple in concept, but, as with all Pacific War amphibious assaults, extraordinarily complicated in the details. He wanted to land Krueger's Sixth Army on the broad beaches at Lingayen Bay, about 110 miles northwest of Manila. Once ashore, the Sixth Army could march down the level plains to assault Manila from the rear. Capturing Manila and its harbor would provide the Americans with a base from which to overrun the remainder of the island at their leisure. There was nothing original about the design—in fact, the Japanese had done the same thing when they attacked Luzon in December 1941—but it played to American strengths in firepower, mobility, and mechanization.

To carry out the amphibious assault on Lingayen Bay, Krueger had at his disposal two corps that committed two divisions apiece to the landing. The first was Palmer Swift's I Corps. Its two divisions were the 6th and 43rd. The 6th Sightseers Division had cut its teeth in its pointblank confrontation with the Japanese at Lone Tree Hill the previous June–July. It may not have demonstrated much tactical finesse there, but it had certainly showed plenty of grit and determination. From there it conducted an unopposed landing at Sansapor–Mar. The Sightseers were a tough, direct, hard-hitting, and tenacious bunch, now led by General Edwin Patrick, who were unlikely to flinch from a fight. It was a good unit, but one which had not worked with other divisions in combat. Swift was fortunate to have it for the big battles he would soon face.

The 43rd Division had undergone its horrific baptism of fire on New Georgia in June–August 1943. It had only won the battle there because other units arrived to help it secure victory. Moreover, the division's high number of combat fatigue cases raised questions about its effectiveness. In August 1943, General Leonard F. Wing assumed command. He was a National Guardsman, one of only a handful to lead a division in combat during the war. He worked hard to retrain and refit the unit for its next battle. After several months in New Zealand, MacArthur ordered the 43rd Division to New Guinea. There

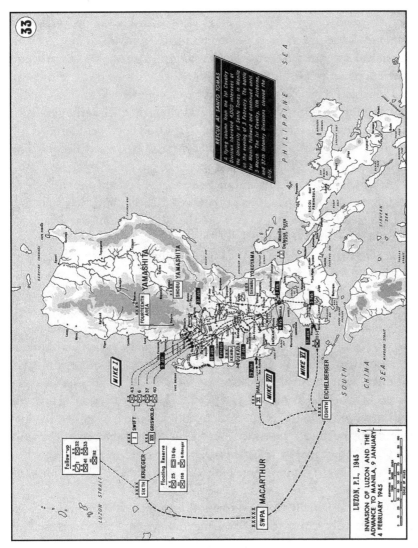

The Invasion of Luzon, January–August 1945.

it impressed the XI Corps chief, Charles Hall, during its minor operations along the Driniumor River. Hall referred to Wing as "a two-fisted kind of chap who is willing to fight."[35] The Luzon invasion would be the 43rd Division's first sustained action in more than a year, and its big opportunity to erase whatever doubts remained in the minds of high-level officers about its abilities.

Krueger also had Oscar Griswold's XIV Corps in his hopper. Griswold had seen plenty of action at New Georgia and Bougainville, and, now that Eichelberger had ascended to lead the new Eighth Army, was MacArthur's most experienced and capable corps commander. Griswold's first division was an old reliable Pacific War standby: Robert Beightler's 37th Buckeyes. It had fought credibly at both New Georgia and Bougainville, during which it had earned Griswold's unwavering support. The Ohio boys were resourceful, inventive, and skilled at their trade. Moreover, the 37th had been killing time on Bougainville ever since it helped repel the ferocious Japanese assault there the previous March, so it was rested and ready. Perhaps the only fly in the ointment was the poor relationship between Krueger and Beightler that extended back to the prewar years. Even so, the 37th Division was a valuable addition to the Luzon invasion force.[36]

Griswold's last division slotted for the Luzon landing was General Isaac Rapp Brush's 40th. The War Department had created it in March 1941 out of the California, Nevada, and Utah National Guards. It was nicknamed "Sunshine" or "Sunburst" and its patch was a twelve-rayed yellow sun superimposed over a blue diamond. It arrived in Hawaii to garrison the Outer Islands in September 1942. Ten months later it moved to Oahu and began amphibious and jungle warfare training. In December 1943 it embarked for Guadalcanal, and from there went in April 1944 to New Britain Island. Its GIs lived for eight months in miserable conditions and saw some limited action against the Japanese. It had been training for the Luzon landing since November. By then its bored and frustrated GIs were more than ready to test their mettle against the Japanese. Whether they would perform well was still in the future when the transport vessels carrying the Sunshiners approached the Luzon shoreline on the morning of 9 January 1945.

MacArthur had originally planned to assail Luzon on 20 December 1944, but the unexpectedly difficult and prolonged Leyte operation, as well as adverse weather and the need to acquire airfields closer to the target, forced him to postpone the invasion. However, on 2–4 January 1945, yet another large American invasion force assembled in Leyte Gulf, this one bound for Lingayen Bay. Getting there required running a gauntlet of kamikaze attacks that damaged twenty-five vessels, but fortunately left the vulnerable troop transports unscathed. As at Leyte, the Japanese declined to expose their men to the American navy's firepower by attempting to defend the beaches. The GIs of the four assaulting divisions therefore landed without serious opposition. Indeed, within days MacArthur had 175,000 troops ashore, ready to grapple with the Japanese army.

Krueger assigned Swift's I Corps the job of protecting the left, or eastern, flank of Griswold's XIV Corps as the 37th and 40th Divisions pushed southward toward Manila. The best way for Swift to do so was for his I Corps to seize the road junction near Rosario that connected the Japanese stronghold of Baguio in the Cagayan Valley with Manila. Once Rosario was in American hands, it would be extremely difficult for the Japanese in the Shobu Group to access the Luzon plain. Swift in turn directed Wing's 43rd Division the task of taking Rosario and reinforced it with the independent 158th Regiment and a regiment from Patrick's 6th Division. Unfortunately, the 43rd Division's initial assaults made little progress. By 17 January, Wing's troops had suffered about 770 casualties and had still not occupied Rosario. An angry Krueger responded by unilaterally relieving Swift's chief of staff and operations officer, inserting the recently arrived 25th Division into the I Corps' front, and ordering Wing to try again. Realizing that Krueger's impatience precluded any tactical subtlety, Wing resorted to direct attacks that gradually ground down the opposing Japanese. Rosario fell on 26 January, at which point the 43rd Division's battalions were at half strength. Wing had achieved his objective, but not on schedule and certainly not in a manner likely to impress anyone.

While Swift's I Corps struggled to secure Rosario, Griswold's XIV Corps was meeting little enemy opposition in its southward march on Manila. Even so, Krueger and Griswold wanted to advance methodically to make sure that the Japanese did not exploit any gap between the two Sixth Army corps. This made perfect military sense, but MacArthur was not thinking exclusively along those lines. Whereas Krueger's concerns were understandably tactical in nature, MacArthur had a more strategic outlook. Some claimed that he wanted to seize the city before his—and, incidentally, Krueger's—26th January birthday, but he most likely wanted to quickly liberate Manila to protect its population from Japanese reprisals and secure the logistical facilities necessary to support Nimitz's upcoming operations against Iwo Jima and Okinawa. He felt that Krueger was unnecessarily cautious. As he saw it, the Japanese did not pose much of a threat to XIV Corps. He explained to one person:

> You know, I want to talk to Walter [Krueger] to see if I can persuade him to go down the plain a little bit faster. I think he feels that every side valley on our east is full of Japanese ready

to come storming out. Well, there are plenty of Japanese back there, but they're defending the Cagayan Valley where they hope to make their last big stand, and they are not going to come charging down into the plain with all that we have here.[37]

MacArthur had, in fact, been frustrated with what he interpreted as Krueger's dilatoriness on Leyte, and he did not want a reoccurrence on Luzon. MacArthur was an impatient man to begin with, and his desire to get to Manila led him to dramatically increase the pressure he exerted on Krueger. The resulting tension between the two officers colored Krueger's relationship with Griswold, Beightler, and Brush and impacted the performance of their units.[38]

At first the XIV Corps' biggest obstacles were destroyed bridges and jubilant Filipinos. However, on 23 January, GIs encountered Japanese troops from the Kembu Group outside of Clark Airbase, about forty-eight miles north of the Philippine capital. Clark Airbase was a major complex that extended for fifteen miles. It contained fifteen runways, as well as numerous taxiways, dispersal areas, hangers, barracks, support buildings, and so forth. Krueger, still under pressure from MacArthur to get to Manila as quickly as possible, wanted Griswold to leave Brush's 40th Division to take care of Clark Airbase while Beightler's 37th Division continued southward. Griswold balked, first because he did not want the Buckeyes to get overextended and then because the green 40th Division proved unable to seize Clark Airbase on its own.

Indeed, the Sunshiners' initial attacks made only moderate progress against Japanese soldiers deployed behind ditches and in fields, and in caves in the ridges overlooking the airbase. This was the 40th Division's first major battle, so it was unsurprising that its men made all sorts of rookie mistakes. The division's historian remembered the drearily repetitive process necessary to root out stalwart Japanese defenders: "With deadly accuracy the caves were blasted until sealed or silenced. Our artillery concentrations, setting fire to the hillsides, disclosed individual rifle and machine gun pits when the camouflage was burned away. Six-inch naval guns similarly emplaced were neutralized in the same manner. As infantry advanced, small arms fire and hand grenades were used to clean out the positions, and flame thrower teams destroyed possible survivors in the larger caves."[39] After five days of frustration, Griswold risked Krueger's wrath by sending most of the 37th Division to help out the Sunshiners. This did the trick, and Clark Airbase was secured on 1 February. Nearby Fort Stotsenberg fell to the Buckeyes two days earlier. The engagement cost the Buckeyes and Sunshiners around 710 casualties.

Seizing Clark Airbase was a major accomplishment. Once the Army Air Forces moved in—or, more accurately, returned—and made the necessary repairs, it became much easier for the Americans to extend their air power throughout Luzon. Even so, the triumph had a somewhat sour aftermath. Although the 37th Division demonstrated again why it was such an effective unit, the 40th Division emerged with a more ambivalent reputation. On the positive side of the ledger, it performed adequately in its first major action, even if the 37th Division eventually had to help it out. It made no mistakes serious enough to cost it victory, did not suffer excessive losses, and won in ten days of hard fighting. This was certainly Griswold's view. As far as he was concerned, the Sunshiners had done as well as could be expected. On the other hand, Krueger had a different take. He was deeply disappointed with the 40th Division's showing, mostly because it did not secure Clark Airbase on a schedule that satisfied the impatient MacArthur. He called the 40th Division his worst, later foisted it on Eichelberger's Eighth Army, and disparaged and browbeat Brush so much that Brush eventually refused to serve in the Sixth Army. Indeed, Krueger leaned hard on Griswold to fire Brush, but Griswold refused. The fight for Clark Airbase was not, in short, an unvarnished success for the Sunshiners.[40]

MacArthur's frustrations with Krueger's slow advance on Manila continued throughout January and into February. Although MacArthur talked darkly of relieving Krueger, he did not. The two men were old friends, and anyway MacArthur usually refrained from removing officers from their commands. This being the case, MacArthur instead focused on working around Krueger to get to Manila quickly. To do so, MacArthur had a couple of arrows in his quiver. One was Robert Eichelberger and his Eighth Army. By now Eichelberger believed that Krueger was boorish, unreasonable, hypocritical, and demeaning. Indeed, by the time the Americans assailed Leyte, Eichelberger's dislike of Krueger had metastasized into full-blown hatred. MacArthur was aware of Eichelberger's enmity toward his old Sixth Army boss and had become adept at playing the two men off against each other for his own benefit. Eichelberger was then headquartered in Leyte, overseeing the mopping up of the remaining Japanese forces on the island. MacArthur decided to insert Eichelberger into the Luzon operation by giving him the opportunity to seize Manila ahead of Krueger's Sixth Army.

MacArthur ordered Eichelberger to use Joe Swing's elite 11th Airborne Division to attack Manila from the south. Everyone admired the Angels. It may have played a relatively minor role in the fight for Leyte, but it seemed like a unit with great potential. Eichelberger, always alert for a chance to best his despised rival Krueger, jumped at the opportunity. On 31 January, two regiments from the 11th Airborne Division landed at Nasugbu on Luzon's west coast, about fifty-five miles south of Manila, followed by a scattered parachute drop by the division's third regiment on 3 February at nearby Tagaytay Ridge. Eichelberger's high hopes of beating Krueger to Manila, though, were dashed when the Angels encountered heavy Japanese opposition the next day along the Paranaque River, just south of the city, at the so-called Genko Line. Airborne divisions lacked heavy weapons to begin with, and the Angels were still understrength from their stint on Leyte. As a result, they lost the race to Manila and ended up instead embroiled in a battle for Nichols Airfield. By then they had suffered about 335 casualties, 150 of whom had been injured parachuting onto Tagaytay Ridge. On 10 February, MacArthur placed the 11th Airborne in Griswold's XIV Corps and sent Eichelberger back to Leyte to plan for the liberation of the central and southern Philippines.

The 11th Airborne Division received considerable praise for its actions. Eichelberger recommended it for a presidential citation and later wrote, "The 11th Airborne [Division] was living up to its reputation. The troops stood up unflinchingly under artillery fire and performed flawlessly. In twenty-eight hours ashore they had advanced nineteen miles on foot."[41] MacArthur was equally laudatory, rating the 11th Airborne Division second only to his beloved 1st Cav Division in effectiveness. Even Krueger grudgingly complimented it. However, the fact was that although the Angels might have looked impressive and fought well, they lost the race to Manila. But in the military, as in so many aspects of life, a good reputation can compensate for unfulfilled expectations. A few weeks later, the 11th Airborne garnered more praise in a daring and skillfully conducted raid on the Japanese internment camp at Los Baños that resulted in the liberation of 2,000 westerners. It subsequently fought in southern Luzon against the Shimbu Group before moving northward to help eliminate the Shobu Group.[42]

MacArthur's other available arrow was Verne Mudge's 1st Cavalry Division. It was MacArthur's favorite unit, with plenty of combat experience in the Admiralties and on Leyte, and had come ashore at Lingayen Bay on 27 January. Because of its peculiar organizational structure, it was smaller than a typical infantry division. It was also understrength and tired from its recent exertions on Leyte. Even so, its troopers possessed high morale, great discipline, and a first-rate commander in Mudge. MacArthur saw it as the ideal instrument for reaching Manila quickly. Bypassing Krueger, on 1 February MacArthur told Mudge, "Go to Manila. Go around the Nips, bounce off the Nips, but go to Manila."[43] Although still seventy miles from the Philippine capital, Mudge hurriedly formed two flying columns at Guimba and sent them southward to the left of the 37th Division with orders to avoid enemy contact and get to Manila as rapidly as possible. Fortunately, enemy opposition was light, the locals sympathetic, and the bridges intact. When Krueger realized what MacArthur was doing, he ordered Griswold to put the spurs to Beightler's 37th Division. Griswold gave the Buckeye Division top priority, but it could not overcome blown bridges and the 1st Cav Division's lead. By way of compensation, the Buckeyes did seize the San Miguel Brewery, whose gallons of beer was to the tired and thirsty GIs worth a dozen Manilas. On 3 February, the troopers seized a bridge over the Tuliahan River, breached Manila's northern outskirts, liberated the 4,000 civilians interned at Santo Tomas University, and swung eastward to cut the city's garrison off from outside help. They had won the race to Manila in a dramatic style that impressed everyone, including Tomoyuki Yamashita, the Japanese army commander in the Philippines.[44]

While the 1st Cav, 11th Airborne, and 37th Divisions were racing toward Manila, MacArthur was also initiating efforts to make sure that the Japanese did not prevent the Americans from using the bay that gave the city much of its strategic value. MacArthur knew from hard experience the stakes involved. He had denied the Japanese access to Manila Bay for months in 1941–42 by holing up with his troops on the nearby Bataan Peninsula. At 530 square miles, the peninsula comprised Manila Bay's western shore, so whoever controlled it controlled the bay. MacArthur worried that the Japanese might steal a page from his playbook by mimicking his strategy. To forestall this, he decided to mount an amphibious landing at the northern base of the peninsula. Once ashore, the GIs could push eastward across the peninsula and seal it off from any retreating Japanese troops. This undertaking would, if successful, go a long way toward opening up Manila Bay once the capital was in American hands.

MacArthur and Krueger assigned this mission to the 38th Division. Created out of the Indiana, Kentucky, and West Virginia National Guards, the 38th Division got its nickname, "Cyclone," from a storm that destroyed the unit's Mississippi tent city in World War I. Its patch was a shield divided vertically into two equal parts, one red and the other blue, with an interlocking white "c" and "y" in the center. Although it was inducted into federal service in January 1941, it did not get overseas until three years later, and it suffered considerable turnover in the process. It then spent six months in Hawaii until MacArthur summoned it to Oro Bay, New Guinea, in July 1944. From there it deployed to Leyte in December, where it saw limited action. Its commander was General Henry Lawrence Cullem Jones, whom Eichelberger referred to as a "queer genius."[45] Whatever Jones's talents, MacArthur and Krueger hesitated to entrust him and his equally green staff to oversee the Bataan operation, so they gave that job to Charles Hall and his XI Corps. They also added a regiment from the veteran 24th Division to provide some experienced ballast.[46]

On 29 January, 35,000 GIs from the 38th Division and the 24th Division's 34th Regiment landed unopposed in the San Narciso area. The only casualty was a soldier gored by a water buffalo. Subic Bay and Olongapo fell the next day. Unfortunately, four days later troops advancing eastward across the peninsula encountered approximately 3,000 Japanese in a place called Zigzag Pass. Zigzag Pass was perhaps the most rugged region in Luzon, with dense forest that the Japanese filled with well-camouflaged dirt and log pillboxes, trenches, tunnels, and foxholes. When the 152nd Regiment made no progress against these defenses, Hall brought up the 34th Regiment to reinforce it. In just a few days, the 34th Regiment suffered so many casualties that Hall and Jones had to withdraw it and replace it with the 151st Regiment, followed by the 149th. Although the 34th Regiment was a veteran unit, having fought at Hollandia, Biak, and Leyte, its commander, Colonel William Jenna, called the Zigzag Pass battle among the toughest he had experienced. Indeed, one historian later referred to the 34th Regiment's experience at Zigzag Pass as a "disaster."[47] As for the 38th Division, it suffered from the usual travails of an inexperienced outfit: poor leadership, lack of initiative, coordination problems, inadequate navigation due to poor maps, rumors, an inability to use all available weapons, and so forth. One soldier stated:

> The nights are hell for the men. They're dead tired, but are keeping their spirits up. The advance in the narrow defiles is tortuous and slow because a few Japs can turn loose withering fire from hidden positions overlooking the road. The bamboo forests are so thick we have to get within a few feet of the Japs to see them. It is the kind of fighting where we have to go in and root them out with grenades.[48]

Neither Krueger nor Hall had much sympathy for and understanding of the 38th Division's plight. The fact that the Cyclone boys were undergoing their baptism of fire and were therefore likely to make plenty of rookie mistakes did not seem to cross their minds. Nor did they connect the division's woes with the extraordinarily difficult terrain in which it was battling. Hall informed Krueger:

> As you know, this country is exceedingly rugged having deep ravines with sharp ridges and nearly all heavily wooded. Movement through it is slow and envelopment difficult. In this terrain all of our information, including aerial photographs, guerrilla reports and our own visual observation shows an extremely well fortified and strongly defended position. In addition, the enemy has obviously sited and registered his automatic weapons and artillery on every road bend and all commanding ground in this area …. It is the best fortified place that I have ever seen.[49]

Even so, both generals wanted the battle won quickly and were unwilling to accept even reasonable excuses and delays. Hall's inaccurate belief that the

38th Division's casualties were minimal reinforced his impatience. As far as Hall was concerned, the problem was that Jones could not manage the 38th effectively. After several days of growing frustration and haranguing, on 6 February Hall relieved Jones. He acknowledged Jones's personal courage and loyalty, but claimed that he did so because of a "… lack of aggressiveness on the part of his division, unsatisfactory tactical planning and execution and inadequate reconnaissance measures. He failed to produce the results with his division which might be reasonably expected. I do not consider his handling of the division in action to be satisfactory."[50]

Krueger replaced Jones with General William Chase, a 1st Cav Division brigade commander who had successfully defended the airfield at Momote in the Admiralties and later played a prominent role in the outfit's recent dash to Manila. Although Krueger had been concerned with Chase's jittery and high-strung attitude on Los Negros, since then Chase had won Krueger's respect. When Chase arrived at the 38th Division's headquarters and looked things over, he was disconcerted with the unit's dispositions, but sympathetic to its plight:

> My first day [as 38th Division commander in the field at Zigzag Pass] was most frustrating because no one knew what was going on or where they were. This was the first taste of combat for most of the division and hence it was subject to all the usual trials and tribulations of inexperienced leadership, confusion, and wild rumor. Many front line platoons did not even have their automatic weapons, machine guns, or mortars, and the riflemen were not using their rifles.[51]

As far as Chase could tell, the lower level officers were fine, but some of the senior ones needed to go. Years later he concluded, "No wonder they were stopped."[52] Fortunately for Chase, he had all three of his regiments on hand and the outnumbered and outgunned Japanese were worn out by nearly a week of heavy combat. Moreover, the 149th Regiment had succeeded in linking up with the XIV Corps and had positioned itself to hit the Japanese from the east. It therefore took Chase only two days to destroy most of the remaining Japanese in Zigzag Pass. One soldier remembered: "How did we crack this formidable defense? The same way we've cracked all of them—artillery and mortar fire to keep them down while we maneuvered close enough to blow them out with grenades or burn them out with flame throwers. It was the old, tedious, painful pattern and none of us shall ever forget the 16 days it took to do it."[53] The 38th Division and the attached 34th Regiment suffered around 1,400 casualties in the process. Although Chase noted proudly that the engagement turned the 38th Division into a tough veteran unit, the cost was disturbingly high. By way of return on this expensive investment, the 38th Division facilitated the clearing of Manila harbor by other units in subsequent operations.[54]

At the same time that the 38th Division was learning the hard way how to fight at Zigzag Pass, the 37th Buckeye Division was receiving a difficult education of its own. In its case, though, the classroom was the urban hell of Manila. Although Yamashita had not intended to contest the city and had ordered its evacuation, he had no authority over the 16,000 naval personnel there whose commander opted to fight to the death, joined by 4,000 trapped soldiers. They blew up bridges, laid barbed wire, constructed machine gun nests, cannibalized stranded warships for weapons, and barricaded themselves in buildings and behind overturned vehicles. They could not win the upcoming battle, but they could certainly make MacArthur pay dearly for his prize. MacArthur initially expected Manila to fall quickly, and had as usual tried to make reality bend to his anticipations by prematurely declaring Japanese opposition at an end. Oscar Griswold, the XIV Corps commander, knew better. He wrote in his diary, "Gen. MacArthur has visions of saving this beautiful city intact. He does not realize, as I do, that the skies burn red every night as they systematically sack the city. Nor does he know that enemy rifle, machine gun, mortar and artillery are steadily increasing in intensity."[55] Whatever MacArthur's delusions on the subject, Griswold recognized that seizing Manila would be a bloody ordeal.

Although the 1st Cav Division helped clear the northeastern part of the city, the 37th Division bore the brunt of the burden of liberating Manila. It was a veteran outfit, having fought at New Georgia, Bougainville, and Clark Airbase, but it had no experience in urban warfare. A fire that swept through northern Manila delayed its attack, but the Buckeyes soon found themselves embroiled in brutal house-to-house and street-by-street combat. Griswold wrote, "The fighting in South Manila is very bitter. Japs organize each big reinforced concrete building into a fortress, and fight to the death in the basement, on each floor, and even to the roof. This is *rough*. I'm getting a lot of unavoidable casualties."[56] MacArthur initially limited the use of airstrikes and artillery in an effort to spare the city and reduce civilian losses, but these restrictions eventually went by the wayside as the battle progressed. GIs used flamethrowers, bazookas, grenades, and satchel charges to root the Japanese out of building after building and resorted to shooting every Japanese corpse they came across just in case of a ruse. They gradually pushed the Japanese back into Intramuros, the old Spanish part of the city of about 160 square acres that was enclosed by big stone walls, some as much as forty feet thick. After a massive bombardment, the

129th and 145th Regiments penetrated the walls and eliminated its residual Japanese defenders. Some mopping up remained, but the engagement was over on 4 March, about a month after it began. The Americans suffered around 1,000 killed and 5,500 wounded, mostly from the 37th Division. MacArthur and Krueger did not appear particularly impressed with the division's performance, though Krueger's indifference might have been tied to his dislike of Beightler. Others, however, were. Indeed, the 37th Division fought quite expertly, systematically, and doggedly to free Manila. The Japanese garrison was practically annihilated. Most tragically, approximately 100,000 Filipino civilians died, many at the hands of the desperate and vindictive Japanese, and the once beautiful city was so obliterated that entire blocks were flattened.[57]

While the 37th Division was experiencing the horrors of urban warfare in Manila, Palmer Swift's I Corps was busy securing the XIV Corps' left flank and severing the supply and communication lines between the Shobu and Shimbu groups. The key to doing so was the town of San José, which dominated the road network connecting the two Japanese strongholds. Swift gave the job of taking San José to two of the sturdiest and hardest-hitting divisions in the army's arsenal: General Edwin Patrick's 6th and General Charles L. Mullins's 25th. The former had cut its teeth at Lone Tree Hill and had landed at Lingayen Bay on the first day of the Luzon invasion. Although elements of the division had seen action since, it had not yet fought on Luzon as an integrated unit with all three of its regiments in a major battle. As for the 25th Division, it had come ashore at Lingayen Bay on 11 January. It was also a veteran outfit, one of the army's best, having seen action on Guadalcanal and New Georgia. It had been cooling its heels at Guadalcanal, New Zealand, and New Caledonia since then, so it was well-rested, up to strength, and ready to go.

Swift's plan to seize San José was simple enough. He ordered the 6th and 25th Divisions to converge on the town, the 6th from the southwest through Muñoz and the 25th from the northwest through Umingan and Lupao. Unfortunately, problems developed soon after the American offensive kicked off on 1 February. Stiff Japanese opposition at Muñoz, Umingan, and Lupao brought both divisions to a halt. Rather than batter away at these Japanese defenses, both Patrick and Mullins ordered their GIs to go around them and strike directly at San José. The 25th Division's historian later referred to it as "hop, skip, and jump type of warfare."[58] It worked; San José fell to the Sightseers without much of a fight on 4 February. Eight days later, elements of the 6th Division reached Luzon's east coast at Baler Bay. All that remained was mopping up the bypassed Japanese troops, an unpleasant and tedious task that invariably followed almost every American victory in the Pacific War. Patrick's and Mullins's willingness and capacity to outmaneuver the Japanese instead of grinding them down through brute attrition demonstrated a tactical sophistication that American generals had not always shown in the Pacific War, one that reflected well on the abilities of the two divisions involved.

The Sixth Army may have seized Clark Airbase during its march on Manila, but the Japanese soldiers in the Kembu Group remained ensconced in the nearby Zimbales Mountains. As far as Krueger was concerned, they constituted a continuing threat to the recently freed airbase, so he ordered Griswold and his XIV Corps to eliminate them. Griswold in turn gave the job to Rapp Brush and his 40th Division. The Sunshiners had helped secure the airbase the previous month, but Krueger had not been impressed with either the division or its commander. His displeasure with Brush grew when he took longer than Krueger thought necessary to start his mission against the Japanese in the Zambales. Brush's offensive, which began on 8 February, resulted in a series of fierce engagements in the thickly forested mountains against die-hard Japanese troops who fought to the death from their caves. Under these circumstances, there was no shortcut to victory, but only the kind of hard and close combat that underscores the brutality of warfare. By 20 February, the Sunshiners had broken the back of enemy resistance in the Zambales. From that point on it was mostly a matter of mopping up the remaining Japanese through dreary, repetitive, and dangerous skirmishing by roving patrols. Charles Hall's XI Corps assumed the responsibility for this task on 23 February. The Sunshiners started the process, but in early March the 43rd Division, veterans of the Rosario fight, relieved them. Ten days later elements of the 38th Division arrived to take over, followed by parts of the 6th Division in early May. When the war ended, only 1,500 Japanese soldiers remained, the rest having died in battle or of hunger, exhaustion, and disease.

MacArthur's Luzon invasion was certainly successful. In about two months, the Sixth Army established a lodgment on Luzon, seized Manila, and almost destroyed the Kembu Group at the cost of around 25,000 casualties. However, the Americans mostly occupied territory that Yamashita never intended to seriously contest. With the exception of the Kembu Group, the Sixth Army had barely touched the Japanese strongholds on the island. It required nine divisions to secure the Luzon plain, Manila, and the Zambales Mountains: the 1st Cav, 6th, 11th Airborne, 24th, 25th, 37th, 38th, 40th, and 43rd. Of these, the 1st Cav and 11th Airborne Divisions played mostly peripheral roles, though they garnered a disproportionate amount of attention. The 38th, 40th, and 43rd Divisions fought grueling battles at Zigzag Pass, Clark Airbase, and Rosario.

Although they all achieved their objectives, usually with some outside help, there was nothing pretty about their performances. This was hardly surprising in the case of the 38th and 40th Divisions because neither had previously experienced sustained combat. On the other hand, the 6th and 25th Divisions fought skillfully in taking San José by outmaneuvering the Japanese. It was the 37th Division, though, that served as the Sixth Army's lynchpin. It landed at Lingayen Bay, spearheaded the drive to Manila, assisted the 40th Division in clearing Clark Airbase, and liberated Manila after a vicious engagement. In doing so, it solidified its position as one of the Pacific War's premier outfits.

Central and Southern Philippines

When MacArthur pledged to liberate the Philippines, he did not mean just the most militarily and politically important parts of the archipelago such as Luzon. He meant all of it—or anyhow as much of it as he could. This included the islands in the central and southern Philippines. He insisted on doing so even though these places possessed little strategic value and contained over 100,000 Japanese troops. Moreover, he did not have explicit permission from the Joint Chiefs of Staff. His reasoning was unclear. He may have wanted to protect American prisoners and Filipino civilians from Japanese retribution, or to provide airbases for a planned Australian assault on nearby Borneo, or to restore American prestige. Whatever MacArthur's motives, conducting the campaign required diverting resources from Krueger's concurrent operations in Luzon. Indeed, MacArthur dispatched all or part of five divisions—the Americal, 24th, 31st, 40th, and 41st—to the central and southern Philippines, as well as plenty of air and naval power which he might have committed to Luzon.

MacArthur gave the job of freeing this region to Robert Eichelberger and his Eighth Army. In a series of brilliant operations that included fourteen major and twenty-four minor amphibious assaults in just forty-four days, often on a logistical shoestring, Eichelberger fulfilled his mission. The Eighth Army's amphibious blitzkrieg included landings on a slew of Filipino islands: Palawan on 28 February (41st Division), Mindanao's Zamboanga Peninsula on 10 March (41st Division), Panay on 18 March (40th Division), Cebu on 26 March (Americal Division), Negros on 29 March and 26 April (40th and Americal Divisions), Sanga Sanga on 2 April (41st Division), Jolo on 9 April (41st Division), Bohol on 11 April (Americal Division), and, finally, Mindanao on 17 April (24th and 31st Divisions). In most cases, the Japanese did not fight on the beaches, but instead retreated inland to make their last stands there against the Americans and Filipino guerrillas. Most of the combat concluded that summer, but significant numbers of Japanese continued to hold out until the end of the war. The tactically dazzling but strategically barren campaign cost the United States some 9,000 casualties and the Japanese a little over 50,000.

MacArthur's headquarters selected from Krueger's Sixth Army the divisions allotted to Eichelberger for his campaign. Although MacArthur's staff officers did so based on factors such as logistics, location, and readiness, Krueger had some input in the decision. Naturally enough, he tried to keep divisions he liked and give up the ones he did not. It was therefore no coincidence that the 1st Cav and 11th Airborne divisions remained with the Sixth Army. Nor was it surprising that the 24th, 40th, and 41st Divisions ended up in the Eighth Army. Krueger made no secret of his dislike of the 40th Division and its commander. He had also soured on the 24th and 41st Divisions due to their performances on, respectively, Leyte and Biak. It would be an exaggeration to state that Eichelberger got the second-rate divisions, but there is an element of truth to it, at least from Krueger's perspective.

The 41st Jungleers Division was the first outfit that Eichelberger used in his campaign. The Jungleers had spearheaded MacArthur's drive across New Guinea's northern coast the previous year until they encountered more Japanese opposition than they could initially handle at Biak. That operation cost the division commander, Horace Fuller, his job and tainted the division's reputation. Since then it had been sitting on the sidelines, so to speak, and had missed both the Leyte and Luzon invasions. Eichelberger, however, liked the 41st Division and its new leader, Jens Doe, though he worried that Doe drank too much. He had inspected it a couple times and was pleased with what he saw. He was therefore happy to use it to assail Palawan. At 200 miles long and thirty miles wide, Palawan was one of the westernmost islands in the Philippines. In American hands, warplanes could reach both Indochina and Borneo. On 28 February, one of the division's regiments, the 186th, landed unopposed on Palawan. Nevertheless, it took almost two months for the regiment to clear the island, with the help of Filipino guerrillas, of its Japanese defenders, at the cost of less than seventy killed or wounded.[59]

After the Palawan assault, elements of the 41st Division went on to land on Mindanao's Zamboanga Peninsula and on several of the Sulu Islands in the central part of the archipelago. In each instance the Jungleers overcame sometimes ferocious Japanese opposition and horrible terrain to achieve their objectives. In all, they suffered about 500 casualties. Although Eichelberger complained that the division was too cautious and lethargic—he compared it unfavorably to the 11th Airborne Division—he was largely happy with its efforts on and off the battlefield. In fact, the division performed competently enough for an outfit committed to missions of minimal strategic significance in a remote part of the conflict.[60]

MacArthur also wanted Eichelberger to seize the four major islands in the Central Philippines: Panay, Negros, Cebu, and Bohol. Eichelberger in turn assigned Rapp Brush's 40th Sunshiners Division the job of taking Panay and northwestern Negros. The Sunshiners had undergone their baptism of fire at Clark Airbase and in the Zambales Mountains against the Kembu Group. Neither Brush nor his division had impressed Krueger much. Krueger thought they were too slow and amateurish, so he was happy to unload the outfit on Eichelberger. Indeed, MacArthur later said to Eichelberger, "You know when he [Krueger] gave you Brush he gave you what he thought was his worst division."[61] Eichelberger, however, liked both Brush and his Sunshiners, though his affinity was undoubtedly motivated at least in part by his knowledge of Krueger's enmity toward the outfit. When he flew to Luzon, he made a point of visiting a dispirited Brush to buck him up and assure him that he would treat him better than Krueger had.[62]

On 18 March, the 40th Division's 185th Regiment came ashore on Panay several miles from the city of Iloilo. Filipino guerrillas had already secured most of the island, so the only remaining obstacle was Iloilo's 2,750-man Japanese garrison, which the 185th overwhelmed in a couple days. This quick victory enabled the regiment to land unopposed on northwestern Negros on 29 March. The local capital of Bacolod fell the next day, but overcoming the 13,500 Japanese troops in the region required hard fighting and the commitment of reinforcements from the 160th and independent 503rd Parachute Regiments. The Sunshiners pushed the Japanese inland until combat tapered off in mid-June. Seizing this part of Negros cost the 40th Division 370 killed and 1,025 wounded. Despite these losses, the Sunshiners' performance won Eichelberger's admiration and called into question Krueger's negative evaluation of the unit. As far as Eichelberger was concerned, the 40th Division demonstrated considerable vigor, aggressiveness, and intelligence. In addition, the outfit had restored local infrastructure too. He noted to his wife, "Rapp's service after taking Panay and Negros is on a very high curve."[63] To drive the point home, especially no doubt to Krueger, Eichelberger decorated Brush for his actions. When Eichelberger inspected the division on 20 April, he reported that the Sunshiners were in such fine spirits that he was not worried about them at all.[64]

Eichelberger used General William H. Arnold's American Division to assail Cebu, Bohol, and southeastern Negros. The American Division had spent most of the Pacific War toiling in obscurity. Indeed, some of its wounded soldiers once asked Eichelberger pointblank why their unit got so little publicity. After its lackluster performance on Guadalcanal, it had assisted the 37th Division in repulsing the Japanese attack on the XIV Corps' defensive perimeter around Empress Augusta Bay on Bougainville. From there it sailed to Leyte to mop up remaining Japanese resistance there, a thankless, tedious, and unglamorous job that still cost the unit some 700 casualties. Neither MacArthur, Krueger, nor Eichelberger had much to say one way or another about the American Division before it embarked on its latest mission. Indeed, Oscar Griswold was just about the only high-level officer who had a kind word for the outfit. Griswold had led the American Division on Bougainville. He told Eichelberger that the American was well-trained and prepared for anything the Japanese could throw at it.[65]

The American Division proved what it was capable of on Cebu. There were 14,500 Japanese soldiers there, most of whom Filipino guerrillas had penned around Cebu City. On 26 March, two regiments from the American Division landed without opposition on the island and easily seized Cebu City the next day. Unhappily, the Japanese had constructed three formidable defensive lines on the high ground overlooking the city and its harbor. As Eichelberger later explained, "The Jap positions that the American Div. had cleaned out was [sic] the most powerful defensive setup I have ever seen. The coral hills were honeycombed with caves and intercommunicating tunnels which were mutually supporting."[66] After battering against the Japanese positions without much success for several days, Arnold sent his recently arrived third regiment on a series of night marches totaling twenty-seven miles around the Japanese right flank. On 13 April, the American Division's GIs attacked the Japanese from both sides. Although their position unraveled, most of the Japanese troops escaped into the mountains, where they remained until the war's end. The battle cost the American Division 410 killed and 1,700 wounded. Moreover, nonbattle casualties, especially tropical and sexually transmitted diseases, sidelined another 8,000 GIs. Despite this somewhat downbeat coda, Eichelberger for one was very happy with the division's performance and decorated Arnold. MacArthur was equally impressed and wrote, "This is a model of what a light but aggressive command can accomplish in rapid exploitation."[67]

Eichelberger's biggest target was the southern Philippines island of Mindanao. At 36,656 square miles, it was a little bigger than Indiana. In terms of infrastructure, it was among the most primitive places in the archipelago. The 41st Division had already landed on Mindanao's Zamboanga Peninsula, but because a narrow mountainous isthmus connected the peninsula to the rest of Mindanao, it may as well have been a separate island as far as Eichelberger's planners were concerned. There were 43,000 Japanese soldiers on Mindanao. Some were located on the north central part of the island, but most were deployed around the southeastern port city of Davao. Horrible terrain, inadequate roads, and Filipino guerrillas made coordination between the two Japanese forces impossible. Although the most obvious place for the Americans to land was near Davao, it was also for that very reason the most heavily defended part of the island. Moreover, the navy lacked sufficient shipping for such an assault because of the demands of the concurrent Okinawa campaign. That being the case, Eichelberger opted instead to come ashore at Illana Bay on Mindanao's west coast and march on Davao overland.

To implement his plan, Eichelberger had two divisions at his disposal. The first was General Roscoe Woodruff's 24th Victory Division. It was a veteran outfit that had fought at Hollandia and on Leyte. Smaller components had also seen action at Biak, Mindoro, Zigzag Pass, and in the opening of Manila Bay. Once it landed on Mindanao, it would be the only division to fight on Leyte, Luzon, and in the southern Philippines. However, the division was still under a cloud for its Leyte performance, and the subsequent mauling of its 34th Regiment at Zigzag Pass had done little to enhance its reputation. On the other hand, there was a growing realization among some, including MacArthur, that the demands Krueger placed on the 24th Division at Leyte had been unfair. Eichelberger tended to give the benefit of the doubt to combat units, and he had great faith in Woodruff, so he was not worried about the 24th Division.[68]

Eichelberger's other division was General Clarence A. Martin's 31st. It had been created out of the Alabama, Florida, Louisiana, and Mississippi National Guards and inducted into federal service in November 1940. It was nicknamed "Dixie" because of its southern roots and its patch was a red-edged white circle with two superimposed back-to-back red "Ds." It had arrived in the Pacific in April 1944, but had seen limited action since. One of its regiments, the 124th, had driven the remaining Japanese troops from the Driniumor River during the fighting there in an attack that won Charles Hall's praise. It had subsequently relieved the 6th Division at Wakde–Sarmi and conducted an unopposed landing at Morotai Island in September 1944. Despite its lack of significant combat experience, it had impressed observers as a promising and an inordinately aggressive unit. Before it went overseas, the army ground forces commander, General Lesley McNair, had written, "[If the] 31st Division does not perform outstandingly in battle, I shall be forced to believe that there is no merit in training, or that the training of the Army Ground Forces has been all wrong ... I remember clearly the last time I saw it in the Louisiana maneuvers, in pouring rain, but with every man stepping along as though it were a summer day."[69] The XI Corps' inspectors had given it the highest rating of any division in the corps when it was stationed in New Guinea. After looking it over, General Clovis Byers, Eichelberger's chief of staff, called it "a good-looking outfit."[70] In short, the 31st had given every indication of becoming a proficient and hard-driving division.[71]

The 24th Division came ashore unopposed at Illana Bay on 17 April. Fortunately for the GIs, the Japanese concluded that this was a diversion and continued to focus on a possible landing at Davao. This enabled the Victory Division's troops to march 100 miles across the island on a rudimentary road in just ten days. By the time the Japanese recognized the seriousness of the threat, it was too late. On 3 May, the Japanese abandoned Davao and retreated to the hills west of the city. There they had constructed a defensive line twenty-five miles long. Although Davao's fall prompted MacArthur to declare victory, rooting the Japanese out of their positions was, in terms of blood spilled, the most difficult part of the operation. Much of the fighting occurred in fields of tall abaca plants used to make Manila hemp. Pushing through their tightly interwoven leaves required a soldier's full weight and left him vulnerable to Japanese fire after he emerged on the other side. To win the battle, Woodruff finally swung his 19th Regiment around the Japanese line to join up with Filipino guerrillas. Together they collapsed the Japanese eastern flank while the other two regiments launched a direct assault. By the time the surviving Japanese melted into the mountains, the 24th Division had lost 350 killed and 1615 wounded.

Although the 24th Division battled the hardest and sustained the most casualties after it seized Davao, its dash across Mindanao attracted the most attention. MacArthur, for instance, told Woodruff that his division had performed this task "in a skillful and efficient manner." Perhaps to make amends for previous negative comments about its actions on Leyte, MacArthur added, "I have heard that your Division was a superior one. It has been confirmed by what I saw here today."[72] Eichelberger was equally pleased. He had figured that it would take the 24th Division a couple of months to fight its way across the island, not a matter of weeks. He praised Woodruff for his skilled leadership, adding that he would like to promote him to corps command. As for the

24th Division, Eichelberger put it high on his list of top units. The division may have disappointed at Leyte, but not on Mindanao.[73]

Five days after the 24th Division landed at Illana Bay, the 31st Division came ashore there too. Its mission was to destroy the Japanese force in north central Mindanao. The only way for the division to get there from Illana Bay was up the Sayre Highway. However, the Dixie boys soon discovered that it could only be called a highway by the most generous definition of the term. Frequent rains turned it into a sea of mud, and the Japanese had destroyed the bridges. Despite the logistical problems that the rudimentary highway caused, the 31st Division succeeded in pushing northward and overcoming Japanese resistance of varying severity. On 10 May, a 40th Division regiment landed at Macajalar Bay on Mindanao's north coast and advanced southward to contact the 31st. Although some mopping up remained to be done, the linking up of the two divisions marked the end of effective organized Japanese resistance in the area. Not surprisingly, such a remote and strategically insignificant operation attracted little notice, but Eichelberger for one appreciated the division's efforts. He wrote, "The speed and skill with which the 31st Infantry Division advanced across extremely difficult terrain occupied by enemy forces to seize objectives and effect juncture with other Eighth Army units reflects highest credit upon officers and men of that command. The soldierly qualities displayed in this action resulted in splitting enemy forces in Mindanao and assuring their destruction. I take great personal pride in these accomplishments of the 31st Infantry Division."[74]

Whatever its strategic merits, it is hard to gainsay Eichelberger's tactical and operational brilliance in the central and southern Philippines. There were plenty of reasons for his success: a gifted commander and staff, ample and effective support from Filipino guerrillas, an increasingly demoralized and hungry enemy, superior firepower and logistics, good intelligence, and air and naval supremacy. However, the performances of the Eighth Army's divisions also played an important role in American victory. These five divisions did not have sterling reputations at the campaign's start. The 31st Division was still green, the Americal Division's record was undistinguished, and the 24th, 40th, and 41st Divisions were tarnished by their actions, respectively, on Leyte, at Clark Airbase, and on Biak. Under Eichelberger, though, they all performed satisfactorily and, in a couple of cases, quite capably. The Americal and 24th Divisions fought particularly well on Cebu and outside of Davao in outmaneuvering the Japanese. It was a shame that these units did not get the opportunity to demonstrate their combat prowess under more worthwhile strategic circumstances.

Luzon: Destroying the Shimbu Group

While Eichelberger's Eighth Army liberated the central and southern Philippines, Walter Krueger's Sixth Army was struggling to clear the remainder of Luzon of Japanese troops. Doing so proved extremely difficult. For one thing, although the Japanese had taken a beating in the six weeks since the Sixth Army landed at Lingayen Bay, the Shimbu and Shobu groups remained extant and relatively intact, ready to contest any American offensive. Moreover, Krueger lacked the strength to fulfill his mission on MacArthur's schedule. MacArthur's decision to divert five divisions to Eichelberger left Krueger with only nine divisions—the 1st Cav, 6th, 11th Airborne, 25th, 32nd, 33rd, 37th, 38th, and 43rd—with which to tackle the large number of Japanese soldiers still on Luzon. As things turned out, that was not enough to secure the island on MacArthur's timetable. Finally, many, but not all, of these Japanese soldiers could have just as easily been left to wither on the vine in their remote mountain strongholds, isolated from the war, but MacArthur insisted that Krueger eliminate them. This commitment demoralized GIs who questioned the strategic value of their missions and interfered with Krueger's efforts to prepare his men for the invasion of the Japanese Home Islands.

Unlike their Shobu Group compatriots isolated in the mountains of northern Luzon, the Japanese soldiers in the Shimbu Group east of Manila constituted a continuing threat because they controlled the dam and reservoir that provided much of the city's fresh water supply. The Americans could not restore and rebuild Manila until they possessed them. Krueger intended to do just that. He ordered an offensive into the Sierra Madre Mountains to seize Wawa Dam on the Marikina River, about twenty miles northeast of Manila. In issuing his directives, though, Krueger made two serious mistakes. First, he severely underestimated the number of Japanese troops remaining in the Shimbu Group. He figured that there were about 20,000 of them when there were actually closer to 50,000 left. More egregiously, he targeted the wrong dam as his top priority. Before the war, Manila authorities had abandoned Wawa Dam and connected their pipelines to Ipo Dam on the Angat River, about fifteen miles to the north. It took Sixth Army staffers nearly two months to realize their error, during which time hundreds of American and Filipino soldiers were killed or wounded fighting for the wrong objective.

Because Krueger lacked sufficient manpower and underestimated Japanese strength, he did not at first commit enough troops to deal with the Shimbu Group. He initially assigned the job to Oscar Griswold's XIV Corps and gave him the 6th Sightseers Division and a brigade from the 1st Cavalry Division.

What these two units lacked in numbers, they made up in quality. The Sightseers had overcome the Japanese on Lone Tree Hill the previous year and had recently outmaneuvered them at San José. As for the 1st Cav Division, it had an extensive and impressive portfolio that included the Admiralties, Leyte, and the dash to Manila. Griswold kicked off his offensive on 20 February. His GIs succeeded in crossing the Mirikina Valley without much trouble, but they ran into serious opposition as they advanced into the overlooking hills. The terrain consisted of rocky limestone pockmarked with natural caves of all sizes for the defending Japanese to use, including one that had thirty-two separate entrances. Repeated American assaults had little success. The 1st Cav Division's commander, Verne Mudge, was seriously wounded and Edwin Patrick, the 6th Division's chief, was killed. Subsequent attacks, especially by the 6th Division, made enough progress to force the Japanese to withdraw to a new line and attempt a futile counterthrust. The all-important dams, though, remained in Japanese hands.

In mid-March, Krueger reorganized his efforts to shatter the Shimbu Group and open Manila's water supply. He had slated the 1st Cav Division to participate in operations in southern Luzon, so he brought in Leonard Wing's 43rd Division to replace the troopers. The 43rd was one of the original four divisions that landed at Lingayen Bay in early January. It then fought in the ferocious battles around Rosario to secure the Sixth Army's eastern flank during the drive to Manila. Wing's division won that engagement through brute force, which was always an expensive and exhausting way to wage war. It had just come off a stint mopping up the Kembu Group, so it was understrength and badly in need of rest. Krueger selected the 43rd for its latest mission over the fresher 38th Division because it was the more experienced outfit. In addition, Krueger sent Charles Hall and his XI Corps to take over for Griswold and his XIV Corps. Krueger hoped that these changes would bring about the result he desired.[75]

Hall and his XI Corps staffers needed little time to acquaint themselves with their new situation. On 15 March, Hall ordered the offensive against the Shimbu Group renewed. Both the 6th and 43rd Divisions encountered the usual heavy opposition. Indeed, the battle was so intense that Hall began worrying about the 6th Division's combat integrity, though the 43rd Division suffered almost as much. Fortunately for the Americans, the Japanese were in even worse shape, so they withdrew part of their forces to yet another defensive line. This retreat opened the door for a direct American attack on the dams. Simply getting into this position, though, cost the 1st Cav, 6th, and 43rd Divisions 435 killed and 1,425 wounded in the thirty-four days of action from 20 February to 26 March.[76]

On 28 March, Hall launched a final offensive against the dams. Unfortunately, by now the 6th Division was in such wretched shape that it did not accomplish much. Weeks of combat had reduced its battalions to half strength. In fact, by the end of April it had lost 1,335 killed and wounded, as well as three times as many nonbattle casualties. It was a spent force that lacked the power to fulfill its missions. To augment the depleted Sightseers, Krueger sent in William Chase's 38th Cyclone Division, which had recently cut its teeth at Zigzag Pass, and a regiment from the always reliable 37th Division. These outfits kicked off their attack on 4 May, and, after heavy fighting, on 28 May they finally seized Wawa Dam. Here, as elsewhere, remoteness and obscurity did little to dampen Japanese fanaticism: "One Japanese who was cornered in a small cave refused to surrender. A phosphorus grenade had no effect on him so a flamethrower was brought up. Thoroughly doused with flame, he finally ran screaming from the cave, in each hand a grenade which he threw deliriously before he expired."[77] By the time Wawa Dam was secured, the two units had suffered 750 casualties.

By now Krueger had learned that Ipo Dam, not Wawa, was the real prize. He gave the job of taking it to Wing's 43rd Division. Wing opted to assail the extreme left of the Japanese line, southeast of the village of Norzagaray. He was assisted by a Filipino outfit called the Marking Regiment, named after its commander's *nom de guerre*. Although Wing intended to use the Filipinos to feint around the Japanese flank, they made such good progress that they succeeded in storming the dam on 17 May, just as elements of the 43rd Division arrived after some hard fighting. Around 590 American and Filipino soldiers were killed or wounded in this final effort. The dams may have fallen, but the Sixth Army still had to mop up the remaining Shimbu Group troops. This task fell to the 38th Division and local Filipinos, and it continued for the rest of the war. During this time, the 38th Division pioneered the use of helicopters to evacuate the wounded from inaccessible areas and of searchlights to illuminate Japanese positions at night. After Japan surrendered, only 6,300 Japanese survivors emerged from the mountains to return to the Home Islands.

The three divisions that contributed the most to the Shimbu Group's destruction were the 6th, 38th, and 43rd. Although all three paid steep prices for their efforts, the 6th Division's story was the most unfortunate. There is no doubt that it fought hard to seize the Wawa Dam, but also unsuccessfully. It demonstrated little of the tactical skills that enabled it to take San José several weeks earlier, but instead relied on direct assaults that wore the division down to a nub. As the division historian remembered:

> The Sightseers who left the Shimbu Line for their new stations in west central Luzon were red-eyed and worn, their faces reflecting the sleepless nights and agonizing days that had been their lot for almost two and one half months on the Shimbu Line, facing the heaviest concentrations of artillery, mortar and rocket fire that the Japs had used in the entire Luzon campaign. The fighting men of the 6th had completed 113 days of uninterrupted combat from the landing on 9 January to their relief on the Shimbu Line on 30 April, the only division in the Pacific to face such concentrated enemy might over so great a period of time without a break.[78]

Much the same could be said of the 43rd Division. By the end of the engagement, its battalions had also been reduced by half and the survivors were scarcely battleworthy. But, unlike the Sightseers, the 43rd Division's GIs could take pride in accomplishment as well as in effort. Although the Marking Regiment actually seized Ipo Dam, it was attached to the 43rd Division when it did so. Of more import, the hard fighting and skillful maneuvering of the 43rd Division's troops made victory possible. The tactical deftness that Wing displayed was a far cry from the unsubtle direct assaults he used at Rosario. Indeed, the difference between the division's performances at New Georgia and Ipo Dam was like night and day. One Sixth Army staff officer later called the 43rd Division's actions "an excellent study of the coordination of arms."[79]

Finally, the 38th Division's role in taking Wawa Dam demonstrated that it had learned much from its Zigzag Pass mistakes and made itself a good unit. Eichelberger was impressed with the outfit when he inspected it after the battle and labeled it "a grand division."[80] So was Hall, who had actually seen the 38th in battle. He wrote to Chase, "The tasks given the [38th] division have been difficult. It has covered a lot of area, fought many good fights and always performed any assigned duty with great credit to itself and to the army. It has never asked odds of anyone, never cried about an assignment, and always accepted a difficult task without complaint …. It has done a very fine job under most difficult conditions and one for which it may well feel proud."[81] But perhaps the greatest tribute to the division's skills came not from an American, but rather from Tomoyuki Yamashita, the commander of all Japanese army troops in the Philippines. According to Krueger, after the war ended Yamashita specifically mentioned and praised the 38th Division.[82]

Luzon: Demolishing the Shobu Group

At the same time that the Sixth Army's XI and XIV Corps were combating the Shimbu Group and Eichelberger's Eighth Army was liberating the central and southern Philippines, Krueger was also grappling with the Shobu Group in northern Luzon. The Shobu Group was the largest and most remote of the three Japanese troop concentrations on the island. It was ensconced in the Cordillera Central Mountains that surrounded the fertile Cagayan Valley. To defend the area, Yamashita deployed his forces in a rough inverted triangle, with apexes at the towns of Baguio, Bontoc, and Bambang. Because the lack of good roads and even navigable trails made the mountains almost impassible, the only easy entrance to the Cagayan Valley from the south was via a road through the Balete Pass.

Krueger originally planned to deploy five divisions against the Shobu Group, one of which would conduct an amphibious assault. However, Eichelberger, Griswold, and Hall siphoned away too many troops for that kind of operation. Rather than postpone or forego his offensive, Krueger opted to scale it back to three divisions under the direction of Palmer Swift's I Corps: the 25th, 32nd, and 33rd. The first two were old Pacific War standbys. Charles Mullins's 25th Division had an exemplary combat record dating back to Guadalcanal. It had most recently proven its worth in defeating the Japanese at San José. Bill Gill's 32nd Division, on the other hand, possessed a more checkered résumé. Although the Red Arrow boys had defeated the Japanese at Buna, Driniumor River, and on Leyte, there had been nothing pretty about its victories. Moreover, when the division arrived on Luzon on 27 January, it was tired and short 4,000 officers and men after its ordeal on Leyte. Almost a third of its personnel had been overseas for three years, and many of them felt that they had done their duty and wanted to go home. They were unlikely to put their lives on the line for what was, in grand strategic terms, really a giant mopping up battle that would not alter the war's outcome. Even so, Krueger used it not only because he respected it, but also because it was all he had available.[83]

General Percy W. Clarkson's 33rd Division was the last army division deployed to the Pacific that saw combat. Nicknamed "Prairie," it was a National Guard outfit from Illinois. Its patch was a simple gold cross superimposed over a black disc. It and the hard-luck 27th Division were the only two National Guard units that the War Department did not overhaul in an effort to purge it of its parochial and incestuous leadership. One Regular Army officer later complained that when he assumed command of a battalion in the division before the United States entered the conflict, he discovered that no one took the training seriously, that the officers all lounged around while the sergeants did all the work. He elaborated, "I found that most of the National Guard officers were fine officers, and they had an interest in the military or they wouldn't have been in the National Guard. The only thing was they were commanding companies where almost every man in the company came from their hometown, and it was tough for them to demand a lot."[84] Although the 33rd Division was inducted into federal service in March 1941, it did not go overseas until the War Department dispatched it to Hawaii in July 1943. From there it went to New Guinea in May 1944, where it saw limited action while keeping an eye on Wakde–Sarmi and Morotai. By then divisional morale had hit rock bottom because its GIs felt that the war was passing them by while they unloaded ships. Indeed, they referred to themselves as the 4F Division, meaning "Finschhafen [New Guinea] Freight Forwarding Force." Even so, Eichelberger was impressed with the division when he inspected it in October 1944. Charles Hall, on the other hand, complained that the outfit had been insufficiently aggressive while occupying Morotai. Whatever the truth of these somewhat contradictory observations, the 33rd Division finally got its chance to prove itself after it landed on Luzon on 10 February.[85]

When Krueger and Swift deployed their units across northern Luzon, they placed the 33rd Division along the west coast, the 32nd Division in the center, and the 25th Division toward the eastern shore. Krueger ordered the latter two to attack toward Bambang, but he also permitted Clarkson's 33rd Prairie boys to advance on Baguio. Considering their inexperience, it was unsurprising that most of the division initially made little progress, despite a willingness to conduct nighttime operations. However, one of Clarkson's regiments encountered almost no enemy opposition as it marched up the coastal road. Clarkson recognized an opportunity to descend on Baguio from the northwest and not only persuaded Krueger and Swift to go along, but also to reinforce him with two regiments from Robert Beightler's always formidable 37th Division. The Buckeyes were just coming off a stint occupying Manila, a tedious chore perhaps, but certainly preferable to the ordeal they went through to capture the city in the first place. On 11 April, the two outfits launched their offensive. The 37th Division overcame last gasp Japanese resistance at Irisan Gorge and seized the town on 27 April. With that, the I Corps kicked one block out from under the Shobu Group. Part of the credit for this accomplishment should go to the 37th Division for providing the knock-out punch that led to Baguio's fall, but a good bit should also go to the 33rd Division for developing the opening and Clarkson for recognizing it.

At the same time that the 33rd and 37th Divisions were fighting for Baguio, Bill Gill's hard-luck 32nd Red Arrow boys were undergoing yet another terrible ordeal to the southeast, one that would rival Buna in terms of casualties and suffering. Its target was Bambang, the second of the Shobu Group's three pillars. Krueger and Swift decided that the best way for the 32nd Division to get there was via the Villa Verde Trail. Originating in the foothills near Santa Maria, the trail extended twenty-seven miles through heights up to 4,000 feet to a crossroads at Santa Fe. Navigating the trail, which was often little more than a primitive footpath, was difficult under the best of circumstances without the added burden of tenacious Japanese soldiers shooting at anything that moved on or near it. Krueger and Swift hoped that the 32nd Division could link up with the neighboring 25th Division at Santa Fe, from where they could strike Bambang. It was a rough assignment for even a robust outfit, much rougher than some initially realized, but Krueger had faith in the Red Arrow boys, writing later, "Repeated visits to the front had made me fully cognizant of the tough conditions facing the 32nd Division, but I was confident that it would overcome all difficulties successfully."[86]

The 32nd Division launched its offensive up the Villa Verde Trail on 21 February. Within days the operation had degenerated into a nightmare. Japanese defenses were stronger than anticipated. There was barely enough room to deploy troops, let alone to maneuver them. Bringing up supplies, weapons, and equipment on the rudimentary track was extremely difficult. Casualties mounted and the advance slowed to a crawl. Fighting was particularly awful at the two Salacsac Passes. Morale among the Red Arrow Division's GIs plummeted under the miserable and frustrating circumstances. As an army historian put it later, "The troops of the 126th and 128th Infantry Regiments were approaching complete mental and physical exhaustion; front-line men with considerable time overseas were becoming supercautious; rotation back to the United States had become the principal topic of conversation at all echelons of the division; the combat troops' aggressive spirit was diminishing rapidly and markedly. With its low strength and its personnel problems, the division was going to find it impossible to make spectacular gains."[87] Here, as elsewhere, superior American firepower and logistics gradually wore the Japanese down and turned the tide. Even so, the 32nd Division did not finally link up with the 25th Division south of Santa Fe until 29 May.

Nothing ever came easy for the 32nd Division. As more than one observer noted, it won all of its major Pacific War battles, but its successes were invariably expensive, controversial, and difficult. The Red Arrow boys usually achieved them through attrition and brute force, not through skillful maneuvering and deft tactics. All these characteristics applied to Villa Verde, but that particular battle was worse in that it was Pyrrhic as well. Villa Verde cost the 32nd Division 825 killed and 2,160 wounded, as well as an additional 6,000 nonbattle casualties. It also almost destroyed the division's already shaky morale. Indeed, Villa Verde rendered the 32nd Division *hors de combat*. Gill agreed later that the victory was not worth the price paid. Krueger did not go that far, but rather instead noted blandly that he was impressed "with the fine performance of the 32nd Division under extremely difficult conditions."[88] The division's long-suffering GIs could take some comfort and pride in Krueger's additional assertion that after the war Yamashita called the 32nd the best unit he faced in the Philippines.[89]

While the 32nd Division struggled at Villa Verde Trail, to the east Charles Mullins's 25th Tropic Lightning Division was pushing toward the Cagayan Valley's entrance at Balete Pass. The 25th Division's mission was easier than that of the Red Arrow boys. For one thing, the division had at its disposal a gravel road to ease the logistical burden. It also had more room to maneuver because the ground was not as formidable as along the Villa Verde Trail. Finally, the 25th Division was in much better shape than the tired 32nd. Before landing at Luzon, the 25th Division had not been in battle since New Georgia, fifteen months previously. It was therefore rested and up to strength when it reached Luzon. To be sure, it had seen action around San José, but not enough to seriously inhibit the outfit's ability to fulfill its latest mission.

When Mullins launched his offensive on 21 February, the 25th Division initially gained plenty of ground. He maneuvered his regiments well and used artillery and air support effectively. Indeed, the division advanced so quickly that on 13 March Swift ordered it to strike directly for Balete Pass. Then things became difficult. Japanese defenses thickened and the heavily wooded ridges made it increasingly problematic for Mullins to deploy his regiments. The division made little progress from 28 March to 23 April. Fortunately, the 27th Regiment found a gap in the Japanese lines that Mullins exploited, and Swift attached a regiment from the 37th Division to help out. Balete Pass fell on 9 May. It took several more weeks, but the division went on to seize Santa Fe on 27 May and link up with the 32nd Division two days later.

At Balete Pass the 25th Division turned in yet another solid performance. The price, however, was not cheap. Opening up Balete Pass cost it 545 killed and 1,650 wounded, as well as more than 4,000 nonbattle casualties. Its GIs demonstrated both a willingness and ability to use maneuver, firepower, and mobility to achieve their objectives. Doing so required no small amount of intelligence, sturdiness, coordination, and determination. As the Sixth Army's operations officer later explained:

> First, this swift thrust up Highway #5 sealed off a large number of Japanese troops which could not be withdrawn to Balete Pass itself. Second, it is an excellent example of the interdependence of the infantry and engineers within the infantry division. Finally it describes in part the efforts of the 25th Infantry Division which, despite prolonged combat, contributed so much to the eventual fall of northern Luzon by literally breaking the back of Japanese resistance in front of and at Balete Pass.[90]

The 25th Division's GIs may not have had the same snap and discipline of other Regular Army outfits, such as the 1st Cav Division, but they were certainly fighters. As one historian later put it, "The 25th Division was the Army at its best."[91]

After losing Baguio and Balmete Pass, the Japanese opted to withdraw from the Cagayan Valley into the Cordillera Central Mountains. Unfortunately, the 25th and 32nd Divisions were in no condition to exploit the gains they had so recently attained. That being the case, Krueger gave the job to Beightler's relatively fresh 37th Division. The 37th had just augmented its already impressive résumé by helping to seize Baguio and Balete Pass. Krueger directed it to push through Luzon toward Aparri on the island's northern tip. Beightler got his GIs moving on 31 May. Because the Japanese were more intent on escaping than confronting the Americans, the Ohio boys made good progress against sporadic opposition. Bambang fell without a fight on 6 June. Twenty days later, the GIs linked up with paratroopers from the 11th Airborne Division who had descended near Aparri on 23 June. Although mopping up continued for the remainder of the war, the occupation of the Cagayan Valley marked for all practical purposes the end of major operations against the Shobu Group. The remaining 65,000 Japanese troops eked out a squalid existence in the mountains until the Japanese surrender.

Overrunning the Cagayan Valley was certainly another feather in the 37th Division's collective cap, but it also contributed to the unhappiness and resentment that affected Beightler and his staff. Beightler believed that his division had not received sufficient publicity for its actions on Luzon. As far as he could tell, the 1st Cav and 33rd Divisions got undeserved credit for taking, respectively, Manila and Baguio. For this he blamed Krueger, with whom he had a long-running feud. Happily for Beightler, on 1 July Eichelberger and his Eighth Army assumed control over operations in Luzon. Eichelberger sympathized with Beightler's plight and liked his division, but he also wryly noted that Beightler was pretty good at self-promotion, calling him a "great advertiser."[92] Beightler's wife, for example, published excerpts from his letters in Ohio newspapers. Moreover, Eichelberger noted that morale among the 37th Division's rank-and-file seemed pretty high, indicating that their mindset did not necessarily reflect that of the higher-ups. It was, however, a sour way for such a proud and effective division to end the war.[93]

Four divisions fought against the Shobu Group: the 25th, 32nd, 33rd, and 37th. The 33rd was the only one that had not yet seen extensive action. Despite its inexperience and ingrained parochialism, it performed surprisingly well. It was the 33rd that developed the opportunity to assail Baguio from the northwest. As its commander proudly noted, "The 33rd [Division] has met all my expectations and I'm sure we have completely satisfied everyone from Gen. MacArthur on down."[94] The 33rd Division may have opened the door to Baguio, but it was the 37th Division that stormed through it. Not only did the Ohio boys deliver the Sunday punch at Baguio, but one of its regiments also helped the 25th Division take Balete Pass. Later, it went on to free the Cagayan Valley. In each instance, the division fought with a competency and professionalism that belied its National Guard origins.

Battling the Japanese in the Shobu Group was hard on all four American divisions, but the 25th and 32nd Divisions had particularly awful experiences, the former before Balete Pass and the latter at the Villa Verde Trail. Of the two units, the 25th Division fought better. It broke through Japanese lines first, suffered fewer casualties, and exhibited more tactical finesse. In so doing, the 25th Division lived up to its splendid reputation. However, the 25th Division had some advantages over the Red Arrow boys that contributed to its greater success. It was in much better shape when the engagements began, had more forgiving ground upon which to operate, and benefited from cooperation with an attached regiment from the 37th Division. When viewed from this perspective, the 32nd Division's accomplishments seem equally impressive.

Conclusions

Of the twenty divisions that the army deployed to the Pacific during World War II, all but the 27th Division served in the Philippines at some point from October 1944 until the end of the conflict. Of those nineteen, all but two—the 81st and 93rd—saw considerable action there. Eight divisions battled on Leyte (the 1st Cav, 7th, 11th Airborne, 24th, 32nd, 77th, 96th, and American), eleven on Luzon (1st Cav, 6th, 11th Airborne, 24th, 25th, 32nd, 33rd, 37th, 38th, 40th, and 43rd), and five in the central and southern parts of the archipelago (24th, 31st, 40th, 41st, and American). Five fought in two of these regions (1st Cav, 11th Airborne, 32nd, 40th, and American) and the 24th Division had the unique distinction of engaging the Japanese in all three. Six divisions experienced their baptisms of fire there (11th Airborne, 31st, 33rd, 38th, 40th, and 96th), but the others were veteran outfits to one degree or another.

With the possible exception of the Leyte invasion, in broad geostrategic terms the Philippines liberation campaign was really just a giant mopping up operation. Once the American navy had beaten its Japanese counterpart at the Battle of Leyte Gulf, the Japanese soldiers in the archipelago were cut off from outside sustenance. From that point they could only get weaker. American victory, therefore, was all but inevitable. The only questions were how long would it take and how many casualties the army would sustain in the process. This means that army divisions that fought in the Philippines should not be evaluated on the basis of defeating the enemy, but rather on how fast and at what cost they did so.

Of the six divisions that saw action for the first time in the Philippines, two—the 38th and 40th Divisions—suffered from the usual teething problems that rookie outfits experienced during the war. They won their battles at Zigzag Pass and Clark Airbase, but it was not easy and they needed outside help in doing so. Both, however, went on to perform well in other engagements in the archipelago. On the other hand, the remaining four—11th Airborne and 96th Divisions on Leyte, the 31st on Mindanao, and the 33rd at Baguio—bucked the trend and fought satisfactorily in their baptisms of fire.

Of the remaining, veteran, divisions that saw considerable action in the Philippines, they generally fulfilled their missions. Some of course did better than others. The 7th Division, for instance, fought marvelously on Leyte, as did the 37th Division on Luzon. The 1st Cav, 25th, 77th, 41st, and Americal Divisions all provided dependable service in their battles. Others had at least one frustrating engagement that knocked the wind out of them: the 6th Division against the Wawa Dam, the 24th Division during the drive down the Ormoc Valley on Leyte, the 43rd Division at Ipo Dam, and the 32nd Division on the Villa Verde Trail. Fortunately for the GIs in all but three of these divisions, the Philippines was the last time they had to put their lives on the line against the Japanese.

CHAPTER FIVE

Closing in on Japan

The Japanese Doorstep

Nimitz and the POA had not been idle while MacArthur was busy liberating the Philippines. In late September 1944, Nimitz traveled to San Francisco to persuade Ernest King to forego an assault on Formosa and instead target the islands of Iwo Jima and Okinawa. Nimitz argued that assailing Formosa would be too costly in time and blood, but that the POA had the resources to attack Iwo Jima and Okinawa. King agreed and got the Joint Chiefs to go along with the idea. Nimitz wanted Iwo Jima, part of the Bonin Islands chain, to provide protection and refuge for the B-29 bombers that had started raiding Japanese cities from the Marianas. Three Marine divisions stormed the island in mid-February and took it after six weeks of vicious fighting that killed and wounded nearly 27,000 leathernecks and practically wiped out the 21,000-man Japanese garrison. Nimitz sought Okinawa, located in the Ryukyus chain, only 350 miles south of Kyushu, as a staging area and jumping off point for the final invasion of the Japanese Home Islands. Because of its obvious strategic importance, the Japanese filled the island with 100,000 well-equipped and well-led soldiers, and planned to support them with thousands of kamikaze suicide planes flying from Japan and Formosa against the American vessels transporting troops to and supporting the operation.

The Japanese had annexed Okinawa in 1879, but its population remained linguistically and culturally distinct. It was at 466 square miles big enough to accommodate all the weapons, supplies, equipment, and personnel the Americans needed for their invasion of Japan. Okinawa was sixty miles long, but its maximum width was only eighteen miles. The northern two-thirds of the island was sparsely populated, mountainous, and heavily forested. Most of its 500,000 inhabitants settled in the flatter and more open southern region,

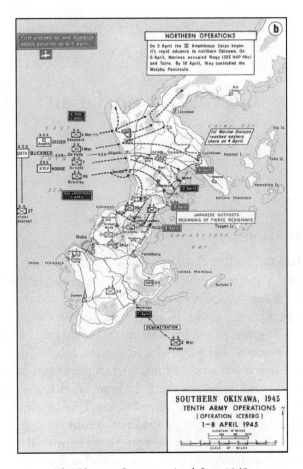

The Okinawa Campaign, April–June 1945.

which included the island's only town, Naha. There, many of them made a living farming sugarcane and sweet potatoes in the temperate climate.

By the time the Americans embarked for Okinawa, the war's outcome was scarcely in doubt. In Europe, Allied armies were in the process of overrunning Germany and finally ending that half of the conflict. Hitler would commit suicide on 30 April, and Germany would surrender a little more than a week later. In the Pacific, the Battle of Leyte Gulf the previous October had rendered the Japanese navy impotent. Moreover, American submarines had sunk much of Japan's merchant marine, making it almost impossible for Japan to import and export anything, or to succor its isolated overseas garrisons. Finally, the Army Air Forces' strategic bombing campaign with its B-29 Superfortress bombers flying out of the Marianas was systematically burning up Japan. One raid on Tokyo in March 1945 destroyed much of the city and killed approximately 80,000 Japanese. While MacArthur was liberating the Philippines, an Anglo-Indian army was recapturing Burma. Unfortunately, the Japanese showed little indication of surrendering on Allied terms. Many American policymakers believed that unless they did so, the Americans might need to launch an all-out invasion of the Home Islands that would undoubtedly kill or wound tens of thousands of American troops—and millions of Japanese.

Nimitz assigned the mission of seizing Okinawa to General Simon Buckner's new Tenth Army. George Marshall had authorized the creation of the Tenth Army and sent Buckner to the POA to lead it to make sure that Marines such as Holland Smith never again commanded army divisions in combat. On the one hand, Buckner was an odd selection for this assignment because he had never led troops into action. By this stage of the war, the army had plenty of combat-hardened corps leaders such as Oscar Griswold and Charles Hall who were fully qualified for such a job, but George Marshall ignored them all and went with Buckner. On the other hand, Buckner was an action-oriented and aggressive officer who had capably fulfilled his previous assignments. That being the case, Marshall believed he deserved the opportunity to run an army in combat. He usually got along well with the navy, whose cooperation he needed, and was sufficiently tactful to work productively with Marine Corps officers as well.

Buckner had at his disposal two corps, the all-Marine III Amphibious and John Hodge's XXIV. Hodge's corps contained four divisions: the 7th, 27th, 77th, and 96th. Three of the four were battle-hardened, albeit understrength, outfits that had proven themselves in action. Archibald Arnold's 7th Hourglass Division may have stumbled to victory at Attu, but it subsequently fought splendidly at Kwajalein and on Leyte. Andrew Bruce's 77th Statue of Liberty Division had a record almost as impressive, with fine performances on Guam and Leyte. Charles Bradley's 96th Deadeye Division was the newest and least experienced of the three, but it had done well on Leyte too. It was fated to see the bitterest fighting on Okinawa. Robert Richardson rated all three as "top units."[1] The three divisions were thoroughly familiar with each other, having battled together on Leyte, and were led by a first-rate officer in Hodge. The only major problem was that they were short several thousand men because of the rigors of the Leyte operation. Even so, Buckner and Hodge could not have asked for better units with which to storm Okinawa.[2]

There were, however, serious questions about the effectiveness of General George W. Griner's 27th Division. The unit was still under a cloud for its alleged deficiencies at Saipan and elsewhere during the Central Pacific offensive.

After it finished mopping up on Saipan, Nimitz had sent it to Espiritu Santo in the New Hebrides for refitting. There, adverse publicity about its record at Saipan sapped its morale. The fact that so many of its personnel had been overseas for almost three years did not help. Many of its GIs had become cynical and weary and wanted to return home. Richardson tried to bring it up to snuff by ordering a retraining program and overhauling its leadership, but that did not bring the results for which he hoped. When Buckner inspected it, he was not impressed. One Marine officer remembered:

> I lived with the brigadier general who commanded the [27th Division] artillery. I forget his name now. And he said, "These damn people don't want to fight." That was an Army officer talking. Gen. Buckner thought he could stir them up a bit by talking to the enlisted men and finding out what was the thing they most would like to do. We'd hoped they'd say "to go and kill Japs." All of them wanted a 30 day furlough to go home.[3]

None of this boded well for the division's fortunes when assigned to the Okinawa operation, and this undoubtedly explained why Buckner gave it such a limited role.[4]

To the Shuri Line

In late March 1945, the last great American invasion fleet of World War II gathered off Okinawa's west coast. It contained 1,200 vessels of various shapes and sizes, including 433 transport ships holding 183,000 men that had embarked from points as far away as Guadalcanal, Hawaii, Leyte, the Marianas, Seattle, and Espiritu Santo in the New Hebrides Islands. On the morning of 1 April, after a preliminary bombardment by ten battleships, nine cruisers, twenty-three destroyers, and 177 gunboats, leathernecks and soldiers from four divisions—from north to south, the 6th Marine, 1st Marine, 7th, and 96th—splashed ashore on Hagushi beach. To everyone's utter amazement and relief, the troops met almost no resistance and quickly established their beachheads. By nightfall around 60,000 Americans were on Okinawa, at the bargain price of twenty-eight killed, 104 wounded, and twenty-seven missing.

Like their comrades in the Philippines and elsewhere, the Japanese on Okinawa fought against overwhelming American materiel superiority without expectation of relief, reinforcement, or victory. Instead, they hoped to delay the Americans for as long as possible so that their compatriots in the Home Islands could prepare for a seemingly inevitable invasion of Japan itself. The Japanese commander on Okinawa, General Mitsuru Ushijima, opted to forego contesting the American landing and make his stand on the southern part of the island. Turning southern Okinawa into a fortress was just one arrow in the Japanese quiver. Kamikazes were another. Kamikazes were not new to the Pacific War, but in this case the Japanese planned to throw 4,000 of these suicide planes at the American vessels off Okinawa. Indeed, the day before the Tenth Army landed on the island, a kamikaze so injured the cruiser USS *Indianapolis* that she had to return to the West Coast for repairs. In the weeks that followed, waves of kamikazes, sometimes hundreds at a time, assailed the American fleet. Although American fighter planes and antiaircraft guns shot the kamikazes down in large numbers, a few almost always got through to crash into the frantically maneuvering ships. By the time the campaign was over, kamikazes killed 4,900 sailors, wounded almost as many, sank twenty-six vessels, and damaged an astonishing 368 more.

For naval officers, the problem was that they could not leave Okinawa's dangerous waters until the Tenth Army secured the island, but Buckner's slow and cautious tactics left them exposed to the kamikazes for a lot longer than they wanted. The kamikaze threat became so serious that on 23 April, Nimitz and several of his lieutenants met with Buckner to urge him to accelerate his efforts. Buckner frostily responded that ground operations were none of the navy's business. Nimitz did not like this one bit and responded, "Yes, but ground though it may be, I'm losing a ship and a half a day. So if this line isn't moving within five days, we'll get someone here to move it so we can all get out from under these stupid attacks."[5] Nimitz did not carry out his threat, but even so, the kamikaze hazard—or, more accurately, the navy's rattled response to it—was something Buckner had to keep in mind.

Buckner's plan called for sending the Marines to clear the northern part of Okinawa while the 7th and 96th Divisions probed southward. Meanwhile, Bruce's 77th Division would occupy offshore islands for anchorages and airfields that would, once secured, help protect the navy from the kamikazes. The Marines required a month to fulfill their objective, during which they engaged in battles of varying intensity, but nothing approaching the bloodletting they would soon face to the south. As for the Old Buzzards, on 16 April they assailed Ie Shima, an island of about nine square miles three and a half miles west of Okinawa's Motobu Peninsula. Ie Shima was full of scrub trees, high grass, and cultivated fields, much of which was on a plateau ideal for the airfield that the Americans wanted to construct there as soon as possible. Seizing it required all three of Bruce's regiments and five days of some of the Pacific War's most vicious combat. Japanese resistance was skillful as usual, but even more fanatical, and included civilians taking up arms to help them out. Here Ernie Pyle, the famous war correspondent, was killed. General Edwin H. Randle, the 77th Division's assistant commander, later stated, "It is a damned highly fortified position with caves three stories deep, each house concrete with machine guns in and under. Whole area of village and circumference of mountain a maze of machine gun, mortar, and gun positions little affected by artillery fire we have poured on."[6] By the time the engagement ended on 21 April, the 5,000-man Japanese garrison was practically exterminated. The 77th Division, for its part, sustained 1,120 casualties in this otherwise supplementary engagement.

Despite such heavy losses in such a short period of time, the 77th Division once again proved itself one of the army's best Pacific War outfits. Here as elsewhere, the Old Buzzards showed considerable professionalism, persistence, and determination as they methodically and remorselessly ground down Ie Shima's Japanese defenders. Reflecting on the battle shortly after it ended, Bruce stated simply, "The last three days of this fighting were the bitterest I ever witnessed."[7] This would not be true for long.

Indeed, the GIs in Arnold's 7th and Bradley's 96th Divisions would certainly have disagreed with Bruce's assessment. After cutting across Okinawa's thin waist, both divisions wheeled southward, the 96th to the west and the 7th to the east, and advanced toward the Shuri Line, the main Japanese defensive position on the island. As things turned out, merely getting there was an exhausting ordeal. It took four days and 1,500 casualties for the two divisions simply to reach the Shuri Line's outer defenses. The key to breaching these outer ramparts was Kakazu Ridge, where the Japanese had taken up position in the caves and crevices. An 8–10 April assault on the ridge by the 96th Division not only failed, but cost one of its regiments, the 383rd, an astonishing two thirds of its strength. In return, the disastrous attack helped to provoke an equally unsuccessful Japanese counterattack on 12–14 April.

Mulling things over, a concerned Hodge prevailed upon Buckner to send him Griner's 27th Division to buttress his depleted outfits. Hodge then redeployed his units across the island, with the 27th Division along the western shore, the 96th in the middle, and the 7th along the east coast. Once he had his divisional ducks in a row, on 19 April the XXIV Corps launched an all-out attack on the Shuri Line's outer battlements that included plenty of naval, air, and artillery support. The first day accomplished little more than swelling the butcher's bill. The 27th Division in particular struggled to fulfill its missions. On 20 April alone it suffered 506 casualties, the most any division lost in a single day on Okinawa. At one point it had expended its reserves, lost contact with the neighboring 96th Division, and failed to clear out Japanese soldiers behind its lines. In addition, an armor-infantry attack went awry when the infantry lost touch with the armor, resulting in the destruction of twenty-two tanks. Despite these and other problems, the Americans took Kakazu Ridge on 21 April and gradually pushed the Japanese back to the Shuri Line proper. However, this fell far short of Buckner's and Hodge's hopes; only now were the Americans coming to grips with the heart of the Japanese position.

Buckner and Hodge were disappointed with the 27th Division. In fact, they pulled it out of the line in early May and sent it to fulfill its original mission of serving as the island's garrison force. Buckner was usually a diplomatic man not given to boat-rocking, so he took pains to assure everyone, including Griner, that this redeployment had nothing to do with the division's battlefield performance. The Tenth Army's deputy chief of staff, Marine General Oliver Smith, later remembered Buckner's attempt to explain to a group of journalists:

> Well, Gen. Buckner told them the truth, but it wasn't exactly what he believed. He said that, after all, in the initial planning the 27th Division had been designated as the island command division—that's correct—and that now there was an opportunity to put them on that job, and he was taking them out to take over the territory from the 6th Marine Division. I don't think he ever convinced the correspondents, but that's what he told them, anyway.[8]

The ploy worked well enough that Richardson wrote Marshall a few months later:

> I am glad to tell you that the 27th Division performed ably and most credibly. They were complimented by General Buckner, although they were only in the line seventeen days. Hodge told me it was never Buckner's intention to put them in the line but to use them as a garrison force. However, he decided to enter them, much to their gratification, and when they were withdrawn they were much chagrined. The withdrawal was in no way an indication of their inability to perform.[9]

Buckner's actions, though, belied his sugary words. During the three-month-long Okinawa campaign, he rotated his other divisions in and out of the line, but not the 27th; it remained on garrison duty, even though the other divisions were sorely in need of rest and refitting. Moreover, few army officers in the know voiced much support for the division. Some Marine officers, for their part, then and later condemned the unit. The fact was that for all the gallantry the individual GIs in the division demonstrated on Okinawa, the outfit as a whole did not retrieve its reputation there.[10]

As for the 7th and 96th Divisions, they did about as well as could be expected by driving the Japanese back to the Shuri Line. After all, both divisions were understrength and facing skilled defenders in well-placed positions that were almost immune from artillery fire and airstrikes. Moreover, both of their commanders were hospitalized that month, Bradley with nervous exhaustion and Arnold with appendicitis. Although Buckner complained about the 7th

Division's excessive caution and the 96th Division's heavy casualties, he was largely satisfied with both units. Unfortunately for the Tenth Army, the worst was yet to come.[11]

Breaking the Shuri Line

Once the Tenth Army reached the Shuri Line, the Okinawa campaign degenerated into a brutal slugfest between American and Japanese forces that involved little operational finesse. This was partly by Buckner's design. When some officers suggested an amphibious assault behind Japanese lines on Okinawa's southern tip, Buckner rejected the idea as too logistically complicated and difficult. He preferred to go about winning the campaign in a safe and systematic manner by employing maximum firepower and materiel against the Japanese. He referred to his tactics as "corkscrew and blowtorch," meaning using demolitions to crack open Japanese fortifications and flamethrowers to roast their occupants. Buckner hoped that this methodical approach would keep American casualties low, but that did not turn out to be the case. Instead, it merely added to the bloodshed and savagery that already characterized the Pacific War.

In late April and early May, Buckner redeployed his forces. He summoned the Marine III Amphibious Corps from northern Okinawa and placed it opposite the Shuri Line on the western side of the island. Next to it, on Okinawa's eastern shore, he put the XXIV Corps' divisions: the 7th, 77th, and 96th. After repelling a 4 May enemy counterattack that cost the Japanese 5,000 casualties, on 11 May the Tenth Army launched its offensive against the Shuri Line. Although Buckner hoped for a coordinated and disciplined assault by all his units, the battle quickly deteriorated into disconnected, barbarous, and costly fights for individual heights with innocuous or exotic names such as Sugar Loaf, Dakeshi, Wana, Chocolate Drop, Wart, Flattop, Dick, Oboe, and Conical. One after another, the leathernecks and GIs pried the Japanese out at heavy cost to both sides. Because so many line officers became casualties, noncoms took over platoon-sized rifle companies. The turnover among the green replacements was especially heavy because the new men lacked the combat savvy of their predecessors. One 77th Division sergeant, for example, wrote:

> Our 30 replacements showed great courage, but were too new to the job. One of them saw two Nips who got a sergeant 30 feet away, but his finger froze on the trigger. Another saw Japs standing on the horizon and shouted wildly for an older man to shoot them while his own rifle lay in his hands. Another saw enemy a few yards from his hole, aimed and fired an empty rifle. In the excitement, he had emptied his magazine and had forgotten to reload.[12]

Despite these problems, the leathernecks and GIs got the job done, but there was nothing subtle or elegant about their tactics. The Marines seized deserted Naha on 23–24 May and entered Shuri Castle five days later.

By then the remaining 30,000 Japanese soldiers had begun withdrawing to the very southern part of the island to make their last stand there. They were helped by heavy rains in late May that turned the roads into mud and grounded aircraft. The battlefield now looked like World War I's Western Front, with corpses and the war's detritus everywhere. When the skies finally cleared on 5 June, the Tenth Army pushed southward and burned the Japanese out of their remaining strongholds. Doing so entailed another 8,100 American casualties. Among these was Simon Buckner, killed on 18 June by coral rock fragments from a nearby shellburst as he observed a Marine unit, just as organized Japanese resistance ended. His successor, General Joseph Stilwell, declared the campaign over on 2 July.

The Okinawa campaign was the Pacific War's bloodiest. American casualties were almost 50,000, including 12,500 killed. The army alone suffered 4,400 dead, 19,100 wounded, and 15,600 nonbattle losses. Specific numbers for the individual army divisions were 10,893 for the 7th Division, 5,224 for the 27th, 7,126 for the 77th, and 10,247 for the 96th. Around 110,000 Japanese troops perished, as well as perhaps a fourth of Okinawa's civilian population, over 100,000 people. In return for all this carnage, the Americans got the island, which would have been essential had an invasion of the Japanese Home Islands proven necessary. Mercifully, this was not the case.

Overcoming the Shuri Line involved little operational refinement by either side. It was instead a straight up brawl during which the Americans and Japanese duked it out across the island. Under these circumstances, tactical innovations mattered more than usual. Here, as on Leyte, Andrew Bruce's 77th Division proved superior to other army units. Bruce was one of the army's most creative thinkers in the Pacific. He preferred to fight alone, as at Ie Shima, and disliked working with other divisions. Either way, though, he was more likely than most division commanders to think outside the box. Buckner said of Bruce's ideas, "Two of the fifteen are okay. The rest are impossible."[13] That may or may not have been true, but on Okinawa any notion that might provide an advantage was worth its weight in gold. Bruce and his Old Buzzards became adept at the slow-but-steady approach of systematically achieving limited objectives. For example, they seized lightly defended hills from where their artillery could shell the hard-to-target reverse slopes of major Japanese positions and engaged in night attacks. Such ingenuity made the 77th the most effective division on Okinawa. Indeed, even Marine officers were impressed with its performance.[14]

The 7th and 96th Divisions also fought well in breaking the Shuri Line, though not as creatively as the 77th. Both suffered heavy casualties in the process. Richardson, Buckner, and Hodge all rated Arnold as the XXIV Corps' top commander, an indication of the respect that they had for his Hourglass boys. As for the 96th Division, it had some of the XXIV Corps' toughest assignments along the Shuri Line, and fought especially well at Conical Hill. Both divisions demonstrated considerable durability and determination in the face of terrible adversity.[15]

Contemporaries and historians of the Okinawa campaign have directed a disproportionate amount of criticism toward Buckner. Many argue that his unimaginative and conventional approach to the battle cost too much time and blood. On the other hand, there has been little analysis of the performance of the army's divisions. The 27th Division's record on the island should raise questions about its effectiveness, but few people have addressed them. Buckner's efforts to downplay the issue no doubt contributed to this collective amnesia, as did a desire to avoid scapegoating and denigrating GIs who had already sacrificed so much for victory.

The other three XXIV Corps divisions—the 7th, 77th, and 96th—had fought together previously during the Leyte operation and had acquired good reputations that the Okinawa campaign did not alter. The 77th Division did particularly well, but the other two also showed a professionalism and remorselessness that helped to achieve victory.

Operation *Downfall*

By the end of the Okinawa campaign, preparations for the climactic assault on the Japanese Home Islands were well under way. Codenamed "Downfall," the plan was divided into two parts. The first, dubbed "Olympic," called for Krueger's Sixth Army to invade the southernmost Japanese island of Kyushu in November 1945. MacArthur's headquarters assigned eleven army divisions to participate in it: the American, 1st Cav, 11th Airborne, 25th, 33rd, 40th, 41st, 43rd, 77th, 81st, and the new 98th. MacArthur hoped to occupy Kyushu's lower third and use it as a logistical base to facilitate the implementation of *Downfall's* second component, "Coronet." For *Coronet*, Eichelberger's Eighth Army and General Courtney H. Hodges' First Army would land near Tokyo in March 1946. Some of the divisions allotted to *Coronet* would come from Europe, but the 6th, 7th, 27th, 31st, 32nd, 37th, 38th, and 96th Divisions would also participate. The objective was to destroy Japan's ability to resist, replace its government, and subjugate the country.

There is no evidence that American planners considered divisions' reputations or commanders' preferences while formulating *Downfall*. Krueger, for example, got some of his favorite divisions, such as the 1st Cav and 11th Airborne, but he also had to take the 40th and 41st, neither of which he had ever expressed much affection for. Instead, logistics played the biggest role in their selections. The obvious exception was the 93rd Division. Of all the Pacific War's army divisions, the 93rd was the only one that did not receive a combat assignment for *Downfall*. Although MacArthur had promised to use it like any other division, he made no effort to live up to that pledge. The 93rd remained the army's neglected stepchild until the war's end. Fortunately for the Americans, the atomic bombings of Hiroshima and Nagasaki in August 1945 and Soviet intervention in the conflict persuaded the Japanese government to surrender, rendering *Downfall* mercifully academic.

Conclusions

The Relevance of Evaluating Divisions

The twenty divisions that the army deployed and used in the Pacific War were integral to its ultimate success. Even in the Pacific's oceanic expanse, seizing terrain mattered, and only ground troops—soldiers or leathernecks—could do that. Although the army designed most of its divisions to be as uniform and interchangeable as possible, this was not the reality because these units were composed of human beings. Each division was different in myriad ways, including qualitatively. They all had their own organizational cultures, histories, traditions, and modi operandi. These variances make it possible to evaluate and rate them. Doing so is a tricky, divisive, and subjective task, but also worthwhile for several reasons. For one thing, it is impossible to understand the Pacific War's land battles, operations, and campaigns without assessing the divisions that fought in them. If these divisions had been as unvaried as the army wanted, it would not matter, but they were in fact sufficiently dissimilar to affect the outcomes. For instance, Buna is incomprehensible without acknowledging the 32nd Division's greenness. Similarly, Kwajalein was a clear-cut American triumph in part because the 7th Division was a well-trained and battle-hardened outfit. In short, divisional characteristics go a long way toward explaining the army's Pacific War victory.

Moreover, the composition and performance of these divisions reveals much about the army's role in American society. Although the army was in some ways distinct from society, it was still part of it. This interaction between the two was especially important in wartime when the bond between the army and American society became so crucial to protecting national security. For example, the fact that the War Department accepted and designated National Guard divisions, and *then* tried with middling success to mold them into something resembling Regular Army or draftee outfits, indicates that the army deferred to civilian authorities who insisted on maintaining the National Guard's identity. Likewise, the army's treatment of the all-black 93rd Division reflected the racism of the era and the army's reluctance to challenge these mores, but also its willingness to make gestures toward change that some civilian leaders demanded. Although the army's subservience to the society that created it sometimes meant that it acted in ways that were not always militarily wise, this was necessary to preserve the relationship that made the army's overall success possible.

Finally, the army's experience with these divisions provides contemporary lessons. There is nothing easy about creating large organizations and molding them into entities capable of achieving defined goals, even with solid leadership, good intentions, adequate resources, and clear objectives. As army generals discovered, organizations such as divisions develop their own distinct collective personalities, cultures, and routines that may or may not help them fulfill their missions. No one, for instance, intended for the 27th Division to become such a controversial outfit, but it did, and once that happened, army officers had a hard time recognizing the problem, let alone formulating an effective antidote. Simply comprehending this fact can help leaders use their organizations effectively by assigning them tasks that they are capable of achieving. The upshot is that just as it is impossible to understand and assess a league without discussing the merits of the participating teams, the same is true of the army's Pacific War divisions.

Indicators of Divisional Quality

Divisional quality, like beauty, is often in the eye of the beholder. The army's Pacific War divisions were complex units that consisted of innumerable and constantly changing organizational parts. One regiment might show improvement over the course of a campaign, while at the same time an artillery battery's efficiency might deteriorate. While it is important to keep these nuances in mind, this does not invalidate efforts to evaluate divisions in the aggregate. Although there is no one objective and surefire way to measure a division's effectiveness, there are a variety of available methodological tools that can illuminate divisional quality. No one is perfect, but, put together, they give a three-dimensional view of divisions that clarifies the question of which ones were the best.

One obvious methodological tool is statistics. Carried to its extreme, this means inputting into a computer numerical data about divisions such as ground gained and lost, casualties sustained and inflicted, days in combat, ammunition expended, citations earned, and so forth. With enough data, a computer should produce some sort of divisional rating. Doing so can provide interesting information, but its value leaves much to be desired. For one thing, it is not as objective as advertised. Programmers select which data to use and how much weight to give each variable, both of which are subjective decisions. Is ground acquired more important than casualties exacted? In addition, there is no guarantee that complicated data hastily catalogued is even accurate. For example, any estimate of Japanese losses in some engagements is just that—an estimate—and is open to debate. Finally, it overlooks intangible but undeniably important factors such as leadership and morale that are impossible to quantify objectively. How much is a Robert Beightler, Andrew Bruce, or Palmer Swift worth? Statistics may be useful, but they are not necessarily determining or even true.

Another way with which to evaluate divisions is through the sentiments of the high-level commanders who oversaw them in combat. These included the heads of theaters, field armies, and corps, men such as MacArthur, Nimitz, Halsey, Richardson, Buckner, Krueger, Eichelberger, Swift, Hall, Patch, Griswold, and Hodge. These officers trained, deployed, maneuvered, and fought these divisions across the Pacific, during which time they sometimes developed decided opinions about them. It was not unusual for them to have their favorites. MacArthur and Krueger, for example, rated the 1st Cav Division as their best. Eichelberger was partial to the 11th Airborne Division, Hodge valued the 7th and 77th, and Griswold liked the American and 37th Divisions. Because these men were theoretically the army's best and brightest whose career fortunes rose or fell on the performance of these units, their views deserve a good bit of respect. As with statistics, though, this method is not foolproof. Some generals were blinded by sentimentality or inaccurate information. MacArthur's affection for the 1st Cav Division, for instance, was based as much on his fond childhood memories of the outfit as any objective assessment of its quality. Although the initial consensus was that the 24th Division stumbled badly on Leyte, more mature thinking convinced many officers that it had in fact done as well as could be expected. Even so, this methodological tool offers valuable insights into the merits of the divisions.

Another, related, technique for evaluating divisions is to examine the opinions of the division commanders to see what they said about these outfits—their own and others. The pitfalls are obvious. These men had a proprietary interest in painting their divisions in the brightest possible colors for both contemporaries and historians. They were also sometimes willing to denigrate other divisions to vivify the comparative contrast with their own. For example, Joseph Swing, the 11th Airborne Division's commander, was quite chauvinistic about his paratroopers. Robert Beightler was a shameless, albeit frustrated, self-promoter of his 37th Division. At the same time, some of these men were strikingly honest about their division's shortcomings, even if only to discredit their predecessors by establishing a paper trail. William Gill was remarkably candid about the 32nd Division's problems after its Buna nightmare. Similarly, William Chase wrote disarmingly about the 38th Division's woes at Zigzag Pass. The fact that these officers were understandingly prejudiced toward their units does not disqualify their analyses.

Most officers and enlisted men were too distant from the various headquarters and too ignorant of operations to knowledgeably opine on the quality of divisions. There were, however, two exceptions. One was staff and liaison officers who worked closely with division, corps, field army, and theater commanders and traveled from headquarters to headquarters. This gave them access to plenty of information and gossip. For example, Eichelberger's chief of staff, General Clovis Byers, kept a diary during the war full of headquarters chatter, including news about divisions. Other officers acted as sounding boards, such as Roger Egeberg, who served as MacArthur's physician and confidante. Although these men sometimes merely echoed the thinking of their patrons in their memoirs and postwar interviews, most had definite and insightful observations about a wide variety of subjects, including the performance of divisions.

Outside observers constitute another group with knowledgeable and valuable views on the performance of the army's Pacific War divisions. These men were not part of the American army, but were rather navy, Marine Corps, and foreign officers. They had access to high-level American combat commanders and their staffs, knew army plans, understood all things military, and were generally intelligent, thoughtful, and observant men. They included naval officers such as Nimitz and Halsey, Marines like Holland Smith and his staffers, and Australian and New Zealander military personnel. Finally, Japanese officers on the receiving end of the American military machine such as Yamashita later voiced their opinions of the quality of the divisions they faced. Holland Smith, for example, was quite vocal in his criticisms of the 27th Division and praise of the 77th. After the war, Yamashita expressed his admiration for the 1st Cav, 32nd, and 38th Divisions. These individuals did not necessarily understand all aspects of the army's culture and challenges, but they provided unique and often incisive outsider perspectives about army divisions that should be taken into account in evaluating them.

Leadership is another useful gauge of divisional quality. A division whose commander was elevated to run a corps is evidence that he was helming a good outfit. Conversely, a division whose commander was relieved might indicate a poor unit. During the Pacific War, six division chiefs were fired from their posts for failure on the battlefield: the 32nd Division's Forrest Harding at Buna, the 7th Division's Albert Brown at Attu, the 43rd Division's John Hester on New Georgia, the 27th Division's Ralph Smith on Saipan, the 24th Division's Fred Irving on Leyte, and the 38th Division's Henry Jones at Zigzag Pass. Their removals reflected problems within these divisions that negatively impacted their battlefield performances. On the other hand, five division heads were promoted to corps command: the Americal Division's Alexander Patch and John Hodge, the 1st Cav Division's Palmer Swift, the 25th Division's J. Lawton Collins, and the 7th Division's Charles Corlett. There are, though, problems with this criterion. The most obvious is that perception sometimes mattered more than reality. For example, George Marshall appointed Patch to run the XIV Corps because he mistakenly believed that the Americal Division performed better on Guadalcanal than was actually the case. Indeed, it is odd that the Americal Division, one of the Pacific War's less distinguished outfits, produced two corps commanders. In addition, most of these promotions were based on a commander's record in just one battle, and one victory does not constitute a pattern of success that marks a superb division. Generally speaking, though, generals ascending the army's hierarchy ran good divisions.

A division's performance in its first operation is also an indicator of its abilities. After all, this was when a division was most likely to make serious mistakes due to its inexperience. A division that fights well in its baptism of fire will probably continue to do so in the future. Although American naval, air, and materiel superiority throughout the Pacific War's counteroffensive all but guaranteed a division's success, some made mistakes so serious as to either threaten their triumphs or require additional help to secure them. Unfortunately, the list of army divisions that stumbled in their first combat outings is depressingly long: the 32nd Division at Buna, the Americal on Guadalcanal, the 7th on Attu, the 43rd on New Georgia, the 27th on Makin and Saipan, the 40th at Clark Airbase, and the 38th at Zigzag Pass. Other divisions committed errors which, while not sufficiently grievous as to jeopardize the battle's outcome, are still worth noting. These include the 37th Division on New Georgia, the 6th at Lone Tree Hill, the 81st on Angaur, and the 33rd before Baguio. This leaves only a minority of divisions that emerged reputationally unscathed from their first major engagement as a unit: the 25th Division on Guadalcanal, the 1st Cav in the Admiralties, the 24th at Hollandia, the 77th on Guam, the 11th Airborne and 96th on Leyte, and the 31st on Mindanao. The fact that these divisions succeeded right out of the chute speaks well of them, and should certainly factor into determining which ones were the army's most proficient.

Finally, the opinions of historians about the divisions matter. Although the army's role in the Pacific War has not received as much historiographical attention as that of the navy and Marine Corps, someone with historical training has examined almost every facet of the conflict to some extent: battles and campaigns, strategy and tactics, weaponry, intelligence, logistics, commanders, culture, and so forth. These experts often form knowledgeable opinions about divisional performance that deserve to be respected, even if expressed only tangentially. This is especially true of divisions that participated in the more famous and controversial parts of the conflict, such as the 32nd Division at Buna and the 27th Division on Saipan. To be sure, historians are as subject to prejudice, bias, intellectual sloppiness and laziness, groupthink, carelessness, mendacity, and ignorance as anyone else. Hopefully, however, examining a wide range of historical work produces a nuanced and thoughtful consensus about divisions.

No one methodological approach in evaluating the army's divisions is infallible; they all have their flaws. However, using most or all of them provides a redundancy that helps to compensate for the shortcomings of each. Even then, any analysis of the divisions, while worthwhile, will remain inherently subjective. Ultimately, rating divisions means offering an informed opinion over which honest people can disagree, and which may change based on new evidence or thinking. That is the nature of the historiographical beast.

Rating the Divisions

The army deployed six Regular Army divisions to the Pacific during World War II: the 1st Cav, 6th, 7th, 11th Airborne, 24th, and 25th. Of these, three can make a claim to being the most proficient Regular Army division in the conflict. The first is the 1st Cav. Innumerable high-level officers, including MacArthur, lauded it for its discipline, efficiency, and bearing. Indeed, it is difficult to find someone with a bad word for it. Its first commander, Palmer Swift, went on to lead the I Corps on Luzon and many officers considered his successor, Verne Mudge, the best divisional leader in the Pacific. Its ten Distinguished Unit Citations were more than any other division except for the 11th Airborne, 32nd, and 77th Divisions. There was more to the 1st Cav than just talk and awards. It saw more than 500 days of combat, a number surpassed in the Pacific War only by the Americal, 32nd, and 37th Divisions. It fought superbly in its debut in the Admiralties, making it one of a handful of divisions to perform well in its baptism of fire. From there it did yeoman service on Leyte. Then, without much rest, it went to Luzon and spearheaded the Sixth Army's drive on Manila. It spent the remainder of the conflict battling the Shimbu Group and clearing southeastern Luzon. It never suffered a major setback or failed to achieve its objectives. Although the 1st Cav did not see as much of the hard grinding combat as other units, its accomplishments certainly place it at the top of any list of the best Pacific War divisions.

The 7th Hourglass Division can also make a good case for being the army's best Pacific War Regular Army division. It may have stumbled in its baptism of fire on Attu, but it won the battle and went on to amass a long and stellar record that no other division surpassed. Among other things, it conducted four major amphibious assaults. At Kwajalein it overcame approximately 5,000 dug-in Japanese soldiers on a tiny island on schedule and with acceptable losses. Indeed, many saw its performance there as a model for future amphibious operations. On Leyte it showed that it could also maneuver and fight defensively. After coming ashore, it seized the airfields around Burauen, crossed the island before any other American unit, fended off a ferocious Japanese attack at Shoestring Ridge, and drove up the coast to link up with the 77th Division near Ormoc. Finally, on Okinawa it demonstrated a remarkable sturdiness and determination by engaging from beginning to end in that long brutal slugfest against the best Japanese army of the conflict. Although its first leader in action, Albert Brown, was relieved on Attu, its subsequent commanders were men of caliber. Charles Corlett's performance on Kwajalein was so impressive that George Marshall promoted him to run a corps in Europe. Many considered his replacement, Archibald Arnold, one of the war's best division heads. The XXIV Corps chief, John Hodge, under who the 7th Division served on Leyte and Okinawa, initially complained that the outfit was too independent and wedded to direct assault, but later rated it the best in his corps. Richardson agreed. Even Krueger called it a fine unit, as did Buckner. It accumulated nine Distinguished Unit Citations in its over 200 days of combat. No division battled for so long against such stubborn defenders with as much success as the Hourglass division.

Finally, an argument can be made that the 25th Tropic Lightning Division was the most proficient Regular Army division in the Pacific War. Like the 1st Cav and 7th Divisions, plenty of high-level officers lauded it, including most notably George Marshall. The 25th Division also had a commander, J. Lawton Collins, who performed so well that he was elevated to run a corps and became arguably the army's greatest World War II combat commander. During the conflict, the 25th Division earned a reputation as a skillful, remorseless, and hard-hitting outfit. It fought well in its first action on Guadalcanal and then bore the brunt of the awful mopping up operations on New Georgia. After a long interlude, it went to Luzon. Unlike Guadalcanal and New Georgia, Luzon was large enough for the 25th Division to maneuver effectively. It bypassed Japanese strongpoints to help the 6th Division seize San José, thus severing the link between the Shobu and Shimbu groups. Later it outmaneuvered the Japanese again to break through to Balete Pass. The 25th Division never had the snap and finish of the 1st Cav Division's troopers or the 11th Airborne Division's paratroopers, but it made up for this in its performance. Although it served in combat for only 165 days, less than all but a handful of Pacific War divisions, it fulfilled difficult missions in a timely and efficient manner.

The other Regular Army divisions in the Pacific War did well, but their performances did not rise to the level achieved by the 1st Cav, 7th, and 25th Divisions. The 6th Sightseers Division was a solid and durable outfit whose leader in New Guinea, Franklin Sibert, later led a corps. Although the 6th Division won its first battle at Lone Tree Hill, it did so only after one of its battalions got trapped near the summit. The Sightseers went on to Luzon to skillfully outmaneuver the Japanese and take San José, but were practically rendered combat ineffective in their efforts to reduce the Shimbu Group. As for the 11th Airborne Division, it was an elite unit of whom top-level officers spoke highly. It may not have seized Manila after it landed and parachuted onto Luzon, but it certainly impressed observers with the élan and courage its GIs demonstrated. Its subsequent brilliant raid on the Japanese internment camp at Los Baños merely solidified its good reputation. However, it did not have as long or acquire as distinguished a combat record as the 1st Cav, 7th, and 25th Divisions. Finally, the 24th Division was unable to sustain its fine start at Hollandia. On Leyte it ran into so much trouble that Krueger relieved its commander and pulled it out of the line, though later many officers concluded that it did about as well as could be expected. The Victory boys' later commendable efforts in the central and southern Philippines were not enough to place them ahead of the other, more successful, Regular Army divisions.

Among the ten National Guard divisions committed to the Pacific War, the 37th Division was head and shoulders above the rest. The army deployed such a high percentage of its National Guard divisions to the Pacific because they were among the few units organized and trained enough to send overseas to confront the Japanese rampage across the Pacific in 1941–42. Although the 37th was led by a nonprofessional, it amassed a superior wartime record. Its performance in its first battle on New Georgia was hardly flawless, but it did not make many mistakes there serious enough to jeopardize the operation's outcome. A few months later, at Bougainville, the Ohio boys successfully repelled the Japanese attack on the Empress Augusta Bay beachhead. Because the Americans were fighting from behind defensive positions against the outgunned and outnumbered Japanese, they could hardly lose, so the 37th Division's accomplishment was not noteworthy. However, the division came into its own on Luzon. There it landed on Lingayen Beach, helped the 40th Division take Clark Airbase, and, most impressively, eliminated the Japanese from Manila in a month of savage urban combat. Later it assisted in demolishing the Shimbu and Shobu groups and cleared the Cagayan Valley. Considering its record, it is small wonder that it so impressed men such as Griswold and Eichelberger. It also served more days in combat than any Pacific War Division except for the Americal. Reliable, efficient, adaptable, and thoroughly competent, the 37th Division never failed to achieve its major objectives.

None of the other National Guard divisions in the Pacific—the Americal, 27th, 31st, 32nd, 33rd, 38th, 40th, 41st, and 43rd—fought as well as the 37th. Most of them stumbled in their baptisms of fire: the 32nd at Buna, the Americal on Guadalcanal, the 43rd on New Georgia, the 27th on Makin and Saipan, the 38th at Zigzag Pass, and the 40th at Clark Airbase. Although the 31st Division showed great promise at Mindanao, it did not see nearly as much action as the 37th. As for the 41st, it certainly possessed a long and honorable record, but its difficulties on Biak tainted its reputation. Moreover, some of these divisions generated controversy that the 37th avoided. In the end, all these divisions performed well, but the 37th Division simply did better.

Only a small number of draftee divisions served in the Pacific: the 77th, 81st, 93rd, and 96th. Of these, the 77th was undoubtedly the best. It amassed more Distinguished Unit Citations—sixteen—than any other Pacific War army division. In addition, it was led by Andrew Bruce, probably the most creative divisional commander the Japanese faced. Almost every high-level officer who saw the 77th in action praised it. It fought so well on Guam in its first outing that even Marine officers commended it. Later, on Leyte, it delivered the knock-out punch with its amphibious assault near Ormoc that put paid to Japanese efforts to forestall American conquest of the island. Finally, on Okinawa it seized Ie Shima in a brutal battle and helped break the Shuri Line. Army officers had expected much from the 77th even before it shipped overseas, and happily its GIs delivered in every battle in which they participated.

The other selectee divisions did not match the 77th Division's accomplishments. The 81st Division showed potential, but its Pacific War record was limited to Angaur/Peleliu. Although the 96th was a reliable outfit that fought well on Leyte and Okinawa, its performance was simply not as extensive or impressive as the Old Buzzards'. Finally, the army's racism prevented the 93rd Division from demonstrating its worth. Its combat experiences were limited to patrolling and mopping up in New Guinea and the Philippines.

The Pacific War has faded from American historical memory. For even the historically literate, that part of World War II consists of Pearl Harbor, the Marine Corps, Douglas MacArthur, the Battle of Midway, and the atomic bomb. There certainly is not much knowledge of or interest in the army's contributions, including that of its twenty combat divisions. This is unfortunate because the army played such an important role in winning the conflict. Although the divisions might seem like a random series of numbers, these numbers represent the collective efforts of hundreds of thousands of people who sacrificed their time, energy, and, in all too many cases, their lives to rid the world of fascism. In doing so, they generated a rich history that tells much about the army and twentieth-century America. Whether it is the 32nd Division's hard-luck struggle at Buna, the interservice controversies surrounding the 27th Division's actions, the racism that relegated the 93rd Division to the military backburner, or the 77th Division's innovative tactics on Leyte, these units encapsulated an American way of war that helped determine World War II's outcome.

List of Pacific War Army Divisions

1st Cavalry Division

Nickname:	First Team, Hell for Leather
Date Activated:	August 1921
Departed Overseas:	May 1943
Wartime Commanders:	Innis Swift, April 1941–August 1944
	Verne Mudge, August 1944–July 1945
	William Chase, July 1945–December 1948
Regiments:	5th Cavalry
	7th Cavalry
	8th Cavalry
	12th Cavalry
Days in Combat:	521
Casualties:	4,055
Major Operations:	Admiralty Islands, Leyte, Luzon

6th Infantry Division

Nickname:	Red Star, Sightseers
Date Activated:	October 1939
Departed Overseas:	July 1943
Wartime Commanders:	Clarence Ridley, January 1941–August 1942
	Durward Wilson, September 1942–October 1942
	Franklin Sibert, October 1942–August 1944
	Edwin Patrick, August 1944–March 1945
	Charles Hurdis, March 1945–April 1946
Regiments:	1st Infantry
	20th Infantry
	63rd Infantry
Days in Combat:	306
Casualties:	2,370
Major Operations:	Wakde–Sarmi, Sansapor–Mar, Luzon

7th Infantry Division

Nickname:	Hourglass Division
Date Activated:	July 1940
Departed Overseas:	April 1943
Wartime Commanders:	C. H. White, August 1941–October 1942
	Albert Brown, October 1942–April 1943
	Charles Corlett, April 1943–February 1944
	Archibald Arnold, March 1944–September 1945
Regiments:	17th Infantry
	32nd Infantry
	184th Infantry
Days in Combat:	208
Casualties:	9,212
Major Operations:	Attu, Kwajalein, Leyte, Okinawa

11th Airborne Division

Nickname:	Angels
Date Activated:	February 1943
Departed Overseas:	April 1944
Wartime Commander:	Joseph Swing, February 1943–February 1946
Regiments:	187th Glider Infantry
	188th Glider Infantry
	511th Parachute Infantry
Days in Combat:	204
Casualties:	2,431
Major Operations:	Leyte, Luzon

24th Infantry Division

Nickname:	Victory Division
Date Activated:	October 1941
Wartime Commanders:	Durward Wilson, October 1941–July 1942
	Frederick Irving, August 1942–October 1944
	Roscoe Woodruff, November 1944–November 1945
Regiments:	19th Infantry
	21st Infantry
	34th Infantry
Days in Combat:	210
Casualties:	6,995
Major Operations:	Hollandia, Biak, Leyte, Luzon, Central and Southern Philippines

25th Infantry Division

Nickname:	Tropic Lightning
Date Activated:	October 1941
Wartime Commanders:	Maxwell Murray, October 1941–May 1942
	J. Lawton Collins, May 1942–January 1944
	Charles Mullins, Jr., January 1944–May 1948
Regiments:	27th Infantry
	35th Infantry
	161st Infantry
Days in Combat:	165
Casualties:	5,425
Major Operations:	Guadalcanal, New Georgia, Luzon

27th Infantry Division

Nickname:	New York
Date Activated:	October 1940
Departed Overseas:	March 1942
Wartime Commanders:	Ralph Pennell, November 1941–October 1942
	Ralph Smith, November 1942–May 1944
	George Griner, June 1944–December 1945
Regiments:	105th Infantry
	106th Infantry
	165th Infantry
Days in Combat:	110
Casualties:	6,533
Major Operations:	Makin, Eniwetok, Saipan, Okinawa

31st Infantry Division

Nickname:	Dixie
Date Activated:	November 1940
Departed Overseas:	March 1944
Wartime Commanders:	John Persons, November 1940–September 1944
	Clarence Martin, September 1944–December 1946
Regiments:	124th Infantry
	155th Infantry
	167th Infantry
Days in Combat:	245
Casualties:	1,733
Major Operations:	Driniumor River, Morotai, Central and Southern Philippines

32nd Infantry Division

Nickname:	Red Arrow
Date Activated:	October 1940
Departed Overseas:	May 1942
Wartime Commanders:	Irving Fish, October 1940–March 1942
	Edwin Harding, March 1942–January 1943
	William Gill, February 1943–February 1946
Regiments:	126th Infantry
	127th Infantry
	128th Infantry
Days in Combat:	654
Casualties:	7,268
Major Operations:	Buna–Gona, Saidor, Driniumor River, Leyte, Luzon

33rd Infantry Division

Nickname:	Prairie
Date Activated:	March 1941
Departed Overseas:	July 1943
Wartime Commanders:	Samuel Lawton, March 1941–May 1942
	Frank Mahin, May 1942–July 1942
	John Millikin, August 1942–September 1943
	Percy Clarkson, October 1943–November 1945
Regiments:	123rd Infantry
	130th Infantry
	136th Infantry
Days in Combat:	139
Casualties:	2,426
Major Operations:	Luzon

37th Infantry Division

Nickname:	Buckeye
Date Activated:	October 1940
Departed Overseas:	May 1942
Wartime Commander:	Robert Beightler, October 1940–December 1945
Regiments:	129th Infantry
	145th Infantry
	148th Infantry
Days in Combat:	592
Casualties:	5,960
Major Operations:	New Georgia, Bougainville, Luzon

38th Infantry Division

Nickname:	Cyclone
Date Activated:	January 1941
Departed Overseas:	January 1944
Wartime Commanders:	Daniel Sultan, April 1941–April 1942
	Henry Jones, April 1942–February 1945
	William Chase, February 1945–July 1945
	Frederick Irving, August 1945–November 1945
Regiments:	149th Infantry
	151st Infantry
	152nd Infantry
Days in Combat:	210
Casualties:	3,464
Major Operations:	Luzon

40th Infantry Division

Nickname:	Sunburst, Sunshine
Date Activated:	March 1941
Departed Overseas:	August 1942
Wartime Commanders:	Ernest Dawley, September 1941–April 1942
	Rapp Brush, April 1942–July 1945
	Donald Myers, July 1945–April 1946
Regiments:	108th Infantry
	160th Infantry
	185th Infantry
Days in Combat:	265
Casualties:	3,025
Major Operations:	Luzon

41st Infantry Division

Nickname:	Jungleers
Date Activated:	September 1940
Departed Overseas:	March 1942
Wartime Commanders:	Horace Fuller, December 1941–June 1944
	Jens Doe, June 1944–December 1945
Regiments:	162nd Infantry
	163rd Infantry
	186th Infantry
Days in Combat:	380
Casualties:	4,260
Major Operations:	Sanananda, Salamaua, Hollandia–Aitape, Wakde, Biak, Central and Southern Philippines

43rd Infantry Division

Nickname:	Winged Victory
Date Activated:	February 1941
Departed Overseas:	October 1942
Wartime Commanders:	John Hester, August 1941–July 1943
	Leonard Wing, August 1943–October 1945
Regiments:	103rd Infantry
	169th Infantry
	172nd Infantry
Days in Combat:	370
Casualties:	6,026
Major Operations:	New Georgia, Driniumor River, Luzon

77th Infantry Division

Nickname:	Statue of Liberty, Old Buzzards
Date Activated:	July 1940
Departed Overseas:	March 1944
Wartime Commanders:	Robert Eichelberger, March 1942–June 1942
	Roscoe Woodruff, June 1942–May 1943
	Andrew Bruce, May 1943–February 1946
Regiments:	305th Infantry
	306th Infantry
	307th Infantry
Days in Combat:	208
Casualties:	9,212
Major Operations:	Guam, Leyte, Okinawa

81st Infantry Division

Nickname:	Wildcat
Date Activated:	June 1942
Departed Overseas:	July 1944
Wartime Commanders:	Gustave Franke, June 1942–August 1942
	Paul Mueller, August 1942–January 1946
Regiments:	321st Infantry
	322nd Infantry
	323rd Infantry
Days in Combat:	166
Casualties:	2,314
Major Operations:	Angaur, Peleliu

93rd Infantry Division

Nickname:	Blue Helmets
Date Activated:	May 1942
Departed Overseas:	January 1944
Wartime Commanders:	Charles Hall, May 1942–October 1942
	Fred Miller, October 1942–May 1943
	Raymond Lehman, May 1943–August 1944
	Harry Johnson, August 1944–September 1945
Regiments:	25th Infantry
	368th Infantry
	369th Infantry
Days in Combat:	175
Casualties:	133
Major Operations:	Solomon Islands, New Guinea, Central and Southern Philippines

96th Infantry Division

Nickname:	Deadeye
Date Activated:	August 1942
Departed Overseas:	July 1944
Wartime Commander:	James Bradley, August 1942–February 1946
Regiments:	381st Infantry
	382nd Infantry
	383rd Infantry
Days in Combat:	200
Casualties:	8,812
Major Operations:	Leyte, Okinawa

American Division

Date Activated:	May 1942
Wartime Commanders:	Alexander Patch, May 1942–December 1942
	Edmund Sebree, January 1943–May 1943
	John Hodge, May 1943–April 1944
	Robert McClure, April 1944–October 1944
	William Arnold, November 1944–December 1945
Regiments:	132nd Infantry
	164th Infantry
	182nd Infantry
Days in Combat:	600
Casualties:	4,050
Major Operations:	Guadalcanal, Bougainville, Leyte, Central and Southern Philippines

Endnotes

Introduction

1   Robert L. Eichelberger, with Milton McKay, *Our Jungle Road to Tokyo* (New York: Viking Press, 1949), 254; Robert L. Eichelberger to his wife, 6 July 1945, *Dear Miss Em: General Eichelberger's War in the Pacific, 1942–1945*, ed. Jay Luvaas (Westport, Connecticut: Greenwood Press, 1972), 290; Clovis Byers diary, 7 July 1945, Clovis Byers Collection, Hoover Institution, box 36, folder 1.

2   Harry Lemley, interview by Gerald F. Feeney, 1974, *Armed Forces Oral Histories: Army Senior Officer Oral Histories* (Frederick, Maryland: University Publications of America, 1989), section 2, 12 (hereafter cited as *ASOOH*).

3   George Marshall, 7 December 1956, *George C. Marshall Interviews and Reminiscences for Forrest C. Pogue*, ed. Larry I. Bland (Lexington, Virginia: George C. Marshall Research Foundation, 1991), 255–56.

4   For various views of the National Guard, see Holland M. Smith and Percy Finch, *Coral and Brass* (New York: Charles Scribner's Sons, 1949), 168–70; Marshall, 28 September 1956, *Marshall Interviews*, 578; Graves Erskine, interview by Benis M. Frank, 1975, Marine Corps Oral History Collection, Marine Corps History Division, 320 (hereafter cited as MCOHC); Fred L. Walker, 3 September 1941 and 21 February 1944, *From Texas to Rome: A General's Journal* (El Dorado Hills, California: Savas Beatie, 2021), 2–4, 300; Omar N. Bradley, *A Soldier's Story* (New York: Henry Holt and Co., 1951), 14; J. Lawton Collins, interview by Charles Sperow, 1972, *ASOOH*, vol. 1, 85; George Decker, interview by Dan H. Ralls, 1972, *ASOOH*, section 2, 5, 41; Arthur Collins, Jr., interview by Chandler Robbins III, 1982, *ASOOH*, 90–91; Matthew Ridgway, interview by John M. Blair, 1971–72, *ASOOH*, section 2, 87–88.

5   George Patton, *War As I Knew It* (Boston: Houghton Mifflin Co., 1947), 325–26.

6   Dwight Eisenhower, *At Ease: Stories I Tell to Friends* (Garden City, New York: Doubleday and Co., 1967), 253.

Chapter 1

1   For examples of contemporaries praising the 164th Regiment's performance, see J. Lawton Collins, *Lightning Joe: An Autobiography* (Baton Rouge, Louisiana: Louisiana State University Press, 1979), 147; Alexander Archer Vandegrift, as told to Robert B. Asprey, *Once a Marine: The Memoirs of General A. A. Vandegrift, United States Marine Corps* (New York: Ballantine Books, 1964), 186–87; Francis D. Cronin, *Under the Southern Cross: The Saga of the Americal Division* (Washington, D.C.: Combat Forces Press, 1951), 57; Merrill B. Twining, *No Bended Knee: The Battle for Guadalcanal* (New York: Ballantine Books, 2004), 167. See also Robert Luckey, interview by Benis M. Frank, 1973, MCOHC, 152.

2   Gerald Thomas, interview by Benis M. Frank, 1966, MCOHC, 170.
3   Ralph Wismer, interview by Benis M. Frank, 1979, MCOHC, 18; Samuel B. Griffith, Jr., *The Battle for Guadalcanal* (New York: J.B. Lippincott Co., 1963), 231; Eric Bergerud, *Touched with Fire: The Land War in the South Pacific* (New York: Viking, 1996), 192.
4   J. Lawton Collins interview, *ASOOH*, vol. 1, 102.
5   J. Lawton Collins interview, *ASOOH*, vol. 1, 101–102; William F. Halsey and J. Bryan III, *Admiral Halsey's Story* (New York: McGraw-Hill Book Co. 1947), 377; John Miller, Jr., *Guadalcanal: The First Offensive* (Washington, D.C.: Center of Military History, 1995), 212, 217–18; Robert F. Karolevitz, ed., *The 25th Division in World War 2* (Baton Rouge, Louisiana: Army and Navy Publishing Co., 1946), 17; Russell F. Weigley, *Eisenhower's Lieutenants: The Campaign of France and Germany, 1944–1945* (Bloomington, Indiana: Indiana University Press, 1981), 100.
6   Karolevitz, *25th Division in World War 2*, 51.
7   Bergerud, *Touched with Fire*, 199.
8   Marshall, 21 November 1956, *Marshall Interviews*, 370; Halsey, *Halsey's Story*, 140; Miller, *Guadalcanal*, 305; Richard B. Frank, *Guadalcanal* (New York: Random House, 1990), 552; Alan Rems, *South Pacific Cauldron: World War II's Greatest Forgotten Battlegrounds* (Annapolis, Maryland: Naval Institute Press, 2014), 49; Karolevitz, *25th Division in World War 2*, 17, 51; Keith E. Bonn, *When the Odds Were Even: The Vosges Mountains Campaign, October 1944–January 1945* (Novato, California: Presidio Press, 1994), 70; Cronin, *Southern Cross*, 102.
9   Samuel Milner, *Victory in Papua* (Washington, D.C.: Center of Military History, 1989), 91–92.
10 Eichelberger to V. L. Peterson (unsent), 19 January 1943, Robert L. Eichelberger Papers, Perkins Library, Duke University, reel 44.
11 Eichelberger to Peterson (unsent), 19 January 1943, *Dear Miss Em*, 61–62; Eichelberger, *Jungle Road*, 22–23; William H. Gill, as told to Edward Jaquelin Smith, *Always a Commander: The Reminiscences of Major General William H. Gill* (Colorado Springs, Colorado: The Colorado College 1974), 49–50; George C. Kenney, *General Kenney Reports: A Personal History of the Pacific War* (Dayton, Ohio: Air Force History and Museums Program, 1997), 32, 91–92; Byers diary, 5 September 1942, Byers Collection, box 36, folder 1; Decker interview, *ASOOH*, section 2, 40; Milner, *Victory in Papua*, 133, 137–38; Hugh J. Casey, *Engineer Memoirs: Major General Hugh J. Casey, U.S. Army* (Washington, D.C.: Office of Engineers, 1993), 254; Edwin Harding to Douglas MacArthur, 7 December 1942, Richard Sutherland Papers, Douglas MacArthur Memorial Archives and Library, RG-30, reel 1002; Eichelberger to MacArthur, 29 September 1942, Sutherland Papers, RG-30, reel 1002; Bergerud, *Touched with Fire*, 211–12; Eichelberger to his wife, 21 February 1943, Eichelberger Papers, reel 44.
12 Harold Riegelman, *Caves of Biak: An American Officer's Experiences in the Southwest Pacific* (New York: The Dial Press, 1955), 18.
13 Kenney, *Kenney Reports*, 150–51, 157; Milner, *Victory in Papua*, 137, 202; Casey, *Engineer Memoirs*, 254; Eichelberger to MacArthur, 19 February 1943, Sutherland Papers, RG-30, reel 1002; Eichelberger to Richard Sutherland, 3 December 1942, Sutherland Papers, RG-30, reel 1002; Paul P. Rogers, *The Good Years: MacArthur and Sutherland* (New York: Praeger, 1990), 313.
14 Quoted in Jay Luvaas, "Buna, 19 November 1942–2 January 1943: A 'Leavenworth Nightmare,'" *America's First Battles, 1776–1965*, eds. Charles E. Heller and William A. Stofft (Lawrence, Kansas: University Press of Kansas, 1986), 211.
15 Gill, *Always a Commander*, 52.

16 Gill, *Always a Commander*, 43, 49–50, 53; Byers diary, 22 March and 21 May 1943, Byers Collection, box 36, folder 1; Eichelberger to Walter Krueger, 2 July 1943, Eichelberger Papers, reel 44.

17 Eichelberger, *Jungle Road*, 22.

18 Eichelberger, 12 December 1944, *Dear Miss Em*, 176–77; Gill, *Always a Commander*, 45; Byers diary, 11 and 13 December 1944, Byers Collection, box 36, folder 1; Eichelberger to Peterson (unsent), 19 January 1943, Eichelberger Papers, reel 44.

19 Kenney, *Kenney Reports*, 175; Harry A. Gailey, *The War in the Pacific: From Pearl Harbor to Tokyo Bay* (Novato, California: Presidio, 1995), 215; Sutherland to Horace Fuller, 28 February 1943, Sutherland Papers, RG-30, reel 1006; Archibald Roosevelt to MacArthur, 26 July and 7 August 1943, Sutherland Papers, RG-30, reel 1006; John Sloan Brown, *Draftee Division: The 88th Infantry Division in World War II* (Lexington, Kentucky: The University of Kentucky Press, 1986), 26; John C. McManus, *Island Infernos: The U.S. Army's Pacific War Odyssey, 1944* (New York: Caliber, 2021), 138; "41st Infantry Division," n.d., Bonner Fellers Papers, Douglas MacArthur Memorial Archives and Library, box 1, folder 5.

20 Eichelberger to Krueger, 26 November 1943, Walter Krueger Papers, United States Military Academy, box 8.

21 Eichelberger to Krueger, 6 December 1943, George Decker Papers, United States Army Heritage and Education Center (hereafter USAHEC), box 2.

22 R.W. Coane to MacArthur, 29 June 1944, Sutherland Papers, RG-30, reel 1002; Eichelberger to his wife, 5 May 1945, Eichelberger Papers, reel 47; Fuller to Krueger, 30 May 1944, Decker Papers, box 2; Eichelberger to Krueger, 10 and 21 November 1943, Decker Papers, box 2.

23 Chester Nimitz, 26 November 1942, *Command Summary of Fleet Admiral Chester W. Nimitz, USN (Graybook)*, vol. 2, accessed at http://www.ibiblio.org/anrs/docs/Volumes/Nimitz_Graybook%20Volume%202.pdf.; Edwin P. Hoyt, *The Glory of the Solomons* (New York: Stein and Day, 1983), 143, 319; John Costello, *The Pacific War* (New York: Quill, 1982), 412; Ronnie Day, *New Georgia: The Second Battle for the Solomons* (Bloomington, Indiana: Indiana University Press, 2016), 83; Bergerud, *Touched with Fire*, 230, 446; Rems, *South Pacific Cauldron*, 65. For after-the-fact concerns about the 43rd Division, see Collins, *Lightning Joe*, 168–69; Marshall to Robert Richardson, 5 August 1943, George Marshall Papers, Pentagon Office, George C. Marshall Foundation, box 82, folder 43; Halsey, *Halsey's Story*, 161.

24 William H. Arnold, interview by Warren R. Strumpe, 1975, *ASOOH*, 111.

25 Oscar Griswold diary, 12 July 1943, Oscar Griswold Papers, USAHEC, box 1.

26 George Carroll Dyer, *The Amphibians Came to Conquer: The Story of Admiral Richmond Kelly Turner*, vol. 1 (Washington, D.C.: Department of the Navy, 1972), 586; John Miller, Jr., *Cartwheel: The Reduction of Rabaul* (Washington, D.C.: Center of Military History, 1959), 124. Arnold interview, *ASOOH*, 111; Griswold diary, 13 and 25 July 1943, Griswold Papers, box 1.

27 Lesley McNair to Marshall, 7 October 1941, Marshall Papers, Pentagon Office, box 76, folder 31.

28 Marshall, 28 September 1956, *Marshall Interviews*, 578; H. E. Gardiner, 18 March 1942, *1,271 Days a Soldier: The Diaries and Letters of Colonel H.E. Gardiner as an Armor Officer in World War II*, ed. Dominic J. Caraccilo (Dahlonega, Georgia: University of North Georgia Press, 2021), 25; Peter R. Mansoor, *The GI Offensive in Europe: The Triumph of American Infantry Divisions, 1941–1945* (Lawrence, Kansas: University Press of Kansas, 1999), 58–59; Brown, *Draftee Division*, 26.

29 Griswold diary, 6–25 August 1943, Griswold Papers, box 1.

30 Day, *New Georgia*, 201; Bergerud, *Touched with Fire*, 228–29; Brian Altobello, *Into the Shadows Furious: The Brutal Battle for New Georgia* (Novato, California: Presidio Press, 2000), 327; Collins, *Lightning Joe*, 166.

31 Marshall to Richardson, 5 August 1943, Marshall Papers, Pentagon Office, box 82, folder 43.

32 For some analyses of the 43rd Division's troubles on New Georgia, see Collins, *Lightning Joe*, 168–69; Halsey, *Halsey's Story*, 161; Arnold interview, *ASOOH*, 111; Hoyt, *Glory of the Solomons*, 143, 319; Costello, *Pacific War*, 412; Ronald H. Spector, *Eagle Against the Sun: The American War with Japan* (New York: The Free Press, 1985), 236; Bergerud, *Touched with Fire*, 230, 446; Rems, *South Pacific Cauldron*, 55; Altobello, *Into the Shadows*, 319.

33 Byers diary, 6 and 8 November 1943, Byers Collection, box 36, folder 1; Bergerud, *Touched with Fire*, 228; Rems, *South Pacific Cauldron*, 81.

34 Marshall to MacArthur, 20 December 1943, Douglas MacArthur Papers, War Department Correspondence, RG-4, reel 594.

35 Halsey, *Halsey's Story*, 140; Bergerud, *Touched with Fire*, 200, 228–29; Collins, *Lightning Joe*, 175–76; Rems, *South Pacific Cauldron*, 81; Eric Hammel, *Munda Trail: The New Georgia Campaign, July–August 1943* (Pacifica, California: Pacifica Military History, 1989), 129.

36 Cronin, *Southern Cross*, 119.

37 Griswold to Eichelberger, 28 April 1945, Eichelberger Papers, reel 46.

38 Marshall to Millard Harmon, 18 March 1944, *The Papers of George Catlett Marshall*, vol. 4, ed. Larry I. Bland (Baltimore, Maryland: John Hopkins University Press, 1981), 355; Harry A. Gailey, *Bougainville, 1943–1945: The Forgotten Campaign* (Lexington, Kentucky: The University Press of Kentucky, 1991), 178–82.

39 Arnold interview, *ASOOH*, 125–26; Harmon to Marshall, 30 May 1944, Marshall Papers, Pentagon Office, box 70, folder 7; Rems, *South Pacific Cauldron*, 186, 188; Gailey, *Bougainville*, 178–82.

40 MacArthur to Marshall, 4 March 1945, MacArthur Papers, RG-4, reel 594.

41 Marshall to MacArthur, 9 August 1944 and 2 March 1945, MacArthur Papers, RG-4, reel 594; MacArthur to Marshall, 9 August 1944 and 4 March 1945, MacArthur Papers, RG-4, reel 594; Walter White to MacArthur, 8 March 1945, Sutherland Papers, RG-30, reel 1006; White to Franklin Roosevelt, 8 March 1945, Sutherland Papers, RG-30, reel 1006.

42 Eichelberger to his wife, 19 July 1945, Eichelberger Papers, reel 47.

43 Courtney Whitney, *MacArthur: His Rendezvous with History* (New York: Knopf, 1964), 107.

44 John E. Hull, *The Autobiography of General John Edwin Hull, 1895–1975* (M. Anderson, 1978), 104–105; John E. Hull, interview by James W. Wurman, 1974, *ASOOH*, section 6, 15–17.

45 James Collins, interview by Wade Hampton, n.d., *ASOOH*, section 2, 40.

46 The quote is from Frazier Hunt, *The Untold Story of Douglas MacArthur* (New York: Devin-Adair, 1954), 318. See also Marshall Memorandum for the Record, 3 March 1943, *Marshall Papers*, vol. 3, 578; William Chase, *Front Line General: The Commands of William C. Chase* (Houston, Texas: Pacesetter Press, 1975), 29–30, 41–42; Kenney, *Kenney Reports*, 359; James Collins interview, *ASOOH*, section 2, 39; Riegelman, *Caves of Biak*, 174; Thomas Handy, interview by Edward Knoff, Jr., Thomas Handy Papers, USAHEC, vol. 1, section 3, 28; Byers diary, 28 July 1943, Byers Collection, box 36, folder 1; "1st Cavalry Division," n.d., Fellers Papers, RG-44, box 1, folder 5; Daniel Barbey, *MacArthur's Amphibious Navy: Seventh Amphibious Force Operations, 1943–1945* (Annapolis, Maryland: United States Naval Institute, 1969), 145–46.

47 Krueger, 28 March 1944, Congratulatory and Other Messages, Krueger Papers, box 25.

48 Eichelberger, *Jungle Road*, 168; Walter Krueger, *From Down Under to Nippon: The Story of the Sixth Army in World War II* (Washington, D.C.: Combat Forces Press, 1953), 53; Miller, *Cartwheel*, 350; Hull interview, *ASOOH*, section 6, 15–17; MacArthur to Krueger, 20 March 1944, Sutherland Papers, RG-30, reel 1002; Rems, *South Pacific Cauldron*, 197; Gailey, *War in the Pacific*, 278; Kevin C. Holzimmer, *General Walter Krueger: Unsung Hero of the Pacific War* (Lawrence, Kansas: University Press of Kansas, 2007), 141.

Chapter 2

1   Eichelberger to his wife, 27 June 1945, Eichelberger Papers, reel 47.
2   Stetson Conn, Rose C. Engelman, and Byron Fairchild, *Guarding the United States and Its Outposts* (Washington, D.C.: Center of Military History, 2000), 277; Brian Garfield, *The Thousand-Mile War: World War II in Alaska and the Aleutians* (Garden City, New York: Doubleday, 1969), 253–54.
3   Marshall to Richardson, 5 August 1943, Marshall Papers, Pentagon Office, box 82, folder 43.
4   Memorandum for Ernest King, 29 July 1943, *Marshall Papers*, vol. 4, 73.
5   Richardson to Marshall, 12 August 1943, Marshall Papers, Pentagon Office, box 82, folder 43.
6   Robert Richardson diary, 24 October 1943, Robert Richardson Papers, USAHEC, box 1A.
7   Erskine interview, MCOHC, 320.
8   For various opinions about the 27th Division, see Smith and Finch, *Coral and Brass*, 118–19, 168–70; Erskine interview, MCOHC, 321; MacArthur to Marshall, 28 September 1943, MacArthur Papers, RG-4, reel 594; Sutherland to Marshall, 28 September 1943, Sutherland Papers, RG-30, reel 1005; Costello, *Pacific War*, 436; Memorandum for Ernest King, 29 July 1943, *Marshall Papers*, vol. 4, 73; Richardson to Marshall, 12 August 1943, Marshall Papers, Pentagon Office, box 82, folder 43.
9   Smith, *Coral and Brass*, 126.
10 For analysis of the 27th Division's performance, see Smith, *Coral and Brass*, 125–28; Thomas interview, MCOHC, 207; Omar Pfeiffer, interview by Lloyd Tatem, 1974, MCOHC, 249; S. L. A. Marshall, *Bringing Up the Rear: A Memoir*, ed. Cate Marshall (San Rafael, California: Presidio, 1979), 69–70; Costello, *Pacific War*, 436; Spector, *Eagle Against the Sun*, 267; Edwin P. Hoyt, *Storm Over the Gilberts: War in the Central Pacific, 1943* (New York: Mason/Charter Publishers, 1978), 116, 148; Gailey, *War in the Pacific*, 257.
11 Arthur Collins interview, *ASOOH*, 118.
12 Charles Corlett comments, 13 January 1948, Charles Corlett Papers, USAHEC, box 2.
13 Marshall, *Bringing Up the Rear*, 77–78.
14 Corlett Report, 13 January 1948, Corlett Papers, box 2.
15 Richardson, unpublished memoirs, Richardson Papers, box 1A, chapter 17, 12.
16 Marshall to Eisenhower, 17 February 1944, *Marshall Papers*, vol. 4, 306.
17 Charles Corlett, *Cowboy Pete: The Autobiography of Major General Charles H. Corlett*, ed. William Farrington (Santa Fe, New Mexico: Sleeping Fox Enterprises, 1974), 102; Richardson to Marshall, 9 February 1944, Marshall Papers, Pentagon Office, box 82, folder 43; John Hodge to Richardson, 2 November 1944, Marshall Papers, Pentagon Office, box 82, folder 47; Henry I. Shaw, Jr., Bernard C. Nalty, and Edwin T. Tumbladh, *Central Pacific Drive: History of U.S. Marine Corps Operations in World War II*, vol. 3 (Washington, D.C.: Government Printing Office, 1966), 179; Arthur Collins interview, *ASOOH*, 118; Spector, *Eagle Against the Sun*,

270–71; S. L. A. Marshall, *Island Victory* (Washington, D.C.: Infantry Journal, 1944), 194; McManus, *Island Infernos*, 54; Corlett, "Cowboy Pete" (unpublished manuscript), Corlett Papers, 209.

18   Smith, *Coral and Brass*, 146.

19   Erskine interview, MCOHC, 347.

20   Smith, *Coral and Brass*, 168.

21   Richardson, unpublished memoirs, Richardson Papers, box 1A, chapter 15, 10.

22   Smith, *Coral and Brass*, 168–70, 197–98; Dyer, *Amphibians Came to Conquer*, vol. 2, 929–30; Philip A. Crowl, *Campaign in the Marianas* (Washington, D.C.: Center of Military History, 1993), 41.

23   For the Marine perspective on the 27th Division's problems, see Smith, *Coral and Brass*, 170–71, 197–98; Erskine interview, MCOHC, 322–23; Louis Jones, interview by Thomas E. Donnelley, 1973, MCOHC, 134; John McQueen, interview by Benis M. Frank, 1973, MCOHC, 90; Vandegrift, *Once a Marine*, 263; Holland Smith to Vandegrift, 18 July 1944, Holland Smith Papers, Auburn University Libraries; Crowl, *Campaign in the Marianas*, 178–79.

24   Quoted in Crowl, *Campaign in the Marianas*, 258.

25   Smith, *Coral and Brass*, 176–77.

26   For a good discussion on this, see Crowl, *Campaign in the Marianas*, 191–201. See also Richardson diary, 26 June 1944, Richardson Papers, box 1A; Richardson, unpublished memoirs, box 1A, chapter 15, 11; Simon Buckner diary, 5, 17, 18, 19, 26 July 1944, Simon Buckner Papers, Dwight D. Eisenhower Library, part 2.

27   Dyer, *Amphibians Came to Conquer*, vol. 2, 928.

28   Quoted in Crowl, *Campaign in the Marianas*, 192.

29   "The Generals Smith," *Time*, 18 September 1944, 66–68.

30   The quote is from Edmund G. Love, *The 27th Division in World War II* (Washington, D.C.: Infantry Journal Press, 1949), 522. See also Love, *27th Division*, 289; Shaw, et al., *Central Pacific Drive*, vol. 3, 319; Crowl, *Campaign in the Marianas*, 192.

31   McQueen interview, MCOHC, 90.

32   For a strong defense of the 27th Division at Saipan, see Harry A. Gailey, *Howlin' Mad vs. the Army: Conflict in Command, Saipan 1944* (Novato, California: Presidio Press, 1986).

33   Smith, *Coral and Brass*, 197–98; McQueen interview, MCOHC, 90; Vandegrift, *Once a Marine*, 263; Dyer, *Amphibians Came to Conquer*, vol. 2, 928; Crowl, *Campaign in the Marianas*, 179, 195.

34   Alan Brooke, 24 June 1942, *War Diaries, 1939–1945: Field Marshal Lord Alanbrooke*, eds. Alex Danchev and Daniel Todman (Berkeley, California: University Press of California Press, 2001), 271.

35   Quoted in *Ours to Hold It High: The History of the 77th Infantry Division in World War II* (Washington, D.C.: Infantry Journal Press, 1947), 18.

36   Quoted in McManus, *Island Infernos*, 401.

37   Roscoe Woodruff manuscript, Roscoe Woodruff Papers, Dwight D. Eisenhower Library, box 1, 8, 10–12; Mark Clark diary, 16 July 1942, Mark Clark Diaries, The Citadel Archives and Museum, vol. 1, 26, accessed https://citadeldigitalarchives.omeka.net/collections/show/20; Marshall to Eichelberger, 28 June 1942, Marshall Papers, Pentagon Office, box 66, folder 41; *Ours to Hold It High*, 18, 21, 24; Eichelberger, *Jungle Road*, xxii.

38   *Ours to Hold It High*, 84.

39   Smith, *Coral and Brass*, 218.

40 John H. Chiles, interview by D. Clayton James, 1977, Harry S. Truman Library, 24; Mansoor, *GI Offensive in Europe*, 72–73; McManus, *Island Infernos*, 440; Paul Mueller to Hodges, 2 March 1943, Courtney Hodges Papers, Dwight D. Eisenhower Library, box 7; Eichelberger to his wife, 10 June 1945, Eichelberger Papers, reel 47; Richardson diary, 25 July and 7 August 1944, Richardson Papers, box 1A.
41 Quoted in McManus, *Island Infernos*, 458–59.
42 Oliver Smith, interview by Benis M. Frank, 1973 interview, MCOHC, 157.
43 For Marine views of the 81st Division on Peleliu, see Lewis Fields, interview by Thomas E. Donnelley, 1976, MCOHC, 125; Frederick Henderson, interview by Benis M. Frank, 1976, MCOHC, 365–66; Merwin Silverthorn, interview by Benis M. Frank, 1969, MCOHC, 319, 340. See also Bobby C. Blair and John Peter DeCioccio, *Victory at Peleliu: The 81st Infantry Division's Pacific Campaign* (Norman, Oklahoma: University of Oklahoma Press, 2011), 254.
44 Richardson to Marshall, 18 January 1945, Marshall Papers, Pentagon Office, box 82, folder 49.

Chapter 3

1 Quoted in Stephen R. Taaffe, *MacArthur's Jungle War: The 1944 New Guinea Campaign* (Lawrence, Kansas: University Press of Kansas, 1998), 31.
2 Eichelberger to Peterson (unsent), 21 August 1943, *Dear Miss Em*, 74; Marshall, 28 September 1956, *Marshall Interviews*, 578; Byers diary, 23 July, 31 October, 19 November 1943, Byers Collection, box 36, folder 1; Krueger to MacArthur, 19 June 1944, Sutherland Papers, RG-30, reel 1002; Coane to MacArthur, 29 June 1944, Sutherland Papers, RG-30, reel 1002; Eichelberger to his wife, 21 August 1943, Eichelberger Papers, reel 44; Eichelberger to his wife, 5 May 1945, Eichelberger Papers, reel 47; "41st Infantry Division," n.d., Fellers Papers, RG-44, box 1, folder 5.
3 Eichelberger to Krueger, 15 August 1943, Eichelberger Papers, reel 44.
4 Eichelberger to Peterson (unsent), 21 August 1943, *Dear Miss Em*, 74; Byers diary, 24 November 1943, Byers Collection, box 36, folder 1; Eichelberger to Krueger, 24 and 30 September 1943, Eichelberger Papers, reel 44; Eichelberger to his wife, 21 August 1943, Eichelberger Papers, reel 44; Eichelberger to his wife, 31 December 1945, Eichelberger Papers, reel 45; "24th Infantry Division," n.d., Fellers Papers, box 1, folder 5; Richardson diary, 27 July 1943, Richardson Papers, box 1A.
5 MacArthur, 24 April 1944, Congratulatory and Other Messages, Krueger Papers, box 25.
6 Eichelberger to his wife, 23 April and 2 May 1944, Eichelberger Papers, reel 45; Eichelberger to his wife, 3 August 1944, Eichelberger Papers, reel 46.
7 Eichelberger, *Jungle Road*, 168; Woodruff manuscript, Woodruff Papers, 58; Byers diary, 22 April 1942, Byers Collection, box 36, folder 1; Krueger to MacArthur, 2 July 1944, Sutherland Papers, RG-30, reel 1002; MacArthur to Krueger, 24 April 1944, Sutherland Papers, RG-30, reel 1002; Eichelberger to his wife, 23 April and 15 May 1944, Eichelberger Papers, reel 45.
8 Charles Hall to Krueger, 17 May 1944, Decker Papers, box 2.
9 Decker interview, *ASOOH*, section 2, 40–41; Bruce Palmer, Jr., interview by James E. Shelton and Edward P. Smith, 1975, *ASOOH*, 325–26, 339; Eichelberger to his wife, 5 August 1944, Eichelberger Papers, reel 46; Eichelberger to his wife, 20 June 1045, Eichelberger Papers, reel 47; Krueger to MacArthur, 2 July 1944, MacArthur Papers, RG-4, reel 593.
10 Krueger to MacArthur, 2 July 1944, MacArthur Papers, RG-4, reel 593.
11 Palmer interview, *ASOOH*, 326.

12 Krueger to MacArthur, 16 June 1944, Sutherland Papers, RG-30, reel 1002.

13 Riegelman, *Caves of Biak*, 139.

14 Decker interview, *ASOOH*, section 2, 22–23; Krueger to MacArthur, 5, 8, 16 June 1944, MacArthur Papers, RG-4, reel 593; MacArthur to Krueger, 14 June 1944, MacArthur Papers, RG-4, reel 593; MacArthur to Krueger, 5 June 1944, Sutherland Papers, RG-30, reel 1007; Fuller to Krueger, 30 May 1944, Decker Papers, box 2.

15 Eichelberger to his wife, 25 July 1944, Eichelberger Papers, reel 46.

16 Taaffe, *MacArthur's Jungle War*, 169–70.

17 Eichelberger to his wife, 29 July 1944, Eichelberger Papers, reel 46; Byers diary, 18 June 1944, Byers Collection, box 36, folder 1.

18 Eichelberger, 10 and 20 March 1945, *Dear Miss Em*, 232, 236; Eichelberger, *Jungle Road*, 244–45; Marshall, 28 September 1956, *Marshall Interviews*, 578; Byers diary, 20 October 1944, Byers Collection, box 36, folder 1; Decker interview, *ASOOH*, section 2, 40–41; William F. McCartney, *The Jungleers: A History of the 41st Infantry Division* (Washington, D.C.: Infantry Journal Press, 1948), preface; Eichelberger to his wife, 21 February and 14 March 1945, Eichelberger Papers, reel 46.

19 "32nd Infantry Division," n.d., Fellers Papers, RG-44, box 1, folder 5.

20 Gill, *Always a Commander*, 43, 45, 51–53; Byers diary, 22 March and 21 May 1943, Byers Collection, box 36, folder 1; Eichelberger to Krueger, 2 and 19 July, 15 August 1943, Eichelberger Papers, reel 44.

21 MacArthur to Krueger, 10 August 1944, Sutherland Papers, RG-30, reel 1002.

22 Julian Cunningham and Philip Hooper, interview by Robert R. Smith, 8 April 1947, Office of the Chief of Military History Collection, box 43 (temporary), 2.

23 Clyde Eddleman, interview by L.G. Smith and M.G. Swinder, 1975, *ASOOH*, section 5, 9–10; Decker interview, *ASOOH*, section 2, 40–41; Eichelberger to his wife, 9 August 1944, Eichelberger Papers, reel 46; Taaffe, *MacArthur's Jungle War*, 204; Bergerud, *Touched with Fire*, 225; Hall interview, 27 March 1947, Office of the Chief of Military History Collection, box 43 (temporary), 5; Hall to Krueger, 18 July 1944, Decker Papers, box 2.

24 Taaffe, *MacArthur's Jungle War*, 222.

Chapter 4

1 Byers diary, 22 November 1944, Byers Collection, box 36, folder 1; MacArthur to Marshall, 19 July 1944, MacArthur Papers, RG-4, reel 594; Paul Freeman, interview by John N. Ellis, 1973–74, *ASOOH*, section 1, 73; Eddleman interview, *ASOOH*, section 2, 30–31; Griswold diary, 28 February 1945, Griswold Papers, box 1.

2 Gill, *Always a Commander*, 75; Roscoe Woodruff reminiscences, D. Clayton James interviews, Mitchell Memorial Library, Mississippi State University, 4; Frederick Irving to Sutherland, 20 January 1945, Sutherland Papers, RG-30, reel 1003; Eichelberger to his wife, 21–22 November 1944 and 8 April 1945, Eichelberger Papers, reel 46.

3 Marshall, *Bringing Up the Rear*, 80.

4 Richardson to Marshall, 1 August 1944, Marshall Papers, Pentagon Office, box 82, folder 46.

5 Hodge to Richardson, 2 November 1944, Marshall Papers, Pentagon Office, box 82, folder 47; Richardson to Marshall, 18 January 1945, Marshall Papers, Pentagon Office, box 82, folder 49; M. Hamlin Cannon, *Leyte: The Return to the Philippines* (Washington, D.C.: Center of Military History, 1993), 244–48.

6 Eichelberger to his wife, 16 January 1945, Eichelberger Papers, reel 46.

7   MacArthur to Chester Nimitz, 17 September 1944, MacArthur Papers, RG-4, reel 589; Stanley L. Falk, *Decision at Leyte* (New York: W.W. Norton and Co., 1986), 97.

8   Quoted in Cannon, *Leyte*, 214.

9   Woodruff manuscript, Woodruff Papers, 57, 59; Gill, *Always a Commander*, 75; Byers diary, 22 November 1944, Byers Collection, box 36, folder 1; Irving to Sutherland, 20 January 1945, Sutherland Papers, RG-30, reel 1003; Eichelberger to his wife, 30 April 1945, Eichelberger Papers, reel 46; Eichelberger diary, 5 January 1945, Jay Luvaas Papers, USAHEC, box 10b, folder 10; Cannon, *Leyte*, 244–48.

10 Irving to Sutherland, 20 January 1945, Sutherland Papers, RG-30, reel 1003.

11 Eichelberger to his wife, 30 April 1945, Eichelberger Papers, reel 46.

12 Eichelberger to his wife, 8 April 1945, *Dear Miss Em*, 247; Woodruff manuscript, Woodruff Papers, 59; Gill, *Always a Commander*, 75; Woodruff reminiscences, 4, 6; Irving to Sutherland, 20 January 1945, Sutherland Papers, RG-30, reel 1003; Eichelberger to his wife, 8 April 1945, Eichelberger Papers, reel 46.

13 Krueger, *From Down Under*, 316; Byers diary, 21 September 1944, Byers Collection, box 36, folder 1; Eichelberger to his wife, 10 January, 18 February, and 30 April 1945, Eichelberger Papers, reel 46.

14 Hodge to Robertson, 2 November 1944, Marshall Papers, Pentagon Office, box 82, folder 47; MacArthur to Richardson, 29 October 1944, Sutherland Papers, RG-30, reel 1002.

15 Eichelberger to his wife, 30 December 1944, 31 January, 2 and 7 February, 10 March 1945, *Dear Miss Em*, 189, 207, 208, 212, 232; Krueger, *From Down Under*, 316; Brown, *Draftee Division*, 18; Edward M. Flanagan, Jr., *The Angels: A History of the 11th Airborne Division 1943–1946* (Washington, D.C.: Infantry Journal Press, 1948), 11, 66; Sixth Army, *Report of the Leyte Operation*, 62, accessed at http://collections.pvao.mil.ph/Collections/ BataanDiary/Box_1478/ReportontheLeyteOperation-SixthArmy.pdf; Eichelberger to his wife, 4 March 1945, Eichelberger Papers, reel 46; Eichelberger to his wife, 11 August 1945, Eichelberger Papers, reel 47.

16 Krueger, *From Down Under*, 177; Richardson to Marshall, 30 December 1944, Marshall Papers, Pentagon Office, box 82, folder 48; MacArthur to Nimitz, 17 September 1944, MacArthur Papers, RG-4, reel 589; Eddleman interview, *ASOOH*, section 5, 9–10; Andrew Bruce to his wife, 14 December 1944, Andrew Bruce Papers, USAHEC, box 2; McManus, *Island Infernos*, 535–36.

17 Eichelberger to his wife, 13–14 December 1944, Eichelberger Papers, reel 46.

18 Eichelberger, 16 and 26 December 1944, *Dear Miss Em*, 178, 185; Richardson to MacArthur, 30 December 1944, Marshall Papers, Pentagon Office, box 82, folder 48; Freeman interview, *ASOOH*, section 1, 72; Bruce to his wife, 14 December 1944, Bruce Papers, box 2.

19 Cronin, *Southern Cross*, 225.

20 Eichelberger, 12 December 1944, *Dear Miss Em*, 176–77.

21 Byers diary, 11 and 13 December 1944, Byers Collection, box 36, folder 1; Paul P. Rogers, *The Bitter Years: MacArthur and Sutherland* (New York: Praeger, 1990), 35.

22 The figures are from Cannon, *Leyte*, 368.

23 Hodge to Richardson, 2 November 1944, Marshall Papers, Pentagon Office, box 82, folder 47.

24 Eichelberger, 12 December 1944, *Dear Miss Em*, 176–77; Richardson to Marshall, 30 December 1944, Marshall Papers, Pentagon Office, box 82, folder 48; Richardson to Marshall, 18 January 1945, Marshall Papers, Pentagon Office, box 82, folder 49; Decker interview, *ASOOH*, section 2, 40–41; MacArthur to Richardson, 29 October 1944, Sutherland Papers, RG-30, reel 1002; McManus, *Island Infernos*, 535–36; Holzimmer, *General Walter Krueger*, 203–204.

25 Quoted in McManus, *Island Infernos*, 535–36.

26 Eichelberger, 12 December 1944, *Dear Miss Em*, 176–77; Eichelberger to his wife, 16 and 26 December 1944, *Dear Miss Em*, 178, 185; Krueger, *From Down Under*, 177; Byers diary, 1 January 1945, Byers Collection, box 36, folder 1; Richardson to Marshall, 30 December 1944, Marshall Papers, Pentagon Office, box 82, folder 48; Richardson to Marshall, 18 January 1945, Marshall Papers, Pentagon Office, box 82, folder 49; Freeman interview, *ASOOH*, section 1, 72; Eddleman interview, *ASOOH*, section 5, 9–10; Bruce to his wife, 14 December 1944, Bruce Papers, box 2.

27 Hodge to Richardson, 2 November 1944, Marshall Papers, Pentagon Office, box 82, folder 47.

28 Richardson to Marshall, 30 December 1944, Marshall Papers, Pentagon Office, box 82, folder 48; Richardson to Marshall, 18 January 1945, Marshall Papers, Pentagon Office, box 82, folder 49; Byers diary, 26 December 1944, Byers Collection, box 36, folder 1.

29 Eichelberger to his wife, 26 December 1944, Eichelberger Papers, reel 46.

30 Eichelberger to his wife, 30 December 1944, *Dear Miss Em*, 189; Joseph Swing to Peyton March, 30 December 1944, *Dear General: World War II Letters*, ed. Dale F. Yee (Palo Alto, California: 11th Airborne Division Association, 1987), 15; Decker interview, *ASOOH*, section 2, 40–41; Eichelberger diary, 11 August 1945, Luvaas Papers, box 10b, folder 10.

31 Bertram C. Wright, *The 1st Cavalry Division in World War Two* (Paducah, Kentucky: Turner Publishing Co., 2000), 99.

32 Byers diary, 22 November and 29 December 1944, Byers Collection, box 36, folder 1; Irving to Sutherland, 20 January 1945, Sutherland Papers, RG-30, reel 1003.

33 Eichelberger to his wife, 8 April 1945, *Dear Miss Em*, 247; Eichelberger to his wife, 30 April 1945, Eichelberger Papers, reel 46; Woodruff manuscript, Woodruff Papers, 59; Cannon, *Leyte*, 244–48.

34 Eichelberger to his wife, 12 and 16 December 1944, *Dear Miss Em*, 176–78; Byers diary, 11 December 1944, Byers Collection, box 36, folder 1; Rogers, *Bitter Years*, 35; Gill, *Always a Commander*, 106.

35 Hall to Krueger, 24 July 1944, Decker Papers, box 2.

36 Byers diary, 6 November 1943, Byers Collection, box 36, folder 1; John Kennedy Ohl, *Minuteman; The Military Career of General Robert S. Beightler* (Boulder, Colorado: Lynne Rienner Publishers, 2001), 140–41.

37 Roger Egeberg, *The General: MacArthur and the Man He Called "Doc"* (New York: Hippocrene Books, 1983), 114–15.

38 Griswold diary, 14 January 1945, Griswold Papers, box 1.

39 United States Army, *40th Infantry Division* (Baton Rouge, Louisiana: Army and Navy Publications Co. 1946), 111.

40 Eichelberger to his wife, 25 March and 18 April 1945, Eichelberger Papers, reel 46; Eichelberger to his wife, 8 and 15 June 1945, Eichelberger Papers, reel 47; Griswold diary, 9 February 1945, Griswold Papers, box 1.

41 Eichelberger, *Jungle Road*, 192.

42 Eichelberger, 4 March 1945, *Dear Miss Em*, 230; Swing to March, 21 and 24 February 1945, *Dear General*, 18–19; Willoughby to Eichelberger, 4 March 1945, Eichelberger Papers, reel 46.

43 Quoted in Costello, *Pacific War*, 532.

44 Krueger, *From Down Under*, 316.

45 Eichelberger to his wife, 18 February 1945, Eichelberger Papers, reel 46.

46 Krueger to MacArthur, 15 January 1945, Sutherland Papers, RG-30, reel 1002.

47 B. David Mann, *Avenging Bataan: The Battle of ZigZag Pass* (Raleigh North Carolina: Pentland Press, 2001), 159.

48 United States Army, *38th Infantry Division: "Avengers of Bataan," Luzon Campaign, Battle Pictures, Overseas Pictorial, Division Roster* (n.p. 1947), 15. See also William Jenna to Sutherland, 11 February 1945, Sutherland Papers, RG-30, reel 1003.

49 Hall to Krueger, 4 February 1945, Decker Papers, box 2.

50 Hall to Krueger, 6 February 1945, Decker Papers, box 2. See also Hall to Krueger, 3, 4, and 5 February 1945, Decker Papers, box 2.

51 Chase, *Front Line General*, 102.

52 Chase, *Front Line General*, 102.

53 Quoted in Clyde Eddleman, *Combat Notes*, vol. 10 (Fort Leavenworth, Kansas: Command and General Staff School, 1945), 60, accessed at https://cgsc.contentdm.oclc.org/digital/collection/p4013coll8/id/4662/rec/114.

54 Chase, *Front Line General*, 99–103, 109.

55 Griswold diary, 7 February 1945, Griswold Papers, box 1.

56 Griswold diary, 10 February 1945, Griswold Papers, box 1.

57 Byers diary, 1 March 1945, Byers Collection, box 36, folder 1; Eichelberger, *Jungle Road*, 254; Eichelberger to his wife, 6 July 1945, *Dear Miss Em*, 290; Griswold diary, 23 February 1945, Griswold Papers, box 1.

58 Karolevitz, *25th Division in World War 2*, 108.

59 Eichelberger to his wife, 21 February, Eichelberger Papers, reel 46; Eichelberger to his wife, 5 May 1945, Eichelberger Papers, reel 47; Byers diary, 20 October 1944, Byers Collection, box 36, folder 1.

60 Eichelberger to his wife, 10 March 1945, *Dear Miss Em*, 232; Eichelberger, *Jungle Road*, 244–45; Eichelberger to his wife, 10 and 14 March 1945, Eichelberger Papers, reel 46.

61 Eichelberger to his wife, 25 March 1945, *Dear Miss Em*, 238.

62 Byers diary, 29 October 1944 and 1 March 1945, Byers Collection, box 36, folder 1; Eichelberger to his wife, 12 March 1945, Eichelberger Papers, reel 46.

63 Eichelberger to his wife, 15 June, Eichelberger Papers, reel 46.

64 Eichelberger, *Jungle Road*, 208; Eichelberger to his wife, 25 and 29 March, 2, 8, 20, 21, 30 April 1945, Eichelberger Papers, reel 46.

65 Griswold to Eichelberger, 28 April 1945, Eichelberger Papers, reel 46; Eichelberger diary, 8 April 1945, Luvaas Papers, box 10b, folder 10.

66 Eichelberger diary, 20 April 1945, Luvaas Papers, box 10b, folder 10.

67 The quote is from Cronin, *Southern Cross*, 343. See also Robert Ross Smith, *Triumph in the Philippines* (Washington, D.C.: Center of Military History, 1993), 617; Eichelberger, 25 March 1945, *Dear Miss Em*, 239–40; Arnold interview, *ASOOH*, 158, 165–66; Eichelberger to his wife, 28 and 29 March 1945, Eichelberger Papers, reel 46; Eichelberger to his wife, 22 and 31 May 1945, Eichelberger Papers, reel 47; Eichelberger diary, 6 June 1945, Luvaas Papers, box 10b, folder 10.

68 Eichelberger to his wife, 7 March and 8 May 1945, Eichelberger Papers, reel 46.

69 United States Army, *History of the 31st Infantry Division in Training and Combat, 1940–1945* (Nashville, Tennessee: Battery Press, 1993), 18.

70 Byers diary, 18 October 1944, Byers Collection, box 36, folder 1.

71 For various impressions of the 31st Division, see United States Army, *31st Infantry Division*, 19, 30, 31, 32; Hall to Krueger, 28 July 1944, Decker Papers, box 2.

72 Woodruff manuscript, Woodruff Papers, 79.
73 Eichelberger to his wife, 26 April 1945, Eichelberger Papers, reel 46; Eichelberger to his wife, 1, 3 and 19 May, 20 and 27 June 1945, Eichelberger Papers, reel 47.
74 United States Army, *31st Infantry Division*, 30.
75 Smith, *Triumph*, 377.
76 Smith, *Triumph*, 387.
77 Stanley Frankel, *The 37th Infantry Division in World War II* (Washington, D.C.: Infantry Journal Press, 1948), 354.
78 Division Public Relations Section, *The 6th Infantry Division in World War II, 1939–1945* (Washington, D.C.: Infantry Journal Press, 1947), 122.
79 Eddleman, *Combat Notes*, vol. 10, 29.
80 Eichelberger to his wife, 10 July 1945, *Dear Miss Em*, 291.
81 United States Army, *38th Infantry Division*, 49.
82 Krueger, *From Down Under*, 316; Byers diary, 11 July 1945, Byers Collection, box 36, folder 1.
83 Smith, *Triumph*, 504.
84 Arthur Collins interview, *ASOOH*, 90–91.
85 Byers diary, 29 October 1944 and 9 January 1945, Byers Collection, box 36, folder 1; Arthur Collins interview, *ASOOH*, 88–89; *33rd Infantry Division: The Golden Cross Division* (Paducah, Kentucky: Turner Broadcasting Co., 1996), 16, 20.
86 Quoted in Harold Blakely, *The 32nd Infantry Division in World War II* (Madison, Wisconsin: Combat Forces Press, 1957), 220.
87 Quoted in Smith, *Triumph*, 503.
88 Krueger, *From Down Under*, 307.
89 Krueger, *From Down Under*, 316; Gill, *Always a Commander*, 84; William Gill interview, William Gill Papers, USAHEC, box 1, folder 9, 1–2.
90 Eddleman, *Combat Notes*, vol. 10, 3.
91 Bergerud, *Touched with Fire*, 182.
92 Eichelberger to his wife, 24 July 1945, Eichelberger Papers, reel 47.
93 Eichelberger, *Jungle Road*, 254; Eichelberger to his wife, 30 June, 6 and 10 July 1945, *Dear Miss Em*, 286, 290, 291; Eichelberger to his wife, 27 June, 7 and 20 July 1945, Eichelberger Papers, reel 47; Byers diary, 7 July 1945, Byers Collection, box 36, folder 1; Ohl, *Minuteman*, 140–41.
94 Percy Clarkson to Richardson, 29 April 1945, Marshall Papers, Pentagon Office, box 82, folder 49.

Chapter 5

1 Richardson to Marshall, 18 January 1945, Marshall Papers, Pentagon Office, box 82, folder 49.
2 Oliver Smith interview, MCOHC, 158–59.
3 Oliver Smith interview, MCOHC, 157.
4 Oliver Smith interview, MCOHC, 157; Richardson to Marshall, 21 November 1944, Marshall Papers, Pentagon Office, box 82, folder 47; James and William Belote, *Typhoon of Steel: The Battle for Okinawa* (New York: Harper and Row, 1970), 193; Love, *27th Division*, 520.
5 Quoted in E. B. Potter, *Nimitz* (Annapolis, Maryland: Naval Institute Press, 1976), 375.

6   Roy E. Appleman, James M. Burnes, Russell A. Gugeler, and John Stevens, *Okinawa: The Last Battle* (Washington, D.C.: Center of Military History, 1993), 175–76.

7   Appleman, et al., *Okinawa*, 181.

8   Oliver Smith interview, MCOHC, 168–69.

9   Richardson to Marshall, 5 July 1945, Marshall Papers, Pentagon Office, box 82, folder 52.

10 Buckner, 20, 21, 22, 29 April 1945, *Seven Stars: The Okinawa Battle Diaries of Simon Bolivar Buckner, Jr., and Joseph Stilwell*, ed. Nicholas Evan Sarantakes (College Station, Texas: Texas A&M University Press, 2004), 42, 43, 49; Oliver Smith interview, MCOHC, 159, 168–69; August Larson, interview by Thomas E. Donnelley, 1975, MCOHC, 83; Lemuel Shepherd, interview by Benis M. Frank and Robert D. Heinl, Jr., 1966–67, MCOHC, 107–108; Richardson, unpublished memoirs, box 1A, chapter 20, 9.

11 Buckner to his wife, 8, 10, 14 April, 3 May 1945, *Seven Stars*, 35, 36, 38–39, 51; Buckner, 19 April and 2 May 1945, *Seven Stars*, 42, 50; Appleman, et al., *Okinawa*, 265; Belote, *Typhoon of Steel*, 133, 212.

12 *Ours to Hold It High*, 346.

13 Stilwell, 5 June 1945, *Seven Stars*, 73.

14 Buckner, 3 May 1945, *Seven Stars*, 50; Joseph Stilwell, 5 June 1945, *Seven Stars*, 75; Oliver Smith interview, MCOHC, 159, 164; Larson interview, MCOHC, 83; Appleman, et al., *Okinawa*, 386; Belote, *Typhoon of Steel*, 244.

15 Buckner, 13 and 30 May 1945, *Seven Stars*, 56, 65; Oliver Smith interview, MCOHC, 159; Richardson to Marshall, 5 July 1945, Marshall Papers, Pentagon Office, box 82, folder 52.

Bibliography

Archival Sources

Auburn University Libraries, Auburn, Alabama
Holland Smith Papers

BACM Research/PaperlessArchives.com
After Action Reports Archive: American Military 1770 to 1975
After Action Reports Archive: World War II Archive

Duke University, Perkins Library, Durham, North Carolina
Robert L. Eichelberger Papers

Dwight D. Eisenhower Library, Abilene, Kansas
Papers of
   Simon Buckner
   Courtney Hodges
   Roscoe Woodruff

Hoover Institution, Stanford University, Palo Alto, California
Clovis Byers Collection, Charles Corlett Manuscript

The Citadel Archives and Museum, Charleston, South Carolina
Mark Clark Diaries at https://citadeldigitalarchives.omeka.net/collections/show/20

Douglas MacArthur Memorial Archives and Library, Norfolk, Virginia
Papers of
   Bonner Fellers
   Douglas MacArthur
   Richard Sutherland

Marine Corps History Division, Marine Corps University, Quantico, Virginia

Oral Histories of
Graves Erskine
Lewis Fields
Frederick Henderson
Louis Jones
Victor Krulak
August Larson
Robert Luckey
John McQueen
Omar Pfeiffer
Lemuel Shepherd
Merwin Silverthorn
Oliver Smith
Gerald Thomas
Ralph Wismer

George C. Marshall Foundation, Lexington, Virginia

Papers of George C. Marshall

Mitchell Memorial Library, Mississippi State University, Starkville, Mississippi

D. Clayton James's Interviews
Oral Reminiscences of Roscoe Woodruff

Harry S. Truman Library and Museum, Independence, Missouri

Oral History of John H. Chiles

United States Army Heritage and Education Center, Carlisle, Pennsylvania

Papers of
William Arnold
Andrew Bruce
J. Lawton Collins
Charles Corlett
George Decker
Clyde Eddleman
William Gill
Oscar Griswold
Walter Krueger
Thomas Handy
Jay Luvaas
Sidney Matthews
Robert Richardson
Joseph Swing
Albert Wedemeyer

Office of the Chief of Military History Files
Senior Officers Oral History Program Interviews with Clyde Eddleman

United States Military Academy, West Point, New York

Papers of Walter Krueger

Primary Sources

Alexander, Harold, 1st Earl Alexander. *The Alexander Memoirs, 1940–1945*. Ed. John North. New York: McGraw-Hill Book Co., 1962.

Armed Forces Oral Histories: Army Senior Officer Oral Histories. Frederick, Maryland: University Publications of America, 1989.

Barbey, Daniel. *MacArthur's Amphibious Navy: Seventh Amphibious Force Operations, 1943–1945*. Annapolis, Maryland: United States Naval Institute, 1969.

Bradley, Omar N. *A Soldier's Story*. New York: Henry Holt and Co., 1951.

Brooke, Alan. *War Diaries, 1939–1945: Field Marshal Lord Alanbrooke*. Eds. Alex Danchev and Daniel Todman. Berkeley, California: University of California Press, 2001.

Casey, Hugh J. *Engineer Memoirs: Major General Hugh J. Casey, U.S. Army*. Washington, D.C.: Office of Engineers, 1993.

Chase, William. *Front Line General: The Commands of William C. Chase*. Houston, Texas: Pacesetter Press, 1975.

Collins, J. Lawton. *Lightning Joe: An Autobiography*. Baton Rouge, Louisiana: Louisiana State University Press, 1979.

Corlett, Charles. *Cowboy Pete: The Autobiography of Major General Charles H. Corlett*. Ed. William Farrington. Santa Fe, New Mexico: Sleeping Fox Enterprises, 1974.

Eddleman, Clyde. *Combat Notes*, vol. 10. Fort Leavenworth, Kansas: Command and General Staff School, 1945. Accessed April 10, 2024 at https://cgsc.contentdm.oclc.org/digital/collection/p4013coll8/id/4662/rec/114.

Egeberg, Roger. *The General: MacArthur and the Man He Called "Doc."* New York: Hippocrene Books, 1983.

Eichelberger, Robert L. *Dear Miss Em: General Eichelberger's War in the Pacific, 1942–1945*. Ed. Jay Luvaas. Westport, Connecticut: Greenwood Press, 1972.

Eichelberger, Robert L., with Milton MacKaye. *Our Jungle Road to Tokyo*. New York: Viking Press, 1949.

Eisenhower, Dwight. *At Ease: Stories I Tell to Friends*. Garden City, New York: Doubleday and Co., 1967.

Eisenhower, Dwight. *The Papers of Dwight David Eisenhower: The War Years*, vols. 1–4. Ed. Alfred D. Chandler, Jr. Baltimore, Maryland: The Johns Hopkins Press, 1970.

Gardiner, H. E. *1,271 Days a Soldier: The Diaries and Letters of Colonel H.E. Gardiner as an Armor Officer in World War II*. Ed. Dominic J. Caraccilo. Dahlonega, Georgia: University of North Georgia Press, 2021.

Gill, William H., as told to Edward Jaquelin Smith. *Always a Commander: The Reminiscences of Major General William H. Gill*. Colorado Springs, Colorado: The Colorado College, 1974.

Halsey, William F. and J. Bryan III. *Admiral Halsey's Story*. New York: McGraw-Hill Book Co., 1947.

Hull, John E. *The Autobiography of General John Edwin Hull, 1895–1975*. M. Anderson, 1978.

Hunt, Frazier. *The Untold Story of Douglas MacArthur*. New York: Devin-Adair, 1954.

Kenney, George C. *General Kenney Reports: A Personal History of the Pacific War.* Dayton, Ohio: Air Force History and Museums Program, 1997.

Krueger, Walter. *From Down Under to Nippon: The Story of the Sixth Army in World War II.* Washington, D.C.: Combat Forces Press, 1953.

MacArthur, Douglas. *Reminiscences.* New York: McGraw-Hill Co., 1964.

Marshall, George. *Biennial Reports of the Chief of Staff of the United States Army to the Secretary of War, 1 June 1939–30 June 1945.* Washington, D.C.: Center of Military History, 1996.

Marshall, George. *George C. Marshall Interviews and Reminiscences for Forrest C. Pogue.* Ed. Larry I. Bland. Lexington, Virginia: George C. Marshall Research Foundation, 1991.

Marshall, George. *The Papers of George Catlett Marshall,* vols. 2–5. Ed. Larry I. Bland. Baltimore, Maryland: The Johns Hopkins Press, 1986–2003.

Marshall, S. L. A. *Bringing Up the Rear: A Memoir.* Ed. Cate Marshall. San Rafael, California: Presidio, 1979.

Marshall, S. L. A. *Island Victory.* Washington, D.C.: Infantry Journal, 1944.

Nimitz, Chester. *Command Summary of Fleet Admiral Chester W. Nimitz, USN* (Graybook), vols. 1–8. Accessed April 10, 2024 at http://www.ibiblio.org/anrs/docs/Volumes/Nimitz_Graybook%20 Volume%202.pdf.

Patton, George. *War as I Knew It.* Boston: Houghton Mifflin Co., 1947.

Pyle, Ernie. *Brave Men.* New York: Grosset and Dunlap, 1944.

Riegelman, Harold. *Caves of Biak: An American Officer's Experiences in the Southwest Pacific.* New York: The Dial Press, 1955.

Rogers, Paul P. *The Bitter Years: MacArthur and Sutherland.* New York: Praeger, 1990.

Rogers, Paul P. *The Good Years: MacArthur and Sutherland.* New York: Praeger, 1990.

Sarantakes, Nicholas Evan, ed. *Seven Stars: The Okinawa Battle Diaries of Simon Bolivar Buckner, Jr., and Joseph Stilwell.* College Station, Texas: Texas A&M University Press, 2004.

Sixth Army. *Report of the Leyte Operation.* Accessed at https://cgsc.contentdm.oclc.org/digital/ collection/p4013coll8/id/3170/.

Smith, Holland M. and Percy Finch. *Coral and Brass.* New York: Charles Scribner's Sons, 1949.

Twining, Merrill B. *No Bended Knee: The Battle for Guadalcanal.* New York: Ballantine Books, 2004.

Vandegrift, Alexander Archer, as told to Robert B. Asprey. *Once a Marine: The Memoirs of General A. A. Vandegrift, United States Marine Corps.* New York: Ballantine Books, 1964.

Verblank, William J. *The Story of a Regiment in Action.* Accessed April 10, 2024 at https://cgsc. contentdm.oclc.org/digital/collection/p4013coll8/id/3311/rec/1.

Walker, Fred L. *From Texas to Rome: A General's Journal.* El Dorado Hills, California: Savas Beatie, 2021.

Wedemeyer, Albert C. *Wedemeyer Reports!* New York: Henry Holt and Co., 1958.

Whitney, Courtney. *MacArthur: His Rendezvous with History.* New York: Knopf, 1964.

Yee, Dale F., ed. *Dear General: World War II Letters.* Palo Alto, California: 11th Airborne Division Association, 1987.

Secondary Sources

Altobello, Brian. *Into the Shadows Furious: The Brutal Battle for New Georgia.* Novato, California: Presidio Press, 2000.

Appleman, Roy E., James M. Burns, Russell A. Gugeler, and John Stevens. *Okinawa: The Last Battle.* Washington, D.C.: Center of Military History, 1993.

Belote, James and William. *Typhoon of Steel: The Battle for Okinawa.* New York: Harper and Row, 1970.

Bergerud, Eric. *Touched with Fire: The Land War in the South Pacific.* New York: Viking, 1996.

Blair, Bobby C. and John Peter DeCioccio. *Victory at Peleliu: The 81st Infantry Division's Pacific Campaign.* Norman, Oklahoma: University of Oklahoma Press, 2011.

Bonn, Keith E. *When the Odds Were Even: The Vosges Mountains Campaign, October 1944–January 1945.* Novato, California: Presidio Press, 1994.

Breuer, William B. *Retaking the Philippines: America's Return to Corregidor and Bataan, October 1944–March 1945.* New York: St. Martin's Press, 1986.

Brown, John Sloan. *Draftee Division: The 88th Infantry Division in World War II.* Lexington, Kentucky: The University Press of Kentucky, 1986.

Cannon, M. Hamlin. *Leyte: The Return to the Philippines.* Washington, D.C.: Center of Military History, 1993.

Combat Divisions of World War II. Washington, D.C.: Army Times, 1950.

Conn, Stetson, Rose C. Engelman, and Byron Fairchild. *Guarding the United States and Its Outposts.* Washington, D.C.: Center of Military History, 2000.

Costello, John. *The Pacific War.* New York: Quill, 1982.

Crowl, Philip A. *Campaign in the Marianas.* Washington, D.C.: Center of Military History, 1993.

Crowl, Philip A. and Edmund G. Love. *Seizure of the Gilberts and Marshalls.* Washington, D.C.: Center of Military History, 1993.

Day, Ronnie. *New Georgia: The Second Battle for the Solomons.* Bloomington, Indiana: Indiana University Press, 2016.

Drea, Edward J. *Defending the Driniumor: Covering Force Operations in New Guinea, 1944.* Fort Leavenworth, Kansas: Combat Studies Institute, 1984.

Duffy, James P. *Return to Victory: MacArthur's Epic Liberation of the Philippines.* New York: Hachette Books, 2021.

Dyer, George Carroll. *The Amphibians Came to Conquer: The Story of Admiral Richmond Kelly Turner.* 2 vols. Washington, D.C.: Department of the Navy, 1972.

Falk, Stanley L. *Liberation of the Philippines.* New York: Ballantine Books, 1971.

Falk, Stanley L. *Decision at Leyte.* New York: W.W. Norton and Co., 1986.

Frank, Benis M. *Okinawa: The Great Island Battle.* New York: Elsevier-Dutton, 1978.

Frank, Richard B. *Guadalcanal.* New York: Random House, 1990.

Gailey, Harry A. *Peleliu, 1944.* Annapolis, Maryland: The Nautical & Aviation Publishing Company of America, 1983.

Gailey, Harry A. *Howlin' Mad vs. the Army: Conflict in Command, Saipan 1944.* Novato, California: Presidio Press, 1986.

Gailey, Harry A. *Bougainville, 1943–1945: The Forgotten Campaign.* Lexington, Kentucky: The University Press of Kentucky, 1991.

Gailey, Harry A. *The War in the Pacific: From Pearl Harbor to Tokyo Bay.* Novato, California: Presidio, 1995.

Garfield, Brian. *The Thousand-Mile War: World War II in Alaska and the Aleutians.* Garden City, New York: Doubleday, 1969.

Greenfield, Kent Roberts, Robert E. Palmer, and Bell I. Wiley. *The Organization of Ground Combat Troops.* Washington, D.C.: Center of Military History, United States Army, 1987.

Griffith, Samuel B., Jr. *The Battle for Guadalcanal.* New York: J.B. Lippincott Co., 1963.

Hammel, Eric. *Munda Trail: The New Georgia Campaign, July–August 1943.* Pacifica, California: Pacifica Military History, 1989.

Holzimmer, Kevin C. *General Walter Krueger: Unsung Hero of the Pacific War.* Lawrence, Kansas: University Press of Kansas, 2007.

Hoyt, Edwin P. *Storm Over the Gilberts: War in the Central Pacific, 1943.* New York: Mason/Charter Publishers, 1978.

Hoyt, Edwin P. *The Glory of the Solomons.* New York: Stein and Day, 1983.

Luvaas, Jay. "Buna, 19 November 1942–2 January 1943: A 'Leavenworth Nightmare.'" In *America's First Battles, 1776–1965.* Ed. Charles E. Heller and William A. Stofft. Lawrence, Kansas: University Press of Kansas, 1986.

Mann, B. David. *Avenging Bataan: The Battle of ZigZag Press.* Raleigh, North Carolina: Pentland Press, 2001.

Mansoor, Peter R. *The GI Offensive in Europe: The Triumph of American Infantry Divisions, 1941–1945.* Lawrence, Kansas: University Press of Kansas, 1999.

Mayo, Lida. *Bloody Buna.* Garden City, New York: Doubleday and Co., 1974.

McManus, John C. *Island Infernos: The U.S. Army's Pacific War Odyssey, 1944.* New York: Caliber, 2021.

McManus, John C. *To the End of the Earth: The U.S. Army and the Downfall of Japan, 1945.* New York: Caliber, 2023.

Miller, John, Jr. *Cartwheel: The Reduction of Rabaul.* Washington, D.C.: Center of Military History, 1959.

Miller, John, Jr. *Guadalcanal: The First Offensive.* Washington, D.C.: Center of Military History, 1995.

Milner, Samuel. *Victory in Papua.* Washington, D.C.: Center of Military History, 1989.

Ohl, John Kennedy. *Minuteman: The Military Career of General Robert S. Beightler.* Boulder, Colorado: Lynne Rienner Publishers, 2001.

Potter, E. B. *Nimitz.* Annapolis, Maryland: Naval Institute Press, 1976.

Prefer, Nathan H. *Leyte, 1944: The Soldiers' Battle.* Havertown, Pennsylvania: Casemate Publishers, 2012.

Rems, Alan. *South Pacific Cauldron: World War II's Great Forgotten Battlegrounds.* Annapolis, Maryland: Naval Institute Press, 2014.

Shaw, Henry I., Jr., Bernard C. Nalty, and Edwin T. Tumbladh. *Central Pacific Drive: History of U.S. Marine Corps Operations in World War II,* vol. 3. Washington, D.C.: Government Printing Office, 1966.

Skates, John R. *The Invasion of Japan: Alternative to the Bomb.* Columbia, South Carolina: University of South Carolina Press, 1994.

Smith, Robert Ross. *Triumph in the Philippines.* Washington, D.C.: Center of Military History, 1993.

Smith, Robert Ross. *Approach to the Philippines.* Washington, D.C.: Center of Military History, 1996.

Spector, Ronald H. *Eagle Against the Sun: The American War with Japan.* New York: The Free Press, 1985.

Taaffe, Stephen R. *MacArthur's Jungle War: The 1944 New Guinea Campaign.* Lawrence, Kansas: University Press of Kansas, 1998.

Weigley, Russell F. *Eisenhower's Lieutenants: The Campaign of France and Germany, 1944–1945.* Bloomington, Indiana: Indiana University Press, 1981.

Wyant, William K. *Sandy Patch: A Biography of Lt. Gen. Alexander M. Patch.* New York: Praeger, 1991.

Young, Gordon R. ed. *The Army Almanac: A Book of Facts Concerning the Army of the United States.* Washington, D.C.: Government Printing Office, 1950.

Unit Histories

Arthur, Anthony. *Bushmasters: America's Jungle Warriors of World War II*. New York: St. Martin's Press, 1987.

Blakeley, Harold. *The 32nd Infantry Division in World War II*. Madison, Wisconsin: Combat Forces Press, 1957.

Cronin, Francis D. *Under the Southern Cross: The Saga of the Americal Division*. Washington, D.C.: Combat Forces Press, 1951.

Daly, Edward L. *33rd Infantry Division: The Golden Cross Division*. Paducah, Kentucky: Turner Broadcasting Co., 1996.

Division Public Relations Section. *The 6th Infantry Division in World War II, 1939–1945*. Washington, D.C.: Infantry Journal Press, 1947.

Flanagan, Edward M., Jr. *The Angels: A History of the 11th Airborne Division 1943–1946*. Washington, D.C.: Infantry Journal Press, 1948.

Frankel, Stanley. *The 37th Infantry Division in World War II*. Washington, D.C.: Infantry Journal Press, 1948.

Karolevitz, Robert F., ed. *The 25th Division in World War 2*. Baton Rouge, Louisiana: Army and Navy Publishing Co., 1946.

Love, Edmund G. *The 27th Infantry Division in World War II*. Washington, D.C.: Infantry Journal Press, 1949.

McCartney, William F. *The Jungleers: A History of the 41st Infantry Division*. Washington, D.C.: Infantry Journal Press, 1948.

United States Army. *38th Infantry Division: "Avengers of Bataan," Luzon Campaign, Battle Pictures, Overseas Pictorial, Division Roster*. n.p., 1947.

United States Army. *40th Infantry Division*. Baton Rouge, Louisiana: Army and Navy Publications Co., 1946.

United States Army. *History of the 31st Infantry Division in Training and Combat, 1940–1945*. Nashville, Tennessee: Battery Press, 1993.

United States Army Infantry Division. 77th. *Ours to Hold It High: The History of the 77th Infantry Division in World War II*. Washington, D.C.: Infantry Journal Press, 1947.

Wright, Bertram C. *The 1st Cavalry Division in World War Two*. Paducah, Kentucky: Turner Publishing Co., 2000.

Index

Abuyog, Leyte, 112
Adachi, Hatazo, 97, 98
Admiralty Islands
    background, 36–40
    fighting on, 40–41
    geography and terrain, 38
    results, 41
Agat, Guam, 70
Aislito Airfield, Saipan, 64
Aitape, New Guinea, 84, 85, 86, 88, 96, 97,
    98, 100, 101
Aleutian Islands, 49–52
    geography and terrain, 48
Angat River, Luzon, 144
Angaur, Palau Islands, 73–74
Aparri, Luzon, 152
Army, United States
    relationship with Marine Corps, 8, 46, 47,
        66–67, 72, 78, 157
    relationship with navy, 4
Arnold, Archibald, 110, 115, 120, 157, 160,
    161, 164, 173, 178
Arnold, Henry, 4
Arnold, William, 140, 187
Arundel Island, 27
Asan, Guam, 70
Atolls, 47
Attu, Aleutian Islands
    background, 49–51
    fighting on, 51–52
    geography and terrain, 49
    results, 52
Australia, 5, 6, 7, 9, 10, 11, 14, 15, 18, 19,
    21, 22, 45, 85, 86, 95, 98, 106

Bacolod, Negros, 139

Baguio, Luzon, 127, 148, 149, 150, 152, 153,
    154, 171
Baler Bay, Luzon, 135
Balete Pass, Luzon, 148, 151–52, 153, 174
Bambang, Luzon, 148, 149, 150, 152
Barike River, New Georgia, 25
Bataan Peninsula, Luzon, 131
    Japanese conquest of, 5, 14, 106
Batangas Peninsula, Luzon, 123
Beightler, Robert, 126, 128, 131, 135, 149,
    152, 169, 182
    background and character, ix, 26
    and Bougainville operation, 31, 33
    frustrations, ix, 152
    and New Georgia operation, 27, 29
Bergerud, Eric, 13
Biak, 90, 102, 103, 110, 132, 138, 141, 143,
    175
    background, 88
    fighting on, 92–96
    geography and terrain, 92
    results, 96–97
Bicol Peninsula, Luzon, 123
Bohol, Philippines, 137, 139, 140
Bontoc, Luzon, 148
Borneo, Dutch East Indies, 137, 138
Bosnek, Biak, 92
Bougainville, Solomon Islands, 34, 38, 42, 43,
    44, 83, 100, 101, 118, 126, 134, 140, 174
    background, 30–31
    fighting on, 31–33
    geography and terrain, 30
    results, 33
Bradley, James, 111, 157, 160, 161, 186
Breakneck Ridge, Leyte, 113–14, 115, 122
Brisbane, Australia, 15, 19

Brooke, Alan, 70
Brown, Albert, 49, 171, 173, 178
  relieved of command, 51
Bruce, Andrew, 70, 72, 116, 117, 120–21,
  157, 159, 160, 163, 169, 175, 185
Brush, Rapp, 126, 128, 129, 136, 139, 183
Buckner Board, 66
Buckner, Simon, 66, 157, 158, 159, 160, 162,
  163, 164, 169, 173
  and 7th Division, 161–62, 164
  and 27th Division, 161
  and 77th Division, 163
  and 96th Division, 162
  background and character, 157
Buin, Bougainville, 30
Buka, Bougainville, 30
Buna–Gona, Papua New Guinea, 22
  background, 13–17
  fighting at, 17–18
  geography and terrain, 17–18
  results, 18–20
Burauen, Leyte, 112, 115–16, 120, 173
Butaritari, Makin Atoll, 54
Byers, Clovis, 142, 170

Cagayan Valley, Luzon, 124, 127, 128, 148,
  151, 152, 153, 175
Cape Esperance, Guadalcanal, 11, 12
Carigara, Leyte, 112, 113
Cartwheel, Operation, 20, 21, 23, 30, 36, 42,
  43, 44, 45, 47, 48, 83
Cebu, Philippines, 137, 139, 140, 143
Cebu City, Cebu, 140
Chase, William, 146, 147, 170, 177, 183
  on Admiralties, 40
  at Zigzag Pass, 133
Chichagof Harbor, Attu, 51–52
China–Formosa–Luzon region, 46, 72, 81,
  84, 86, 94, 103, 106, 108
Chocolate Drop, Okinawa, 162
Churchill, Winston, 69
Clark Airbase, Luzon, 124, 128–29, 134, 136,
  137, 139, 143, 154, 171, 175
Clarkson, Percy, 148, 149, 182
Collins, J. Lawton, 171, 173, 180
  background and character, 11
  and Guadalcanal campaign, 11, 12, 13

and New Georgia operation, 27, 29
Combined Chiefs of Staff, 4, 38
Conical Hill, Okinawa, 162
Cordillera Central Mountains, Luzon, 123,
  124, 148, 152
Corlett, Charles, 57, 59, 60, 61, 78, 171, 173,
  178
Coral Sea, Battle of, 6, 7, 14
Coronet, Operation, 164
Cunningham, Julian, 101
Cyclops Mountains, New Guinea, 84

Daguitan River, Leyte, 109
Dakeshi, Okinawa, 162
Davao, Mindanao, 141, 142, 143
Death Valley, Saipan, 64, 65, 68
DeWitt, John, 49–51
Dick, Okinawa, 162
Divisions, U.S. Army
  indicators of quality of, 168–72
  National Guard, xi–xii
  organization, x–xi
  ratings of draftee divisions, 175–76
  ratings of National Guard divisions,
    174–75
  ratings of Regular Army divisions, 172–74
  Regular Army, xi
  relevance of, xiii, 167–68
  selectee (draftee), xii–xiii
Doe, Jens, 22–23, 85, 87, 88, 90, 94, 95, 96,
  138, 184
Downfall, Operation, 164–65
Driniumor River, New Guinea, 115, 122,
  126, 141, 148
  background, 97–100
  fighting at, 100–01
  geography and terrain, 100
  results, 101–02
Dual Drive Offensive, 46, 81, 84, 108
Dulag, Leyte, 111, 112
Dutch East Indies, 3, 5, 35, 48, 105
Dutch Harbor, Aleutian Islands, 48

East Caves, Biak, 96
Eichelberger, Robert, 26, 47, 88, 91, 111,
  119, 126, 131, 137, 144, 148
  and 1st Cavalry Division, 41

and 11th Airborne Division, 116, 121, 130, 169
and 24th Division, 86, 87, 113, 114, 141, 142–43
and 31st Division, 143
and 32nd Division, 15, 18, 19, 20, 98, 114
and 33rd Division, 149
and 37th Division, ix, 152–53, 175
and 38th Division, 147
and 40th Division, 139
and 41st Division, 22, 23, 85, 87, 94, 95, 97, 138–39
and 77th Division, 70, 117–18, 120
and 93rd Division, 36
and advance on Manila, 129–30
and Americal Division, 118, 140
background and character, 15
on Biak, 94–96
at Buna–Gona, 18
relationship with Krueger, 129
Eisenhower, Dwight, xiv
Empress Augusta Bay, Bougainville, 30–33, 43, 100, 140, 174
Engebi, Eniwetok Atoll, 60
Eniwetok Atoll, Marshall Islands, 59–60, 62, 70
Erskine, Graves Robert, 61, 65
Espiritu Santo Island, New Hebrides, 67, 158

Fiji, 6, 11, 26
Finschhafen, New Guinea, 85, 149
Flattop, Okinawa, 162
Flintlock, Operation, 57, 59
Forager, Operation, 62, 69
Formosa, 5, 46, 105, 108, 155
Fuller, Horace, 22–23, 85, 87, 88, 92, 94, 96, 138, 184
resignation, 94–95

Galvanic, Operation, 53, 56
Geelvink Bay, 88, 90, 92
Geiger, Roy, 69, 70, 71, 72, 74, 75
Gifu, Guadalcanal, 10
Gilbert Islands, 47, 48, 52–56, 57, 61, 62, 77, 81
geography and terrain, 53

Gill, William, 19, 98, 100, 101, 102, 103, 114, 115, 122, 148, 150, 151, 170, 181
Griner, George, 157, 160, 161, 180
Griswold, Oscar
and 37th Division, 29, 126, 169, 175
and 40th Division, 129, 136
and 43rd Division, 26
and 93rd Division, 34
and Americal Division, 33, 140, 169
background and character, 26
and Bougainville operation, 31, 33
and Clark Airbase, 128
and Manila, 131, 134
and New Georgia operation, 26–27
Guadalcanal, Solomon Islands, ix, 20, 21, 23, 24, 26, 27, 28, 29, 30, 33, 34, 42, 43, 44, 53, 73, 118, 126, 135, 140, 148, 158, 171, 173, 174, 175
background, 5–8
fighting on, 8–12
geography and terrain, 7
results, 12–13
Guam, Mariana Islands, 61, 62, 78, 111, 116, 120, 157, 171, 175
background, 69–70
fighting on, 70–72
geography and terrain, 69
results, 72
Guimba, Luzon, 130

Hagushi beach, Okinawa, 158
Hall, Charles, 131, 146, 148, 157, 169, 186
and 6th Division, 90, 145
and 31st Division, 141
and 32nd Division, 102, 103
and 33rd Division, 149
and 38th Division, 132–33, 147
and 43rd Division, 126–27
at Driniumor River, 100–02
at Zigzag Pass, 132–34
Halmahera Island, 102
Halsey, William F., Jr., 9, 11, 20, 23, 24, 26, 28, 30, 31, 84, 108, 169, 170
and 25th Division, 29
Handy, Thomas T., 68
Hansa Bay, New Guinea, 84, 86, 87, 97
Harding, Edwin Forrest, 17, 53, 171, 181

relieved of command, 18
Harmon, Millard F., 9, 24, 26, 27, 28
  and 93rd Division, 34
Hawaii, 6, 45, 53, 63, 70, 86, 90, 110, 111,
  126, 131, 149, 158
Henderson Airfield, Guadalcanal, 8, 9, 10, 11,
  12, 13, 43
Hester, John, 24, 27, 28, 53, 171, 184
  relieved of command, 26
Hill 260, Los Negros, 41
Hodge, John, 27, 33, 73, 109, 157, 161
  and 7th Division, 115, 120, 164, 169, 173
  and 24th Division, 114
  and 27th Division, 161
  and 43rd Division, 27
  and 77th Division, 120, 169
  and 96th Division, 121
  and American Division, 31, 187
  background and character, 31, 110
Hodges, Courtney, 164
Hollandia, New Guinea, 88, 92, 96, 97, 103,
  110, 111, 114, 132, 141, 171, 174
  background, 83–86
  fighting on, 86
  geography and terrain, 84
  results, 86–87
Hull, John Edward, 39, 41
Humboldt Bay, New Guinea, 84, 86
Hyane Harbor, Los Negros, 40

Ibdi Pocket, Biak, 96
Ie Shima, Okinawa, 159–60, 163, 175
Illana Bay, Mindanao, 141, 142, 143
Iloilo, Panay, 139
Indianapolis, USS, 65, 159
Intramuros, Manila, 134
Ioribaiwa, Papua New Guinea, 14
Ipo Dam, Luzon, 144, 146, 147, 154
Irisan Gorge, Luzon, 149
Irving, Frederick, 85, 87, 110, 112, 115, 122,
  171, 179, 183
  relieved of command, 113–14
Iwo Jima, Bonin Islands, ix, 127, 155
Japan, 1, 4, 6, 45, 61, 105–06, 108, 157
  culture of, 3–4
Jarman, Sanderford, 64
Jarmin Pass, Attu, 51

Jenna, William, 132
Johnson, Harry H., 36
Joint Chiefs of Staff (JCS), 4, 11, 48, 62, 67,
  84, 108, 137, 155
Jolo, Philippines, 137
Jones, Henry, 131, 171, 183
  relieved of command, 132–33
Kakazu Ridge, Okinawa, 160–61
Kananga, Leyte, 117
Kavieng, New Ireland, 31
Kembu Group, 124, 128, 136, 139, 145
King, Ernest, 4, 7, 46, 67, 108, 155
Kinkaid, Thomas, 49, 51
Kiska, Aleutian Islands, 48, 49, 52, 57
Kokoda Track, 14
Kokumbona, Guadalcanal, 10, 11, 12
Kolombangara Island, 28
Krueger, Walter, 19, 23, 40, 90, 95, 98, 100,
  109, 112, 119, 123, 124, 127, 128, 137,
  144, 147, 149, 164
  and 1st Cavalry Division, 39, 41, 165, 169
  and 6th Division, 91–92
  and 7th Division, 120, 173
  and 11th Airborne Division, 116, 121,
    130, 165
  and 24th Division, 86, 87, 113–14, 122,
    138, 141, 174
  and 32nd Division, 88, 101, 102, 103,
    115, 122, 148, 150, 151
  and 37th Division, 126, 131, 135, 152
  and 38th Division, 131, 132, 135, 145,
    146
  and 40th Division, 129, 136, 138, 139,
    165
  and 41st Division, 85, 87, 88, 94, 97,
    138, 165
  and 43rd Division, 145
  and 77th Division, 116, 117, 120
  and 96th Division, 116, 121
  and American Division, 140
  background and character, 21
Kwajalein, Marshall Islands, 62, 77, 78, 110,
  119, 157, 167, 173
  background, 57–59
  fighting on, 59
  geography and terrain, 57
  results, 59–61

Kyushu, Japan, 155, 164

Lae, New Guinea, 22, 23
Laiana, New Georgia, 27
Landrum, Eugene, 51
Leahy, William, 4
Leyte, Philippine Islands, 61, 76, 126, 127,
    128, 129, 130, 131, 132, 138, 140, 141,
    142, 143, 145, 148, 153, 154, 156, 157,
    158, 163, 164, 169, 171, 172, 173, 174,
    175, 176
    background, 108–11
    fighting on, 111–18
    geography and terrain, 108–09
    mopping up, 118
    results, 118–23
Leyte Gulf, Battle of, 112, 119, 154, 156
Leyte Valley, Leyte, 108, 112
Lingayen Bay, Luzon, 124, 126, 130, 135,
    137, 144, 145, 175
Liscome Bay, USS, 55
Lone Tree Hill, 90, 91, 92, 102, 103, 124,
    135, 145, 171
Lorengau, Manus Island, 40, 41
Los Baños, Luzon, 130, 174
Los Negros, Admiralty Islands, 38, 39, 40,
    43, 133
Lugos, Manus Island, 41
Lunga Point, Guadalcanal, 7
Lupao, Luzon, 135
Luzon, Philippines, ix, 5, 44, 108, 109, 112,
    113, 117, 118, 119, 123–37, 144–53,
    172, 173, 174, 175

Macajalar Bay, Mindanao, 143
MacArthur, Douglas, ix, xi, 5, 11, 21, 29, 38,
    45, 47, 76, 83, 84, 85, 86, 88, 91, 95, 96,
    101, 102, 103, 109, 110, 112 124, 126,
    137, 139, 144, 155, 157, 164, 176
    and 1st Cavalry Division, 39–40, 41, 116,
        130, 172
    and 7th Division, 115, 119, 120
    and 11th Airborne Division, 116, 130
    and 24th Division, 87, 113–14, 122, 141,
        142
    and 27th Division, 54
    and 32nd Division, 15, 17, 18, 19–20, 119

and 33rd Division, 153
and 37th Division, 135
and 41st Division, 87, 94, 97
and 77th Division, 111, 116–17, 119, 120
and 93rd Division, 35, 165
and 96th Division, 111, 121
and Americal Division, 118, 140
background and character, 14
desire to liberate Philippines, 46, 81,
    106–08
and Manila, 127, 128, 129, 130, 131, 134
McCloy, John, 34
McNair, Lesley, 26, 116, 142
McNarney, Joseph T., 68
Maffin Bay, New Guinea, 88, 91
Makin, Gilbert Islands, 53–56, 62, 77, 79,
    171, 175
Manila, Luzon, ix, 1, 14, 106, 123–124, 127,
    128, 129–31, 134–35, 136, 137, 141,
    144, 145, 149, 152, 173, 174, 175
Manokwari, New Guinea, 102
Manus Island, Admiralties, 38, 40, 41
Mariana Islands, 47, 48, 57, 59, 61, 62, 63,
    69, 81, 155, 156, 158
Marikina River, Luzon, 144
Marine Corps, 4, 8, 9, 10, 11, 12, 23–24,
    42, 54, 61, 64, 66–67, 72, 74, 155, 163,
    170, 176
    accolades, ix, 12, 56, 172
    doctrine, 23, 46, 47
Marking Regiment, 146, 147
Marshall, George, xii, 4, 26, 47, 66, 67, 69,
    76, 110, 157, 161, 171
    and 1st Cavalry Division, 39
    and 7th Division, 52, 60
    and 25th Division, 12, 29, 173
    and 27th Division, 53–54
    and 43rd Division, 28
    and 93rd Division, 34, 35
    and Americal Division, 12
Marshall, S. L. A., 56
Marshall Islands, 47, 53, 59, 60, 61, 62, 77,
    81
    geography and terrain, 57
Martin, Clarence, 100, 141, 181
Melbourne, Australia, 1, 6
Middelburg Island, New Guinea, 102

Midway, Battle of, 6, 7, 13, 48, 176
Milne Bay, Papua New Guinea, 90
Mindanao, Philippines, 72, 106, 137, 138, 140–43, 154, 171, 175
Mindoro Island, Philippines, 117, 141
Mokmer Airfield, Biak, 94, 96
Momote Airfield, Los Negros, 38, 40, 41, 43, 133
Morotai Island, 35, 36, 102, 114, 141, 149
Motobu Peninsula, Okinawa, 159
Mount Austen, Guadalcanal, 10, 11, 12, 13
Mountbatten, Louis, 70
Mudge, Verne, 110, 112, 115, 121, 122, 130, 145, 172
Mueller, John, 73, 74, 185
Mullins, Charles, 135, 136, 148, 151, 180
Munda, New Georgia, 23–27, 29
Muñoz, Luzon, 135

Nafutan Point, Saipan, 64, 65, 68
Naha, Okinawa, 156, 163
Namur, Kwajalein Atoll, 57, 59, 60, 78
Nashville, USS, 87
Nassau Bay, New Guinea, 22
Nasugbu, Luzon, 129
National Association for the Advancement of Colored People, 35
National Guard, xi–xii
Navy, United States, 1, 4–5, 6, 38, 46, 47, 48, 53, 66, 69, 74, 76, 77, 81, 84, 92, 94, 103, 105–06, 112, 141, 154, 157, 159, 172
    strategic thinking, 7–8, 45, 155
Negros Island, Philippines, 137, 139, 140
New Caledonia, 6, 9, 11, 24, 26, 76, 116, 135
New Georgia, Solomon Islands, 30, 31, 34, 38, 42, 43, 44, 56, 61, 87, 124, 126, 134, 135, 147, 151, 171, 173, 174, 175
    background, 23–24
    fighting on, 24–27
    geography and terrain, 23
    results, 27–29
New Guinea, 13–23, 81–103
    geography and terrain, 81–83
New Hebrides, 27, 67, 158
New York Post, 35

New Zealand, 24, 30, 98, 124, 135
Nichols Airfield, Luzon, 130
Nimitz, Chester, 5, 8, 20, 47, 48, 52, 53, 56, 57, 59, 60, 66, 69, 70, 72, 77, 84, 108, 110, 127, 155, 157, 158, 169, 170
    and 25th Division, 11, 12
    and 43rd Division, 24
    background and character, 46
Noemfoor Island, 90
Norzagaray, Luzon, 146
Noumea, New Caledonia, 11

Oboe, Okinawa, 162
Okinawa, Ryukyu Islands, 61, 123, 127, 141, 173, 175
    background, 155–58
    fighting on, 158–63
    geography and terrain, 155–56
    results, 163–64
Olongapo, Luzon, 132
Olympic, Operation, 164
Orange, War Plan, 45
Ormoc, Leyte, 112, 113, 115, 117, 120, 173, 175
Ormoc Valley, Leyte, 108, 113, 117, 122, 154
Oro Bay, New Guinea, 22, 39, 131
Orote Peninsula, Guam, 70
Osmeña, Sergio, 111
Owen Stanley Mountains, 14

Pacific Ocean
    geography, 1
Pacific Ocean Areas (POA), 5
Pacific War, x, xvi, 1, 3, 44, 45
    U.S. strategy, 4–5, 106–08
Palau Islands, 47, 48, 72–77, 92, 110
    geography and terrain, 72–73
Palawan, Philippines, 137, 138
Panaon Strait, 112
Panay, Philippines, 137, 139
Papua New Guinea, 13, 14, 38, 42
Parry, Eniwetok Atoll, 60
Patch, Alexander M., 9, 10, 11, 12, 13, 26, 169, 171, 187
Patrick, Edwin, 88, 90, 124, 127, 135, 136, 145, 178
Patton, George, xiv

Pearl Harbor, Oahu, 5, 6, 9, 14, 26, 53, 56, 59, 86, 106, 108, 110, 176
Peleliu, Palau Islands, 73, 74–75, 76, 78, 79, 175
Philippine Islands, 105–54
  geography and terrain, 106
  JCS decision to liberate, 106–08
Philippine Sea, Battle of, 66, 106
Port Adelaide, Australia, 6
Port Moresby, Papua New Guinea, 6, 13, 14, 15, 22, 81
Pyle, Ernie, 159

Quadrant Conference, 38

Rabaul, New Britain, 14, 19, 20, 23, 30, 31, 36, 38, 44, 45, 48, 87, 106
Randle, Edwin, 159
Reckless, Operation, 85, 86, 87, 88, 97
Regular Army, xi
Richardson, Robert, 128, 169
  and 7th Division, 7, 110, 120, 121, 157, 164, 173
  and 24th Division, 86
  and 27th Division, 54, 63, 66, 158, 161
  and 77th Division, 120, 121, 157
  and 81st Division, 73, 76
  and 96th Division, 121, 157
  background and character, 47
  and Holland Smith, 64, 66–67
  and Marine Corps, 47, 66, 110
  and navy, 47
Rockhampton, Australia, 85, 86, 95
Roi, Kwajalein Atoll, 57, 59, 60, 78
Roosevelt, Franklin, xi, 4, 14, 35, 106, 110
Roosevelt Ridge, Battle of, 22, 42, 44, 96, 103
Rosario, Luzon, 127, 136, 145, 147
Rossum, Manus Island, 41
Rupertus, William, 74
  and 81st Division, 75

Saidor, Papua New Guinea, 84, 85, 88
Saipan, Mariana Islands, 56, 61–69, 72, 76, 78, 79, 157, 158, 171, 172, 175
Salamaua, New Guinea, 22, 23, 85
Salami, Los Negros, 40

Samar, Philippines, 112, 122
San José, Luzon, 135–36, 137, 145, 147, 148, 151, 174
San José River, Leyte, 109
San Juanico Strait, 112
San Narciso, Luzon, 132
Sanananda, New Guinea, 17, 18, 22, 42, 96, 103
Sanga Sanga, Philippines, 137
Sansapor–Mar, New Guinea, 102, 124
Santa Fe, Luzon, 150, 151
Santa Maria, Luzon, 150
Santo Tomas University, Luzon, 131
Sarmi, New Guinea, 88, 91, 94, 149
Sayre Highway, Mindanao, 143
Sealark Channel, 7
Sebree, Edmund B., 10, 187
Seeadler Harbor, Los Negros, 38, 40, 41
Shimbu Group, 124, 130, 135, 144–47, 148, 173, 174, 175
Shobu Group, 124, 127, 130, 135, 144, 148–53, 174, 175
Shoestring Ridge, Leyte, 115, 120, 173
Shuri Line, Okinawa, 158–64, 175
Sibert, Franklin, 90–91, 109, 113, 114, 115, 122, 174, 178
Sierra Madre Mountains, Luzon, 123, 124, 144
Singapore, 1, 5, 48, 105
Smith, Holland, 46, 58, 69, 78, 157
  and 7th Division, 58–59, 61
  and 27th Division, 54, 55, 56, 62–63, 64, 67, 170
  on 77th Division, 72, 170
  elevated to Fleet Marine Force commander, 67
  on Makin, 55–56
  on Saipan, 62, 64–66, 68
Smith, Oliver, 161
Smith, Ralph, 53, 54, 67, 68, 171, 180
  relieved of command, 64–65
Smith vs. Smith controversy, 66–69
Solomon Islands, 12, 20, 35, 44, 48, 49, 52, 84, 110
  geography and terrain, 7
Sorong, New Guinea, 102
South Pacific Area (SOPAC), 9

Southwest Pacific Area (SWPA), 5, 14
Spruance, Raymond, 63, 64, 65
Stalemate II, Operation, 73, 76
Stilwell, Joseph, 163
Stimson, Henry, 34, 69
Subic Bay, Luzon, 132
Sugar Loaf, Okinawa, 162
Sump, Biak, 96
Sutherland, Richard, 114
Swift, Innis Palmer, 39, 40, 41, 109, 124, 127, 135, 148, 149, 150, 151, 169, 171, 172, 177
Swing, Joseph, 116, 121, 129, 169, 179

Tabontabon, Leyte, 112
Tacloban, Leyte, 109, 111, 112, 116
Tagaytay Ridge, Luzon, 130
Tanahmerah Bay, New Guinea, 84, 86, 87
Tanapag, Saipan, 65
Tarawa, Gilbert Islands, ix, 53, 54, 55, 56, 57, 58, 59, 62
Task Force 6814, 6
Teardrop, Biak, 96
Terauchi, Hisaichi, 112
Terowie, Australia, 108
Time magazine, 67
Tinian, Mariana Islands, 62, 65, 67, 78
Toem, New Guinea, 88, 90, 94
Toenails, Operation, 23, 24
Tuguegarao, Luzon, ix
Tulagi, Solomon Islands, 7, 8
Tuliahan River, Luzon, 131
Turner, Richmond Kelly, 59, 60, 65

Ulithi, Palau Islands, 73, 74, 76
Umingan, Luzon, 135
Umurbrogol Pocket, Peleliu, 76
Units, U.S. Army
  Corps
    I, 15, 18, 21, 22, 85, 94, 124, 127, 135, 148, 149, 172
    I Amphibious, 24
    III Amphibious, 69, 72, 157, 162
    V Amphibious, 46, 54, 62
    XI, 90, 100, 126, 131, 136, 142, 145
    XIV, 10, 12, 26, 29, 31, 33, 100, 101, 126, 127, 128, 130, 133, 134, 135,
      136, 140, 144, 145, 148, 171
    XXIV, 73, 109, 110, 112, 113, 114, 115, 117, 119, 120, 160, 162, 164, 173
  Divisions
    1st Cavalry, 83, 92, 103, 116, 136, 138, 152
      on Admiralty Islands, 40–41
      advance on Manila, 130–31, 136
      analysis, 41, 42, 43, 44, 85, 116, 118, 120, 121–22, 130, 153, 154, 169, 170, 171, 172–73, 174
      attack on Shimbu Group, 144–46
      background and deployment, 39–40, 177
      and invasion of Japan, 164, 165
      on Leyte, 109, 110, 111, 112, 113, 115, 117, 118, 119, 121–22
      and Manila, 134
    1st Marine, 8, 10, 11, 12, 21, 24, 73, 74, 76, 78, 158
    2nd Marine, 8, 10, 11, 24, 53, 56, 64, 77
    3rd Marine, 24, 30, 31, 69, 70
    4th Marine, 57, 59, 60, 64, 78
    6th "Sightseers", 83, 102, 124, 141
      analysis, 91–92, 103, 136, 137, 146–47, 153, 154, 171, 172, 174
      attack on Shimbu Group, 144, 145, 146
      background and deployment, 90–91, 178
      and invasion of Japan, 164
      at Lone Tree Hill, 91
      at Rosario, 127
      at San José, 135–36
      and Zimbales Mountains, 136
    7th "Hourglass", 47
      analysis, 52, 60–61, 78, 119–20, 154, 160, 161–62, 164, 167, 169, 171, 172, 173, 174
      on Attu, 51–52
      background and deployment, 49–51, 178
      and invasion of Japan, 164

on Kwajalein, 57, 59–60
on Leyte, 110, 112, 115–16, 117
on Okinawa, 157, 158, 159, 160,
    161–62, 163, 164
11th Airborne "Angels", 83, 103, 144,
    152
    advance on Manila, 129–30, 131
    analysis, 121, 130, 136, 138, 139,
        153–54, 169, 171, 172, 174
    background and deployment, 6,
        116, 179
    and invasion of Japan, 164, 165
    on Leyte, 115, 118, 119, 121
24th "Victory", xi, 83, 88, 92, 103,
    138
    analysis, 87, 122, 136, 143,
        153–54, 169, 171, 172, 174
    background and deployment, 6,
        85–86, 179
    at Biak, 94, 95
    at Hollandia, 85, 86–87
    and invasion of Japan, 164
    on Leyte, 109, 110, 111, 112, 113,
        114, 115, 118, 119, 121, 122
    on Mindanao, 137, 141, 142–43
    at Zigzag Pass, 131, 132
25th "Tropic Lightning", xi, 24, 28,
    30, 83, 85, 103, 127
    analysis, 13, 27, 29, 41, 42, 43,
        44, 61, 137, 151–52, 153, 154,
        171, 172, 173–74
    attack on Shobu Group, 144, 148,
        149, 150, 153
    background and deployment, 6,
        10–11, 85, 180
    and Balete Pass, 151–52
    on Guadalcanal, 11, 12, 13, 41
    and invasion of Japan, 164
    on New Georgia, 26, 27, 29
    at San José, 135–36, 137
27th "New York", 47, 77, 78, 148, 168
    analysis, 56, 68–69, 79, 153, 164,
        170, 171, 172, 175, 176
    background and deployment, 6,
        53, 180
    concerns about, 53–54, 55–56,
        62–63

on Eniwetok, 60
and invasion of Japan, 164
on Makin, 54, 55, 56
on Okinawa, 157, 158, 160, 161,
    163, 164
on Saipan, 62, 63, 64–65, 68–69
Saipan aftermath, 66–68
31st "Dixie", 83, 102, 103
    analysis, 143, 153, 154, 171, 175
    background and deployment,
        141–42, 181
    at Driniumor River, 98, 101
    and invasion of Japan, 164
    on Mindanao, 137, 143
32nd "Red Arrow", 21, 22, 24, 83, 85,
    88, 144, 152
    analysis, 19–20, 42, 43, 44, 101–
        02, 103, 119, 122, 153, 154,
        167, 170, 171, 172, 175, 176
    attack on Shobu Group, 148, 149
    background and deployment, 6,
        15, 181
    at Buna–Gona, 14, 15, 18, 19, 20,
        21
    at Driniumor River, 97, 100, 101,
        102
    and invasion of Japan, 164
    on Leyte, 114, 115, 116, 117, 118,
        119, 122
    recovery from Buna–Gona, 98
    and Villa Verde Trail, 150–51
33rd "Prairie", 83, 103, 171, 175
    analysis, 149, 153, 154, 171, 175
    attack on Shobu Group, 144, 149,
        152
    background and deployment,
        148–49, 182
    and invasion of Japan, 164
35th "Santa Fe", 49
37th "Buckeyes", ix, 83, 103
    advance on Manila, 126, 127, 128,
        130, 131
    analysis, 29, 33, 42, 43, 44, 61,
        129, 136, 137, 153, 154, 169,
        171, 172, 174–75
    attack on Shimbu Group, 144, 146
    attack on Shobu Group, 149

background and deployment, 6, 26, 27, 182
and Balete Pass, 151
on Bougainville, 30, 31, 33
and Cagayan Valley, 152, 153
and Clark Airbase, 128, 129
and invasion of Japan, 164
and Manila, 134–35
on New Georgia, 24, 26, 27, 29
38th "Cyclone", 83, 103
  analysis, 136, 137, 147, 153, 154, 170, 171, 175
  attack on Shimbu Group, 144, 145, 146, 147
  background and deployment, 131, 183
  and invasion of Japan, 164
  on Leyte, 131
  at Zigzag Pass, 132–34
  and Zimbales Mountains, 136
40th "Sunshine" or "Sunburst", 83, 103, 143
  advance on Manila, 127
  analysis, 129, 136, 137, 138, 139, 143, 153, 154, 165, 171, 175
  background and deployment, 126, 183
  and Clark Airbase, 128,
  and invasion of Japan, 164
  and Negros, 137, 139
  on Panay, 137, 139
  and Zimbales Mountains, 136
41st "Sunset" or "Jungleers", 21, 83, 103, 137
  analysis, 22, 42, 44, 87, 96–97, 103, 138–39, 143, 153, 154, 175
  background and deployment, 6, 22, 184
  on Biak, 88, 90, 92–94, 95–96
  at Buna–Gona, 14–15, 18, 19
  dissention in, 22–23
  at Hollandia, 85, 86, 87, 97
  and invasion of Japan, 164, 165
  on Palawan, 137, 138
  at Roosevelt Ridge, 22
  on Wakde, 88

on Zamboanga Peninsula, 137, 138, 141
43rd "Winged Victory", 30, 31, 83, 103, 110
  analysis, 28–29, 42, 43, 44, 52, 56, 136, 146, 147, 153, 154, 171, 175
  attack on Shimbu Group, 144, 145–46, 147
  background and deployment, 9, 24, 184
  at Driniumor River, 98, 100, 101
  and invasion of Japan, 164
  at New Georgia, 24–26, 27, 28
  at Rosario, 124, 126, 127
  and Zimbales Mountains, 136
77th "Statue of Liberty" or "Old Buzzards", 47
  analysis, 72, 78, 118, 119, 120, 121, 153, 154, 160, 164, 169, 170, 171, 172, 173, 175, 176
  background and deployment, 69–70, 185
  on Guam, 70–72
  on Ie Shima, 159–60
  and invasion of Japan, 164
  on Leyte, 111, 116, 117–18, 119
  on Okinawa, 157, 162, 163
81st "Wildcats", 47, 118, 153
  analysis, 76, 78–79, 171, 175
  on Angaur, 73, 74
  background and deployment, 73, 185
  and invasion of Japan, 164
  on Peleliu, 74–76
93rd "Blue Helmets", 36, 83, 103
  analysis, 36, 167, 176
  background and deployment, 34, 186
  on Bougainville, 34
  controversy about, 34–35
  and invasion of Japan, 165
96th "Deadeyes"
  analysis, 121, 153, 154, 164, 171, 175
  background and deployment, 111, 186

and invasion of Japan, 164
  on Leyte, 111, 112, 116, 118
  on Okinawa, 157, 158, 159, 160,
    161, 162, 163
98th "Iroquois", 47
Americal, 83, 110
  analysis, 13, 33, 42, 43, 44, 103,
    118, 119, 143, 153, 169, 171,
    172, 175
  background and deployment, 9, 187
  on Bougainville, 30, 31, 33, 34
  on Cebu, 137, 140
  on Guadalcanal, 10, 11, 12
  and invasion of Japan, 164
  on Leyte, 118
Composite Army-Marine (CAM), 11
Field Armies
  Eighth, ix, 36, 97, 114, 118, 129, 137,
    138, 143, 144, 148, 152, 164
  Sixth (Alamo Force), 19, 21, 23, 85,
    90, 94, 102, 109, 112, 113, 115,
    118, 119, 122, 123, 124, 127, 129,
    136, 137, 138, 144, 145, 146, 147,
    148, 152, 164, 173
  Tenth, 157, 159, 161, 162, 163
Regiments
  1st, 91
  4th, 51
  5th Cavalry, 39, 40, 41, 177
  6th Marine, 11
  7th Cavalry, 39, 40, 41, 177
  8th Cavalry, 41, 177
  12th Cavalry, 40, 41, 177
  17th, 59, 115, 178
  19th, 179
  20th, 91, 178
  24th, 34
  25th, 34, 186
  27th, 151, 180
  32nd, 51, 59, 60, 115, 178
  63rd, 91, 178
  103rd, 27, 184
  105th, 54, 65, 180
  112th Cavalry, 98, 100, 101
  124th, 98, 100, 101, 141, 181
  126th, 15, 100, 150, 181
  127th, 18, 97, 98, 100, 101, 181

128th, 15, 100, 101, 150, 181
  129th, 27, 31, 135, 182
  132nd, 9, 10, 187
  145th, 31, 135, 182
  147th, 11
  148th, 27, 29, 31, 182
  149th, 132, 133, 183
  151st, 132, 183
  152nd, 132, 183
  158th, 88, 90, 91, 127
  160th, 139, 183
  161st, 10, 27, 180
  162nd, 22, 85, 88, 92, 94, 96, 184
  163rd, 18, 19, 22, 85, 86, 88, 90, 94,
    96, 97, 184
  164th, 9, 13, 180, 187
  165th, 53, 54, 56, 64, 180
  169th, 25, 27, 184
  172nd, 25, 26, 184
  182nd, 9, 10, 11, 187
  184th, 51, 59, 60, 115, 178
  185th, 139, 183
  186th, 22, 85, 88, 94, 95, 96, 138, 184
  305th, 70, 185
  321st, 73, 74, 75, 76, 185
  322nd, 73, 185
  323rd, 74, 76, 185
  383rd, 160, 186
  503rd Parachute, 139
  Other
    1st Provisional Marine Brigade, 69, 70

Ushijima, Mitsuru, 158

Vandegrift, Archibald, 8
Vella Lavella Island, 28
Villa Verde Trail, Luzon, 150–51, 153, 154
Vogel, Clayton, 24
Vogelkop Peninsula, New Guinea, 102

Wakde Island, New Guinea, 96, 97, 103, 141,
  149
  background, 87–88
  fighting on, 88
  geography and terrain, 88
  results, 91–92
Wana, Okinawa, 162

Wart, Okinawa, 162

Wawa Dam, Luzon, 144, 146, 147, 154

West Caves, Biak, 96

Western Defense Command, 49, 52, 78

Wewak, New Guinea, 84, 85, 86, 87, 97

White, Walter, 35

Wing, Leonard, 124, 126, 127, 145, 146, 147, 184

Woodruff, Roscoe, 70, 122, 141, 142, 179, 185

X-Ray River, New Guinea, 100

Yamashita, Tomoyuki, 112, 123, 124, 131, 134, 136, 148, 170

and 32nd Division, 151

and 38th Division, 147

Zambales Mountains, Luzon, 123, 124, 136, 139

Zamboanga Peninsula, Mindanao, 137, 138, 141

Zanana beach, New Georgia, 24

Zigzag Pass, 136, 141, 146, 147, 154, 170, 171, 175

   background, 131

   fighting on, 132–33

   geography and terrain, 132

   results, 133–34